T0354553

UNDERSTANDING CHANGE

UNDERSTANDING
CHANGE

A PERSONAL AND PROFESSIONAL MANAGEMENT STRATEGY

DR. ALBERT DE GOIAS

iUniverse, Inc.
Bloomington

UNDERSTANDING CHANGE
A PERSONAL AND PROFESSIONAL MANAGEMENT STRATEGY

iUniverse books may be ordered through booksellers or by contacting:

iUniverse
1663 Liberty Drive
Bloomington, IN 47403
www.iuniverse.com
1-800-Authors (1-800-288-4677)

Because of the dynamic nature of the Internet, any web addresses or links contained in this book may have changed since publication and may no longer be valid. The views expressed in this work are solely those of the author and do not necessarily reflect the views of the publisher, and the publisher hereby disclaims any responsibility for them.

Any people depicted in stock imagery provided by Thinkstock are models, and such images are being used for illustrative purposes only.

Certain stock imagery © Thinkstock.

ISBN: 978-1-4759-7028-9 (sc)
ISBN: 978-1-4759-7029-6 (hc)
ISBN: 978-1-4759-7030-2 (e)

Library of Congress Control Number: 2013900050

Printed in the United States of America

iUniverse rev. date: 4/22/2013

I would like to express my deepest appreciation to my loving and gracious wife, Andrea, for her support, encouragement, and philosophical guidance. Without her help and her tolerance of my mood swings when my work deprived me of sleep, the completion of this work would not have been possible.

CONTENTS

PREFACE.. IX

INTRODUCTION.. XIII

CHAPTER 1 THE REALITY OF CHANGE 1

CHAPTER 2 THE RESOURCES YOU HAVE FOR DEALING WITH
CHANGE.. 17

CHAPTER 3 THE EFFECTS OF MODERN CHANGE ON CREATIVITY....41

CHAPTER 4 UNDERSTANDING CHANGE AND DETERMINING ITS
LIMITATIONS 59

CHAPTER 5 DEVELOPING A SECURE IDENTITY...............................83

CHAPTER 6 ORGANIZING YOUR MANAGEMENT SKILLS.................. 111

CHAPTER 7 PERFORMANCE MANAGEMENT.................................. 149

CHAPTER 8 BEING A MANAGER 171

CHAPTER 9 UNDERSTANDING PEOPLE'S REACTIONS TO CHANGE... 185

CHAPTER 10 MOTIVATING PEOPLE TO ACCOMPLISH.....................203

BIBLIOGRAPHY...239

INDEX..241

PREFACE

I AM A PHYSICIAN in active practice, but my interests have always been in the area of the abstract. I was trained academically in mathematics and physics. My reading interest was in philosophy. I went to medical school because it appeared to bridge the gap between physics and philosophy. At university I was also an avid swimmer, swimming a mile every morning before classes; also, I loved to socialize. But my search for information was not satisfied. My exposure was eclectic, giving me a vast range of experiences from which I eventually drew in order to offer the expertise I have used for the past 30 years of work in the field of existential pain. After graduation, I did one-year residencies in psychiatry, neurosurgery and neuropathology, searching for a niche that would satisfy my curiosity. Financial responsibilities, however, led me to private practice.

I thought the demands of private practice would quell my dissatisfaction, but it only opened it differently. While in practice, I noticed that there were a large number of people who suffered pain that could not be diagnosed medically but that affected their health severely. This was not physical pain but existential pain. Nietzsche and Sartre had opened discussions in the area. I explored it because medicine had no answer. My math and physics background allowed me to see it from an abstract perspective; it also allowed me to examine it within the contributions of chaos theory.

I saw that we could not solve the real problem because we were not looking at from where it came. First, it was too complex and too hidden for easy examination; we needed to see it from the abstract perspective of physics. Second, we couldn't reach it to fix it. Third, it did not appear to be as precious as life. Physical illness can kill; mental anguish simply relegated the person to being defined as one who functions at a lower level of competence. Yet in my practice I saw highly functioning people, executives, professionals, athletes and even church ministers who were going through the same angst as those people whom society seemed to have discarded. I decided to do something about it.

It was a tough decision for me. I was leaving an area where I had already achieved a level of respect and competence and going where I would be thought of as a dropout. I had reached the pinnacle of using deep knowledge to fix the most precious aspect of people, their physical health. I was seen as stepping down to use "less knowledge to fix what cannot be fixed, a state that could only be soothed." I wanted to debunk that.

I learned to see the person as a mind or soul, a truly nonphysical force that is more real than the physical matter of the body. It was not really dualism, though I studied the philosophical ramblings of Descartes. I saw it as monism, which is the singularity of the human being as a soul. The body was a discardable tool we used for a limited period. And of course we do discard various parts every day. We replace them automatically. Think of skin, nails and hair as readily identifiable examples.

At first I developed an understanding of the human psyche, researching from the medical, psychological, philosophical and spiritual disciplines. I discovered a strange fact: all people had the capacity to be as great as man can be; they only needed opportunity and direction and the assurance that they had value. The most mentally distressed or repressed people were able to think as well as anyone else; they just couldn't adapt their thoughts as quickly as conditions changed. In highly charged contexts, even successful people were seen to fail and experience mental anguish. The distressed or ill-prepared person was even more so. Treating existential angst, existential emptiness (as Viktor Frankl described it) or existential weakness became the focus of my work, which I then expanded into a treatment format. I offered this perspective to corporate executives who were precious to their companies for their ideas but were getting stymied by fast change during the '80s. Then I went to teachers, probation officers, counsellors, criminal lawyers and finally to recovering drug addicts. The full experience gave me this insight into that complex area of the human psyche and the tools of logic, which are the only tools that can reach that metaphysical area of human existence. I wish to share with you this insight and those tools.

INTRODUCTION

WE LIVE IN TIMES of great change. No one has been adequately prepared for the disruptions this brings daily in our jobs, family life, health, personal relationships or the social interactions within the multicultural melting pots of our urban centres. It is natural that the personal strengths we have learned to rely on will inevitably become stretched, even to breaking point. The result is that accountable people have time only to put out fires, and many of us are beginning to fail at our jobs or relationships, be addicted to the substances and activities that offer trivial respite or be lost in emotional angst we cannot escape long enough before the next stress arrives. These unhealthy moods and inappropriate behaviours can severely jeopardize our social, material or physical well-being. We need to understand them before we try to fix them, or we will be left going around in circles and getting results only for trivial moments.

Any behaviour is a physical response to the imposition of a stress, a natural fight-flight-surrender instinct. But the human being is more than a physical life form that relies on instinct: we think. Rational thought, however, must be nurtured in order to generate both the experience that can be applied immediately and the confidence that new solutions can be created quickly. Without a mature, rational strength and the conviction to define the self by it, many people are forced to rely on physical strengths that are rooted in biological or material assets, or they have nothing at all when these assets are weak or unavailable.

Physical or material attributes work well in a linear model of reality as in the simple conditions of childhood. In a complex reality as is the lot of any adult in today's society, physical strengths become inefficient and easily reach unhealthy levels when used to the extreme.

Unhealthy Behaviours Are the Extreme Expressions of a Natural Response to Stress

Physical strengths are like a shield in battle—not the primary weapon, but a necessary armour. It is not sensible to try to stifle an unhealthy behaviour. Rather, it is necessary to stop a natural response from being taken to the extreme. In a battle, if a soldier chooses to hide behind his shield, removing the shield will only expose him to the onslaught. Instead, we teach him how to use his weapons more effectively. Similarly, the person who shows unhealthy behaviours should focus on developing the composure to deal with reality as reality evolves, not just treat or stifle the behaviour.

Understanding Change is a way of throwing light on the complexities of reality, showing how new events evolve to create new stresses or impose new twists to familiar conditions to make them difficult again. It explores change in a variety of situations—in the work we do, the people we meet and the health we need. It works on the premise that by having understanding, we can be better prepared to deal with stress from a position of enhanced personal strength.

The Process

Understanding Change is a process of stimulating mental strength through expanding understanding. Although many people would rather have compassion and encouragement when they feel overwhelmed by the stresses of their reality, they are more effectively equipped if they can be empowered with the personal strength of understanding and the confidence to create it independently. As an attribute, understanding can turn a previously formidable challenge into an easily managed task. Yet by the time people begin to fall back on an unhealthy habit, they are so weak that they see no ability to depend on themselves to manage more constructively, even with insight. Nonetheless, it is an accepted fact that people are far better served by being stimulated to think than being advised by the most competent counsellor or encouraged by the most considerate manager. The immediate relief afforded by compassion may be completely depleted by the time the next event arrives. And in modern days, the next event often comes before we have had time to recover from the previous one.

Behaviour like aggression (the fight response) can become hostility, violence and physical or sexual control when applied to others; it can be self-mutilation and anorexia when applied to the self. Augmentation (the submit response) can be hazardous when it becomes victimization, codependency or the self-gratification or too much sex, food, booze or drugs. Evasion (the flight response) can be unhealthy when it is revealed as phobias, antisocial acts, irresponsibility or the chronic retreat to carefree pursuits (gambling and shopping). Added to this is the fact that when these actions fail or are ineffective, we can be left feeling hopeless, depressed or completely devoid of purpose.

A Battle Is Best Won When We Truly Understand the Enemy

Therefore it is the intent of this program to stimulate you to manufacture appropriate solutions as the problems arise, even if you cannot see this to be the best course of action while you are suffering the depletions of stress. It offers more than understanding; it offers a formula that allows you to build hope and understanding, even under difficult or oppressive conditions. This is more effective than offering a solution that ceases to apply when the problem changes, or providing support that cannot be accessed when you need help most.

Why Counselling Is Often Ineffective

Ordinarily, when a person who is compromised by the stresses of reality attends a counsellor, she is either provided with a solution, given reassurance that she will find one or offered treatment for the subsequent unhealthy behaviour. This usually pertains to the particular problem she describes. Since stresses from any single area of life—namely work, health or relationships—can evoke stresses in another, it is often impossible to find the real culprit.

Thus when we apply a solution to what may be the most bothersome stress, we still leave ourselves open to the way another area will affect the one we have treated. Sometimes this is displayed as a different stress; often it simply appears as a resistant form of the problem that was treated.

This is a mouthful, but we can see it more clearly when we look at one of the more common examples. When we solve a problem—for example, treating anxiety with a tranquillizer—we soothe the distressed organ system. However, that solution does not fix an associated financial problem. This unresolved problem can appear as a different disorder, or it can cause the anxiety to emerge more intensely and so resist the medication. Then simply increasing the medication may just make matters worse. Now let us look at how we can get around this problem.

WHY HAVING A FORMULA BEATS HAVING A SOLUTION

When a person presents himself to a counsellor, that counsellor arrives at a conclusion by using a formula. The formula belongs to the counsellor because of her skill and study. The counsellor charges for her expertise using this formula that she has but the client doesn't. This is not unlike employing an electrician to fix a problem in your light switch. The electrician uses his skill and training as a formula to allow him to create a solution for your electrical problem, and he charges you for his expertise. He does not bring a ready solution; rather, he assesses the problem and creates an appropriate solution. He does not teach you how to do what he does. Partly this is because the formula is complex, requiring years of study and practice. Partly this is because he needs to sell his solutions in order to make a living. This works well in an electrical problem because an electrical problem is relatively fixed. The solution that is applied is good for some years, perhaps until the wires deteriorate naturally or an unnatural event erodes it. In addition, the electrician can both see the problem and apply his knowledge to fix the problem.

THE POSSESSION OF A FORMULA IS THE SINGLE ADVANTAGE A COUNSELLOR HAS OVER A CLIENT

Unlike the electrical problem, however, life is highly complex. No counsellor has the ability to examine what is really going on in a person's experience, even as the person is sitting in front of the counsellor. In addition, the counsellor's knowledge cannot be applied routinely to each different person. People cannot be categorized by his race, colour, sex or religion. Each person is an individual. Therefore, although counselling is the most desirable route when you want to solve a problem or control behaviour, it can often be misleadingly inappropriate for the particular person or condition. It can also give good solutions but still leave the person ill-equipped for the next event or encounter.

The *Understanding Change* tutorial is based on the knowledge that people have the intelligence to manage their own stresses; they simply need information appropriate to the event. In a changing world, any information can become insufficient or redundant, no matter who you may be. The *Understanding Change* tutorial chooses to share a formula with you so that you can solve problems as they evolve, not after they become established. What you get is a guided tour of life, exploring the apparently unfair impositions that make reality oppressive and discovering the depth of your own resourcefulness, giving you both hope and the fortitude to realize it.

It shows you how to be awake to change so that you can anticipate it in the things you do, the people you meet and the body you use. It is an immense work that can stimulate you to achieve your fullest potential. You can employ it even if you are totally burnt out, de-energized by depression, compromised by antisocial or irresponsible activities or completely addicted to a chemical or alcohol that you may have used to numb the pain, tame the reality or escape to a seemingly less complicated alternative.

You must know that it is more important for you to wake up to life, even if it takes the last bit of energy you have, rather than conserve an energy that will seep away while the world generates more artillery to throw at you tomorrow.

USING *UNDERSTANDING CHANGE*

Understanding Change is a formula. It is not a series of solutions you can follow immediately, because it recognizes that life is complicated. A formula is a way of simplifying that complexity. Learning to fix your own electrical problems requires that you not only know how to wrap the wire around the screw but to examine for other shorts; life also requires your alertness.

Understanding Change will first show you how to regain your strength—your belief in yourself. Then it shows you how to immunize that strength. It shows you how to examine the inconsistencies and instabilities in the world around you so that you can always be awake to events before they become problems. It will do this in relation to the material world, your social encounters and your biological needs.

I choose to offer it in this book because personal counselling is often unavailable to many people, and when it is, the stresses it imposes can make the process tiresome, inconsistent and ineffective. Self-study, however, demands your attention and dedication. I believe that our discussion and the images used to emphasize it will give you a pleasant tour that simplifies a complex reality and stimulates your attention and determination. I know that you would rather be in the presence of a counsellor, even if that person is teaching the formula. However, I also believe that you would be better served by having the ability to view over and over material that allows you to see your world differently and yourself more positively. Counselling then would be the process of coaching you to solidify your own logic to manage your own reality while encouraging you to discuss your interpretations and applications as you process them.

WHY THIS TUTORIAL IS UNIQUE

This dissertation and the technique it embodies differ from other approaches to unhealthy behaviours for four solid reasons. The first reason is that it offers a formula. The technique does not rely on a series of solutions, nor does it rely on the description of the way successful people manage. It does not spend time soothing you. Rather, it accepts that you are your own best therapist, and it trains you to become awake to your full potential without requiring support or fellowship to be effective.

The second is that it shows you how not only to manage a presenting problem but to reduce problems by empowering yourself to create techniques that are yours—and keep doing so as the world changes. This means that you do not simply access the tutorial. You study it, assimilate it and own it. Yet you may not always feel empowered as you examine any particular level. Nonetheless, you *will* notice that you will view life differently and that things that once were seen as stresses will be more easily managed or even welcomed.

The third is that the tutorial empowers you to be more self-accountable. You will not just seek relief by reducing your exposure to stress. In fact, you will notice a greater desire to accomplish. Productivity and enjoyment of work is increased. The ability to relate to people who once were considered to be oppressive or demanding is increased.

The fourth is that although the tutorial is not designed to replace the help you receive from counselling or from medication, you will have a reduced need for these assists. Any change in medication, however, must be supervised by your doctor, even if the medication was self-administered. However, if you feel the need to talk with a counsellor, please do not believe that you have failed to grasp the contents. The decision to have someone with whom you can discuss ideas is not a statement of weakness as much as it is an opportunity to be stimulated from a different perspective.

Regardless, the ultimate reward is that you will free yourself—to function with self-generated confidence, to grow at your own pace and to manage life at your own recognizance even as your world continues to be unfair in its demands and stingy in its praises.

Therefore, please view all the lessons in the tutorial as a journey of discovery. Do not expect any great revelations, only a progressive change in attitude that you will own as you proceed. You may need to view the discussions more than once, both at the initial sitting and at subsequent times that you wish to be stimulated. Digest the contents of each lesson even if you have to stay with one lesson for what may seem to be an inordinate time, and go to the next only when you feel comfortably satisfied with the last discussion you have viewed. Once you are finished with the whole, view them again. You will discover that you will grasp things differently because new thoughts are evoked after you have seen where the discourse is taking you.

Please also feel free to discuss the emotions they evoke with a counsellor or family member. Any emotion is positive because it will stimulate you to think, and it is in thinking that you will own the insights. Your insights will come from you, not from the discussions. Allow yourself to disagree. It is in disagreeing and reconstructing your interpretations that you will develop direction that you own and strengths that you will maintain.

CHAPTER 1

THE REALITY OF CHANGE

WE LIVE IN A difficult and demanding world, because everything about us is constantly changing. We have to know how to adapt to change, or we will always be confronted by issues and conditions that will disrupt our comfort zones and even threaten our very survival. Many people do not always recognize this constant movement until one of these events occurs and they have a huge and perhaps insurmountable problem to tackle.

When we say that we have to face change, however, it sometimes seems like an academic challenge. We feel that it might read more like, "Theory and Analysis of Transformation," or something academically highbrow. But really, when we speak of change here, we refer to everyday situations. Change is as much the spoiling of food by bacteria as it is the experience of a divorce. Do you know that statistically, many people stay married but not always because of love or companionship? They stay because they are afraid of change. They are afraid to be alone, to lose familiar touchstones. They stay because they cannot face the unknown. The devil you know is often less scary than the devil you do not know.

But change is also the new job, the promotion or the new client. Anything that is different is change. A spouse changes his or her feelings and either expresses them or hides them, often not too cleverly. It is change when the feelings are expressed, but it is also change when, unexpressed, those different feelings evoke behaviours or responses that are not familiar or comfortable.

Sometimes we are not aware that we are running from change or that we are afraid. We see the opposite and cling to what is familiar and comfortable, because we can. The longer we stay with what is comfortable, the less we will be able to face the new or—heaven forbid—unprecedented conditions. We cling to the sameness and do not believe we are clinging until we lose it; then, all we see is the loss. That, too, is change. It is not just the imposition; it can be the removal.

Think of the many things that can change, allowing us to lose what we have or get what we don't want. Do you know how often such change is imposed on each person daily? Every second of every minute, change is building somewhere. We may not see the effect until it builds up to a certain level. Do you not think that, before a storm, there is not a build-up of air movement at the molecular level, or temperature change at an imperceptible level, or humidity?

When we do not know how to appreciate the subtle nuances that *will* build into an effect, we can leave ourselves vulnerable. And when we're vulnerable, we can easily fail or spend extra effort trying to prevent, conceal or disregard the failure we could have prevented, if we only knew how.

Anger, drug abuse, prescription drug use, alcoholism, complacency, manipulations, anxiety, depression, phobias and fears, codependency—these are all ways we use to try to stop change or turn away from the effects when they come. Any of these can happen to anybody. But all of these factors can be prevented or even reversed by getting the mental strength to face change comfortably, purposefully and creatively.

If we wish to be better prepared for anything, we should first understand it. When you have something to do that you do not understand, it often appears huge and formidable. When you understand it, it seems small and manageable. Yet it has not changed—what changed was your understanding. It seems that there are always two ways to create balance and enjoy contentment when there is disruption: one is to stop the disruption; the other is to move with it. We have grown up thinking that we have or are getting the resources to stabilize life, and we often direct all our energies toward procuring and using them. We believe it is easier to fix life than to move with it, yet the reverse is truer. It is far easier to adapt to life, and far more rewarding to do so, than to work at stabilizing the world. What we also do not recognize is that if we ever succeed in stabilizing life, the boredom will be so intense that it will offer a greater discomfort than the change we succeeded in taming.

Let us look at change and attempt to understand it from a logical, rational position. If we do, we will first see that there are three distinct areas in everyone's life from which change evolves. One of these is nature, or the material environment. Another is the body, or the personal biological environment. The third is people, or the social environment.

THE PHYSICAL ENVIRONMENT: VAST AND CONSTANTLY CHANGING

As a human being, you relate to your physical environment using five special instruments called senses. If you can see something, hear it, touch it, taste it or smell it, you know that it is there. It is the only way in which you can be aware of the material world and function within it. Without those senses, you may as well be dead.

When something to which you can relate, or which you can measure with your senses, has changed, and that change can be picked up by those instruments, then you are aware of the change. When that change cannot be measured by those instruments, you are not aware of the change even if it has occurred. These senses are sophisticated instruments, yet they are far from perfect.

Just think: you may be able to read the words on this page. However, between this page and your eyes, there are billions of small particles. These particles may be microbes, dust particles or even the molecules of air. We know now that these are real entities even though we did not think so in ancient times. You know that they are real because if there are enough of them joined together, and they form a large enough mass, you will see the mass. Yet you cannot see these small particles. You cannot see a fungus as a microbe, for instance. But if there is a large quantity of these small microbes on a piece of food, you will see the mass. Many people are familiar with the telltale greenish discoloration on a piece of bread that they know to be fungus.

If change occurs at the level of these submicroscopic entities, you cannot be aware of change—at least not until it has accumulated to the stage at which your senses can be stimulated. Even now, change must be taking place in the chair you are occupying or in the floor on which that chair rests. It is because of these invisible changes that you eventually will see the process of aging, the fading of colour in the material, the accumulation of dust on the floor or even the breakdown of supporting structures from the process of wear and tear.

Do you not think that before an earthquake, there is not a buildup of gradual, accumulative changes in the earth's crust? In fact, you know for sure that this is the case. These changes are caused by activities that, in isolation, cannot be recognized by your imperfect instruments. When these activities have caused sufficient change in the objects you can measure, only then can you recognize their presence.

WHY WE ARE USUALLY UNPREPARED FOR CHANGE IN THE MATERIAL ENVIRONMENT

The ability to be aware of all the activities that are occurring in even the most isolated area of this world can be enough to torture any person. Can you imagine how difficult it would be to live in this world if your eyes were accurate enough to let you see everything that exists in the space before them? You would not be able to recognize anything beyond those that are immediately before your eyes. An instrument that is too sensitive can thus be a severe disadvantage; then, the old adage of not being able to see the forest for the trees will take on a truly realistic meaning.

Think about sound. Perhaps while reading this, you may listen carefully to sounds you have not been hearing because they are occurring at a subliminal level. Then you may even imagine the discomforts you will experience if your ears can hear more than those sounds—the chirping of every insect, the squeaking of every joint or the rumble of every breeze. You never will be able to focus on anything important while there is such constant interference from all the activities that are present. Yet no isolated area can begin to reveal even the smallest percentage of the vast range of activities that are occurring in all parts of this immense and varied environment.

WHAT HAPPENS IF YOU IGNORE THE PRESENCE OF THESE ACTIVITIES

You might ask, "Why, then, are these activities allowed to continue unchallenged so that our comfort can be disrupted and our safety threatened? Why can we not use the universal intelligence of mankind and create a dust-free, microbe-free environment that stays familiar and stable?" To some readers, these may be seen as superfluous questions. To many others, however, they are logical and worth consideration. We may not always see the problems in the way they are described by these questions. We do, however, go about trying to rid the world of a particular disease, to establish a homogeneous society or to create materials that will not disintegrate.

You must remember that in the early 1950s, dream designs of the home of the future were suggested with the promise that the next generation would not have to work at keeping the house clean, cooking or washing utensils. They had visions of robots or automatic machines that would provide those opportunities. Theoretically, when the familiar and comfortable environment was disrupted, we would be able to discard the changed material and replace it with a refreshed version of the original. The throwaway society was born.

People did not see this as hanging on to stability. In fact, many people saw it as being capable of accepting change. If you examine it, you will see instead that it was their changing of the changed material so that a sameness could be restored. We have learned, however, that these invisible activities accumulate and stay with us, and more will happen to make tomorrow even more unpredictably different from today than today was from yesterday.

You are seeing the shattering of the utopian dream: pollution that has arisen from accumulated unseen discards, the greenhouse effect from unseen accumulations of carbon dioxide. These are not new things; they have always been there. We have allowed them to accumulate because we believed that, by hiding the change, we would not have to deal with it. Now we have so much of it to deal with that it has become an unmanageable stress on us. You can see that we cannot create such a utopian environment—one that is stable, secure or persistently familiar— because we cannot eliminate those invisible but powerful activities that constantly change it. You also know that we cannot presume that just because we cannot see these activities, they do not exist.

Change is the reason for Heraclitus's statement, "No man swims the same river twice." He said this in about 400 BC, and he was known as Heraclitus the Obscure because of his apparently abstruse thinking.

Think of it: if you can accept the constant and random fluidity of this environment, you will be able to expect the change that it assuredly will bring to your more familiar tasks and structures. Then you will learn to allow your surprise to be generated only when that change does not arise.

THE BODY: A BIOLOGICAL MARVEL IN A DELICATE AND CONSTANTLY CHANGING BALANCE

Take your body as another example. Do you know how much activity is going on in it at this very moment? You can't. Whatever you surmise is only a guess. There is no way for you to know what has happened to the last meal you have eaten—whether it has already been digested, if it is still in the stomach or where in the intestine it may be now. You cannot know what is going on, simply because there are no instruments directed at the inside of your body to tell you this. You may know that your heart is beating because you can place your hand over it and feel the beat. Until you do that or some other action to bring the heartbeat to the outside, it remains an activity that is hidden from you.

Yet, it is good that we cannot be aware of all of these activities. Imagine the severe disadvantage you would have if you were allowed to be aware of all the activities that are occurring in your body at any time. You will not only be confused by problems you cannot fix, but you will make matters worse by interfering with something that might never have become a full problem. You may react in panic if you can "see" the terrifying appearance of an invading bacterium, a task that is handled with calm reassurance by the body's defence system. You may become totally incapacitated when you realize an injury that the body's defences will heal in the course of normal use. You may become entirely confused by the multilevel adjustments that have to be made to the circulatory system to carry the body from the lying, standing and moving positions.

Ponder what the body constantly goes through to heal the numerous insults that the world throws at it every day. You only have to think of the healing process of a broken bone or that of a bruised skin and then realize that this process goes on every day in some internal part of the body, where the injuries are hidden from you. Before the body's threshold has been reached for you to experience the pain of an injured ankle, for example, there will have been small injuries that must have

6

been inflicted on that ankle in the course of your many movements about your environment; the body healed those injuries automatically. Before the pains of an ulcer have been realized, the walls of the stomach will have been repeatedly injured and healed by the body's defence system. If you were to respond with such confused and frequently inappropriate reactions to these events when you are made aware of them, you would see how inappropriate your reactions might be to the normal daily challenges that constantly affect the function of the body.

Muscular Movement: More Than a Simple Force of Tension

Take your muscle cells as an example. They provide you with the ability to move. That is a special function—it is so special that the same group of cells that can allow you to lift a heavy bag of groceries must also be able to let you play a coordinated game of tennis or do a delicate task such as signing your name. What other sophisticated machine can do that? A forklift can move a heavy crate, but it cannot also be used to toss a salad or pack a carton of eggs. In the same way, a machine designed to type a letter cannot also be expected to hammer nails into a piece of wood. This may seem to be an unnecessary argument, but we often expect performance from our muscles that we do not expect from other seemingly more capable instruments.

Have you ever had to do a delicate task such as signing your name after doing something heavy and demanding with your muscles, such as lifting a heavy crate? You may discover a phenomenon called post-tetanic potentiation. Your hand trembles, and you cannot direct a smooth movement at your wrist. It is then that you may realize what constant adjustments are required of those cells that form the muscles—adjustments that originate from activities at the submicroscopic level to allow you the convenience of versatility almost at demand. There are many other functions in the body that depend on an even more sophisticated balancing of activity—blood pressure, as an example—in the vast range of movements through which we must take our bodies.

Why It Is Important for You to Be Aware of These Activities

Can you not imagine, then, that with this great amount of activity that is taking place even while you sleep, there is a great chance that some small imbalance occurring in some isolated area can cause you to experience an unaccustomed pain, unexpected exhaustion or hindered performance? Who can say that there is not, at this very moment, an imbalance of part of the defence system causing a clot to be released into the bloodstream and make its way to your heart? Will it be such a surprise to have that tireless coordination of your circulation fail for one split second and cause you to faint when you stand up? Why do we always expect that these multitudes of small activities will always function so accurately that when something goes awry, we are ready to condemn ourselves as weak and seek remedies to remove that undesired weakness?

In fact, we should learn to accept that multiple changes are constantly occurring within that apparently solid entity we know as our body. We should know that so much change goes on within it that at no time is the body at the same stage of development or health as it might have been a moment earlier. In the same way, we cannot expect a certain stage of development or a level of health for some time in the future. If it is there, we should appreciate it. We could try to influence its presence, however, we should not expect it. Yet we do. We should appreciate the amount of different conditions that must be met in order for our bodies to complete any function, and we should be more tolerant of it when it fails and more appreciative of it when it functions as expected.

PEOPLE: A FREELY MOBILE AND INDEPENDENTLY GENERATED SOURCE OF CHANGE

If you can accept that you cannot be aware of the subtle activities that generate physical change because of the limitations of your instruments, and if you can accept that you cannot become aware of the submicroscopic activities that generate biological change because of the added problem of their being hidden from your instruments, then you are ready to consider the existence of an even less recognizable source of activity that can generate a whole host of new and unprecedented change: this is the constant, pervasive and absolutely invisible activity of human thought.

People cause change too. You know that all too well. In fact, the most annoying type of change that can be imposed on you is that brought on by another person, especially one who exerts significant authority. It may be a change of opinion or allegiance from a person whose support or endorsement you need. It may be an activity directed at changing conditions within your common environment, increasing your workload, causing you to lose something you like or to have to deal with something you do not like. It may be an activity that changes your biological health. He or she may inflict injury or remove a necessary sustenance.

On the other hand, that person can soothe an injury, reduce workload or provide necessary sustenance. He or she can bring support that was not there or create an environment that is more suitable to your needs.

Whether it is a change of a good situation into a bad one or a bad into a good, it still is change. And if that change is caused by the action of another person interfering with the natural course of events, it is "people change."

WHY YOU ARE USUALLY UNPREPARED FOR CHANGE CAUSED BY PEOPLE

Think of being in a room with a group of other people. Do you know how much activity is going on? You cannot. You may presume that all attention is focused on a common topic, be it the speaker, an event or a task. Yet all you have is that perception. At best, you may be right for a small minority of the group.

Some of those people may be thinking of any small aspect of the common environment that strikes their fancy. This can be as simple a variation as the stance of the speaker, the colour of the hair of the person in front of them, a spot on the wall or a vast range of other trivia. Some people's thoughts may be directed at the words the speaker may be saying, or they may be diverted by a memory stimulated by something said or suggested.

You may yourself have experienced a situation when, although you may be following the direction of the other person's ideas intently, some phrase or description allows you to reminisce on an experience you may have had in the past. It may be the description of a town or country, which reminds you of a long-forgotten holiday. It may be the reference to a bank, which may have reminded you that you did not mail the rent cheque that month. At these reminders, your thoughts may digress onto subjects that are unrelated to the discussion at hand.

Some of these people may be focused on a discomfort within their bodies, an experience that they cannot share with anyone else. It may be as simple as a need to go to the bathroom or as complex as the concern that a pain they may be experiencing in the chest can be a heart attack. They may not even be focused on anything, preferring to lapse into a state of unawareness because of exhaustion or boredom.

Any or all of these activities may be taking place, yet there is no way that you can measure them, simply be aware of them or find out where they are directed, for that matter. Many researchers have used various means to guess at other people's thoughts. All of their efforts have been influenced by nothing more than pure speculation. The pallor of a person's cheek, the movement of that person's eyes, the fluctuations of that person's pulse or blood pressure—all indicate only that a change is taking place. Usually these changes are associated with the body's reactions to a pressure that has been imposed on it from the environment.

If there is no observable pressure from the environment, the presence of these changes may suggest that the activity that influenced these changes comes from a source not readily obvious: the other person's thoughts. This may be true. Then again, we know that there are subtle activities within the material environment that are not necessarily obvious but against which the body automatically has to defend itself. Regardless of whether they arise from the person's thoughts, they still do not indicate what those thoughts may be or what may be influencing them.

Like any other change caused by an activity that you cannot measure, other people's hidden thoughts can cause troublesome change. Until a person chooses to express his or her thoughts, those thoughts remain hidden within the person. When those thoughts are expressed, the change they impose is not necessarily related to other readily identifiable events or even the expected progress of existing conditions. That change can be a totally new and unexpected action. The thoughts are hidden, and they are generated from such a wide range of activities that no one can determine with any presumption of accuracy what may be influencing those thoughts. If you also cannot determine what those thoughts are or how much of those thoughts, if any, will be expressed by that person, then it remains an indisputable fact that you never will be able to prepare yourself for the change that another person can perpetrate on you or on the common environment you share with that person. This goes from the boardroom to the bedroom, and as we have been experiencing recently, the action of someone with a terrorist ambition or personal grudge.

WHY YOU SHOULD NOT BE EXPOSED TO ALL OF THE ACTIVITIES THAT FORM OTHER PEOPLE'S THOUGHTS

Just as you are spared the limitations that can arise from being able to experience all the activities that are occurring in nature between you and the subject you wish to observe; just as you are spared the frustration that can arise if you are able to experience the activities the body must evoke in order to maintain its integrity in a changing environment; so, too, you are spared the immense confusion that can take place if you truly were able to experience the multifarious thoughts that people constantly activate. One of the most delightful activities that we can enjoy as human beings is that of communicating with other people. One of the most interesting challenges in which we can indulge, and one that stimulates our most superior talents of reason and logic, is that of exploring and analyzing the thoughts and intents behind an action that another person expresses. The excitement that can be elicited when you have the opportunity to learn from the ideas that another person has been able to develop from his or her experiences and extrapolate into his or her thoughts has no equal.

Imagine how irritated and disappointed you will be to have to go through the trouble to develop some elaborate or intricate plan if everyone else will know about it before you reveal it. How bored would you be if you could communicate with your spouse or friend so easily that before that other person expresses himself or herself, you know what he or she is about to say? There would be no need for you to communicate with the other person; you would already be familiar with whatever that person has to say to you, and he or she would no longer be a challenge or even a source of inspiration to you.

11

How You Know That These Activities Exist

Yet you cannot know that this activity of thought exists! Mankind has developed instruments to measure the presence of submicroscopic particles that form the elements. We have instruments to allow us to measure some of the activities that take place within the body. We even are able to measure the presence of activities that are too small or too transient by measuring the effects of their presence. Yet we have not been able to develop anything that measures the presence of a person's thoughts, or even if that person is thinking. The nearest we have reached is to measure brain wave patterns. Still, we have not been able to associate these with the presence, absence or degree of thought activity. However, you know that the human being thinks, because you can think yourself. You cannot conclude that the other person thinks similarly to you; you can presume it, but that is where it remains, a presumption.

There is something, however, that we have learned to associate with thought. In fact, it is this association that has allowed us to presume that the human being is the only mammal who has a highly developed intelligence. This association is the expression of creative ideas. When a person thinks, he or she has the ability to express a solution to a problem; the result of thinking is the expression of a new idea, not just the revelation of a learned trivia or a practiced response. Any computer or tape recorder can express a range of stored information. Any dog can express a learned response without doing any more than it has been repeatedly taught. Any wild animal can do a complex task by instinct without adapting that response to the great variations that are imposed on it by the changing environment.

The human being, on the other hand, will express something that varies according to the challenge that stimulates the response. We build a house that withstands the freezing cold of the Canadian winter differently from how we build a house that must protect us from the hot monsoons in India.

The Power of the Immeasurable Activity of Thought

Look around you. Every man-made material, every activity that can be controlled by the human being has evolved from the activity of thought. Sure, the basic materials have always been there because mankind can never create something from nothing. However, the ways that the materials have been rearranged to satisfy some useful purpose have all emanated from the activity of thought. The activity of thought may not directly affect these materials; the designs for their rearrangements, however, are the direct results of thought.

The metal that forms a car has always been just a piece of metal, until the concepts formed by the activity of thought allows it to be transformed first into the metal and then into an internal combustion engine. Anthropologists have observed that without such activity, all life forms remain at the mercy of the elements. Those that use only the materials that are available, never shaping or forming them, usually become extinct when those materials have been used up or when they are no longer able to help withstand the elements. Jacob Bronowski, a famous mathematician and biologist and the author of both a book and television series called *The Ascent of Man*, made these observations and showed the difference between instinct in the most sophisticated animals and creativity in man.[1]

If the activity of thought gives rise to the ability to change something else, then thought must be more powerful than that other activity. You know that the activity of the elements is a powerful activity. Therefore, thought must also be a powerful activity. Yet, not only is thought powerful, it is a tirelessly constant activity.

You cannot know when someone else is thinking; therefore you cannot know whether they are *not* thinking. You can, however, know that you are thinking. You know that you are always thinking, even when some observer may believe that you are not. Even when you are asleep, the activity of thought continues. REM sleep, or rapid eye movement sleep, has been associated with the activity of dreaming, yet this may be totally erroneous. If no one can determine the activity of thought when you are awake, and if they also cannot measure it when you are asleep, how can it be presumed that REM sleep occurs when you are dreaming? This, then, can only be a presumption.

The activity of thought is so private, so personal, that it can continue tirelessly as that hidden activity until you are ready to expose it. That

---

1   Jacob Bronowski, *The Ascent of Man* (British Broadcasting Corporation, 1973).

is a powerful force. Even the elements do not have such power; their activities are fully exposed to the materials they can affect. They do not have the advantage of surprise. The materials they affect, therefore, have the opportunity to develop a resistance to the effects of these activities. The activity of thought, on the other hand, does not have to be exposed until the appropriate solution has been devised. This is why we have been able to develop materials that are equal to the pressures imposed on them by the elements, and why we can use them for some time before the elements can destroy those materials. The hidden nature of your thoughts, however, is what allows you to have the ability to gather information until you are satisfied that you can solve a problem without the disadvantage of being contradicted at each stage in the development of that solution. This is a powerful force. If you can accept that power is not only the ability to overwhelm the opposition but can also be the ability to withstand all that the opposition can throw at you, then you will accept that the activity of thought is a force of tremendous power.

WHY YOU NEED PEOPLE'S THOUGHTS AS INDEPENDENT ACTIVITIES

Even though people's thoughts are private, and even though that privacy can cause those people to be formidable forces against you just as they are powerful forces in the environment, you need those activities. Imagine what you would have if that activity did not occur in the people who preceded you in this world. Not only will you be unable to enjoy the toys and instruments that are available for you to use, you will also have little on which to build. If Albert Einstein did not have the benefit of Newtonian algebra or Euclidian geometry, then he could not have developed the more advanced theories of relativity. If instead you had to experience everything personally, you would be so busy reinventing the wheel or rediscovering fire that you would not have any time or opportunity to expand your knowledge. Therefore, the only way that you can truly increase your visions is to take into account the privately developed ideas of other people. Here, the old adage, "It is a wise man who learns even from the fool," makes good sense.

Mankind does not have a universal awareness. You are an individual, and you possess individually generated activities of thought. You share those thoughts at your personal discretion. It is this ability to develop ideas privately and share them at a certain stage of their development that has allowed mankind to be such a powerful force in this vast and formidable environment.

WHY IT IS IMPORTANT TO BE AWARE OF THE EXISTENCE OF THE INDEPENDENT ACTIVITY OF THOUGHT

Great: so people think, and these thoughts are activities that are occurring privately within them, which will be there whether or not you are concerned about them. If that is the case, why bother to try to understand something that was there before you learned about it and which will continue to be there just as independently despite all of your attempts to understand it?

The obvious answer is that although the activity of thought is private, the expression of that thought affects the common environment. The expression of thought, therefore, is a source of change. The activity of thought is the generator of that change. Just as with change that occurs from the activity of the elements, change that comes from the expression of another person's thoughts can disturb or even destroy that which you have grown to know and enjoy. Remember that when a person expresses his or her thoughts, that person is expressing a solution for a part of the vast environment that he or she sees more deeply than another; remember, the power of thought is intensity, not immensity. Appreciate that the imposed change may also be a solution for some problem that you may not have seen within that familiar environment. By appreciating that even as experienced by other people, thought is a private and intense activity, you will be able to accept that the change they can create is not necessarily bad or dangerous. It is a different perspective on a world that is itself in a state of constant change, one that needs change in order to exist. You also will be able to accept that the only way you can get both depth and scope in your understanding of this vast and beautiful world is by fuelling your thoughts with the challenges you derive from the expressions of other people's thoughts.

SUMMARY

It is important to know how pervasive change can exist—not to be neurotic about its presence, but to be aware of it. Ignorance about the presence of something does not preclude its existence. It only makes it less obvious … to you.

This monograph, then, is intended to alert you to the depth of things that are constantly occurring so that, when the accumulated effects are presented to you, you will be better prepared to address them. It is the person who is not taken by surprise who is more capable of adjusting his or her approach to address a new situation confidently. This change evolves from these distinct sources: matter, or the physical reality; the body, or the biological reality; and other people's independently generated thoughts, or the social reality. However, you do not have to examine every material for the expected deterioration, your body for every discomfort or weakness, or your associates for every change of opinion. It is sufficient only to know that these changes are natural so that when they occur, you will know that they do not represent any personal affront to you or any indication that you have been incompetent.

You also must be aware that as much as things may change in directions that are alien to your desires, further change can take them back to their original states or to more acceptable directions. In other words, change as a continuous activity can bring more acceptable conditions as much as it can cause unacceptable ones to evolve. Remember this when dealing with the opinions and allegiances of other people, your own health or the normal activities that make your tasks difficult and sometimes unrewarding.

CHAPTER 2

The Resources You Have for
Dealing with Change

The human being is a singular creature. We are more than the mere mass of protoplasm that you observe to be shaped into a mobile form with limbs, muscles to move those limbs and a brain to direct those muscles. We are thinking, creative existents with feelings and understanding.

We are able to use reason and logic to relate to the world. With the ability to think, we can plan and create solutions to new problems. We can move and shape the world in ways that seem limited only by our personal vision. We can do this along paths that are completely divergent from the natural paths. As human beings, we are able to conquer whatever new challenges the environment can throw at us— and survive them. As an example, the human being has developed the ability to build houses to live in, adapting them to the various weather conditions we have to occupy. Humans have invented pots in which we cook and plates on which we eat. We have developed cars and planes to carry us over great distances, medicines to treat us and computers and other machines to work for us. We have been able to do this without evolving into a distinctly separate species. Each person has the capacity to learn to do any combination of these activities.

On the contrary, other creatures are forced into an existence that is totally dependent on the whims of their environment. Inanimate objects react; they have an effect on the environment just by being in the path of some external activity. However, we do not change our environment purely by reaction. Instinct can allow a spider to spin an intricate web, but a spider will spin a web within a predictable range in which any other member of its species will function. Instinct allows a bee to build a hive that is geometrically the most ideal for its function, but a bee does not attempt to improve on it. What a bee does is no different from what another bee of the same species will do.

Instinct can allow a beaver to gnaw a tree and build a dam, yet a beaver does not take measurements of water flow, detailed observations of high and low watermarks or comparative assessments of the durability of different trees in order to keep improving her dam-building techniques. She simply fells the nearest tree and builds a dam. By such instinct, a beaver in northern Canada will do what a beaver in the American Midwest will do—no more, no less. We, on the other hand, do not create our effects because of instinct alone.

Some mammals that have been considered to be higher in the evolutionary scale have been observed to teach their young certain tricks of healthy survival, which have been passed down each succeeding generation. Yet, after leaving home, the adult will not be much different from another adult of a previous generation, and she will teach the same to her young, and so on.

I am not saying that other species do not adapt to the demands of the environment. They certainly do. A dog, for example, will learn to respond differently from another dog of the same breed in a different home environment. The point, however, is that the dog can learn only as much as it is taught, either by the owner or by the demands from the immediate environment. It does not create new ideas.

THE INTELLIGENT SPECIES

The human being thinks, and thinking is an act of creativity, the use of reason and logic to effect a conclusion. You know that the human being thinks because what is revealed by a person is not just a learned response to a stimulation from the environment, a predetermined conclusion or the reaction from blind instinct. Rather, what comes out of a human being as a result of this act of thinking is a new course of action, one that has been determined specifically for the problem which that person is addressing.

What sets you apart from other animal species is this fact: each new generation of humans does not simply follow on the discoveries and teachings of the previous generation. Instead, as a human being, you use what you are taught only as the base from which you build new and more elaborate ideas. Look at the book you are reading: Both the ink and the paper on which it is printed are improvements on those used in the past generations, and they are far more sophisticated than the parchments used in the Dead Sea Scrolls or the papyrus in Egyptian writings.

It is this ability to think, this capacity for reason and logic that sets you apart from other species and defines you as Homo sapiens. It is the ability to assess an unknown and to understand it, the dynamically active force that seems to become stronger the more it is used, that gives you the power to deal with the demands your changing world throws at you.

You probably are aware of present concerns about artificial intelligence, so you wonder why there is so much fuss about something that you may share with an electronic device. However, you must not interpret artificial intelligence as being artificial reason and logic. Artificial intelligence is the ability to compare the application of new information against stored and dynamically updated patterns. As new computer chips (which can do hundreds of parallel functions over one small circuit) are developed, the speed of computation, and therefore the amount of considerations that will be possible over a given time, will increase dramatically. Then choices will be made from such a large amount of new information and tested against such a large array of stored patterns that comparative decision making will probably be done more effectively by the computer than by the human.

This is not the act of thinking, though. Thinking is more than the consideration of all the possible permutations within a fixed parameter that pertain to an existing challenge—as, for instance, the movements on a chess board. It is more than the ability to choose the most appropriate response from a series of different bits of information stored from previous observations. It is the ability to originate new ideas, create new insights and explore new opportunities.

A QUESTION OF VALUE

If you will recognize a very simple axiom, you will be able to understand what is perhaps the most important factor in the human being's search for survival. Something exists only as long as it remains the thing that it was in the first place. If it has been changed from its original condition, then it is something else; the original object no longer exists.

Inanimate objects have value only if they are capable of satisfying what can be expected of them while still being those objects. This is why apparently similar objects can have very different values. An expensive oak desk has a structure that allows it to function as a useful desk longer than, say, a cheap imitation made from particle board.

The value of some other things can be determined by parameters that are less stable. For example, the value of an explosive charge is not related to how stable it is as much as its degree of instability. The underlying inference is that the value of anything is determined by how well it is able to satisfy the expectations placed on it.

One thing that we hold true about ourselves is that we are individuals. We are just the object we appear to be. Unlike the inanimate object, we have no value just by being. Our value is not measured by how long we can remain intact as a visible object without being destroyed, but by our ability to think and contribute our unique ideas. The value of the human being, therefore, is based on what we can do, what we can contribute to this world. It is this value that has to be satisfied, and when it's satisfied, it gives us the feeling of importance, value or worth.

Look around. Nearly every human being has what you seem to have: two arms, two legs and a torso. Yet they are just tools that each person develops to different levels of usefulness. Some people cannot use them at all; some people have shapelier bodies, prettier faces or longer legs. Yet, as you know, these attributes are only skin deep. A beautiful girl or handsome man who just sits there has little value, and his or her beauty wears thin after a while. Your value is more than just being, more than just existing.

Of course, you already know that you are not just that body by which you are recognized. Thank goodness for that. One thing you know about the body is that, from the time it has been conceived, it starts to break down; perhaps not visibly from the outside, but from the inside. You do not wave good-bye to part of yourself whenever you flush the toilet. You do not reduce yourself as a person whenever you clip your nails and throw the clippings into the garbage. As a human being, you are more than the physical body; you are a thinking, creative mind.

It is the mind that makes you unique. It is the mind that makes you the individual even in a community of homogeneous people, and even next to your identical twin. It is the mind that grows and becomes stronger while the physical body deteriorates through its limited life span.

A Search for Identity

You do not get up in the morning and check with the mirror to determine if the person who is reflected is really you; you know that it is you. If, when you check in the mirror, you see a body that you do not recognize as the one you had the day before, your reaction will not be, "Who is this person?" Rather, you will wonder what happened to your body. You know yourself not by your body but by your awareness, that mind. Think for a moment. You know your thoughts and can change your thoughts. In fact, you may have changed them already by reading this page and starting to think about changing your thoughts. David Bohm, reputed to be one of the most influential physicists of the 20th century, commented, "When we try to analyze our thought processes, that is, think about thinking, we, of necessity, alter what it is we are thinking about."[2]

One fact you know about yourself is that you were born without the range of insight and awareness you have now. You are born knowing nothing, and the mind becomes stronger as you grow. Another thing you know is that even if your body has become bigger and stronger since birth, the tissues of an adult will have become older and less resilient than those of a child. Each attribute seems to be moving in independently opposite directions, one getting more powerful while the other gets weaker. They must, therefore, be two distinct entities.

You also will recognize that there are times when you are physically exhausted while being in high spirits mentally (e.g., after winning a strenuous game), and that even if you are physically rested, when you

---

2   D. Bohm, *Quantum Theory* (Englewood Cliffs, NJ: Prentice-Hall, 1951), 170.

receive depressing news, you still will become mentally distressed. Can this happen if one state is a function of the other? If so, will not the hormone or chemical that produces the mental effect be as exhausted as the rest of the body? Will it not also be as recharged as other chemicals will be when the body is rested? If these two states can function so independently of each other, won't they have to be two distinct states? If you have chosen to protect or promote one in preference to the other, or to push the other when they both are exhausted, then you will have established not only that you recognize their distinct natures, but that you identify with one over the other. In the case of the human condition, you will find that it is easier to push yourself to do something if you are physically exhausted but mentally refreshed than you can if you are mentally depressed but physically rested. You also will recognize that if you are both physically exhausted and mentally depressed you will be more inclined to seek help for your mental state in preference to your physical state, if only one can be addressed.

We must conclude, then, that you are not a body with a mind. That is, the body does not have or possess a mind. A mind, identified as the self, cannot be a tool. Though it is invisible, the mind has to be the master, not the slave or a function of the body. If the soul is also that part of the human existence that is not visible on the outside, and that promotes the person to being a superior species, then it will have to be that entity that we also refer to as the mind. We then can say that you do not have a soul—rather, you *are* a soul, or a mind. You do not *have* a soul or mind. *You,* the soul, have a body.

That is why you compete. That is why you push your body, your tool, to show that you can accomplish a goal even when it hurts your body. It is because you are not the body; you are a mind that uses the body. You have nails; they are tools as part of the body. When you lose a nail, you are no less a person. You simply lose a part of a tool. Thus, the body is not you. The accent is on the definition of the pronoun *you.* You are not what we see, the body. You are the essence. The body is your means of revealing that essence and connecting with the physical reality.

This is not an argument for dualism. Rather, it is monism of a special brand. Richard Dawkins, in his book *The God Delusion*, argues that dualism cannot be acceptable. He suggests that the human form is proven to have evolved through natural selection. "A monist believes that mind is a manifestation of matter."[3] This is not necessarily so. The monist can also accept the existence of mind as the existent. The body is just a tool; it is not part of the human being.

Therefore, what I am suggesting is that the human being is not a mind with a body or a body with a mind. It is a mind, and just that. We use the body like a driver uses a car. There is a driver and there is a car. The driver needs the car to get to a destination. The car needs the driver to direct it. There is no driver-car. The body, the more readily identified form, is not you. It is part of the physical universe and will conform to the laws of the physical universe. This does not necessarily relegate the mind to being some ethereal substance, but it suggests that, as an entity, it must exist outside of the limitations of matter. Evan Harris Walker, a renowned physicist with the Ballistic Research Laboratories of the US Army, offered a logical observation.

> *The physical world (that described by certain type of measurement) is not the totality of the real world. If there are other kinds of measurements, independently of physical measurements, and it appears that there are, and if the physical world of necessity requires all that it contains to be measurable, and it does, there must exist both physical reality and nonphysical reality.*[4]

Stephen Hawking suggested that the universe expanded from the Big Bang. Earth was an effect of that activity—it was not created by God. God may have created the Big Bang.[5] This has been compared to a young boy with an ant farm: he set it up and provided the ingredients, but the ant and the expansion of the ant farm went on naturally.

Dawkins and Hawking are right. The body evolved. This does not exclude the mind as a nonphysical existent, and therefore it does not exclude God as a nonphysical existent; similarly, it cannot prove it. How can we prove the existence of one thing by defining it according to another? The mind or soul is not an extension of the body. It exists and it is the person. Jean Paul Sartre, in his book *Being and Nothingness*, talked

---

3   Richard Dawkins, *The God Delusion* (New York: Bantam Press, 2006).

4   Evan Harris Walker, "The Nature of Consciousness," *Mathematical Biosciences* 7 (1970): 149.

5   Stephen Hawking, *A Brief History of Time* (Bantam, 1988).

about the essence. "The appearance does not hide the essence, it reveals it; it is the essence."[6] This statement requires some interpretation. The important, or perhaps the more identifiable element is the appearance or what we project of ourselves. But is that all there is to us? I show me. What I show reveals me—that is, what I wish to reveal of me. It cannot, therefore, be all of me. We are not looking for the person as a function of the body. We are looking for the person through the things he or she does to display self (e.g., expressions and performance), and that is a fraction, a chosen manifestation of the person.

THE HUMAN DILEMMA

We have seen that the value of any object is its ability to be useful within its limitations, or better yet, to be able to exceed those limitations. We have seen that the human being is more than just a blob of flesh. You are a mind and can think. Therefore, your value must be related to that specific function. You already know that. Whether you have expressed it or not, your main desire is to be respected for the contribution of your mind, not just of your body.

Inanimate objects and other life forms can function comfortably within defined limitations. A flower is a complete flower if it blooms, produces pollen and is able to turn toward the sun. A worker bee has fulfilled its purpose if it gathers nectar, a spider if it spins a web like that of other spiders of the same species. Even the ape and dolphin (species that are considered to be more intelligent than many others), by doing the simple tasks we teach them, can demonstrate that they are able to exceed the limits that define what an ape or dolphin has evolved to be able to do. These objects and life forms, by having a limit, can at least function contentedly within those limits.

You, on the other hand, are an invisible mind and have no measurable limits to tell you that you have reached your fullest potential. Because that mind is a growing entity that can be as great as you train it to be, there is no fixed parameter that can tell you whatever you have achieved is the peak of your potential. Regardless of what you may have achieved, you always will be haunted by the belief that you can do better, that what you have done is not good enough.

---

6   Jean Paul Sartre, *Being and Nothingness* (Washington Square Press, 1956).

One of the greatest minds of science, Sir Isaac Newton, may shed some light on this frustration of the human being. This is even more relevant when we consider that Sir Isaac Newton was acknowledged in some circles as having almost supreme intelligence, and that he was often exemplified as the second coming of the Christ. We may think that he may grow to be arrogant with that distinction, but in his more humble private writings, he said,

"I do not know what I may appear to the world; but to myself I seem to have been only like a boy playing on the seashore, and diverting myself in now and then finding a smoother pebble or a prettier shell than ordinary, while the great ocean of truth lay all undiscovered before me."

Perhaps this sentiment is more simply stated by Albert Einstein, who, when he was complimented by an admirer for being so much more knowledgeable than he, was reported to have said,

"My friend, the difference between what you know and what I know is infinitesimal when compared with the difference between what I know and what I still do not know."

It therefore follows that as a human being, you are obliged to go about forever trying to better your previous achievement, forever wondering if what you are is good enough to satisfy the expectations that you cannot define of an entity that you cannot accurately identify. It is a sad state of affairs to discover that the species that purportedly was created to be masters of the world, to have domain over the lesser creatures, and to "Be fruitful and multiply, and replenish the earth and subdue it; and have dominion over the fish of the sea, and over the fowl of the air, and over every living thing that moveth upon the earth (The Holy Bible authorized King James version, Genesis 1:28)," will so frequently be unhappy and unsure about what he or she has to do, about how worthwhile are his or her accomplishments. The dilemma of the human condition is that the attribute that gives the human being that power, the mind, is so invisible and so inaccessible to conventional means of detection that no one can know with any degree of certainty how capable or how great that mind has become.

25

THE PURSUIT

Because you cannot identify that entity that you know as yourself—and because without knowing that, you cannot define a measure through which you can know when you have achieved your full potential—then what you need is some recognition that what you are or what you have achieved is good enough to be what you should be or should achieve. You need to be accepted, to be considered, to be approved and to be respected. It is a need that permeates every person.

When you get that recognition, acceptance, approval or respect, then you feel good. Call it ego self-esteem, emotions or what you will. The fact is that when you are able to display a competent profile, when the representation you make of yourself to the world is acceptable to that part of the world you are attempting to shape or when it satisfies some authority within it, then you feel good!

Feeling good is a mental experience. You do not feel good in your stomach, toe or head—*you* feel good. That feeling is not localized to any particular part of the body; you already know that such an association cannot exist. You are not a body, not even a part of it. Therefore, what you experience is not a bodily experience. Obviously, when you do not feel good, that bad feeling or absence of good feeling is experienced not in the body but within you, the mind.

To be happy, to be fulfilled and to know that you are good enough to be what you were destined to be—that is your ultimate objective. That is also the objective of every other person, regardless of how he or she elects to attain that objective. You offer your best ideas and put up your best front. You improve on your presentation of yourself. All this is done in order to arrive at that state of being comfortable, of being fulfilled. You can be fulfilled only when you know that what you are is good enough to be what you should be.

Without any other measure, without any other way of knowing that you have satisfied your objective, you must rely on a measure that is as ethereal as the subject it measures: that feeling of fulfilment. One way you know that you can receive that feeling is through the feedback from the world, the feedback of recognition, acceptance, approval or respect. The pursuit, then, is to be able to get recognition for what you can do or show you can do. If, to succeed at that, you must represent yourself to be strong enough to deal with the challenges that draw out the best of you, so be it. Your immediate pursuit then becomes that of discovering the strengths you may have to allow you to make a strong representation of yourself in the issues that challenge you.

You can see the possible directions in which this can lead you. The simple equation is that to be happy or fulfilled, what you show of yourself must be acceptable to the world or that part of it to which you show yourself. Because you are a hidden entity, what you truly are cannot be assessed by the world. What is assessed is that part of your strengths you make visible to the world.

BEAUTY AND STAMINA: YOUR MOST VISIBLE ATTRIBUTES

The sweet, cuddly package that you were when you were born; the resemblance you had to the people who were responsible for your birth, your parents; the human appearance of your body—these all formed the parameters by which you first were assessed. In fact, the very first assessment was made to ensure that you as a baby were truly a human being. From that first observation, the assumption is made that therein lies a person. No one could ever be sure that a baby is a person until that baby starts revealing a personality of its own. Yet the assumption is made simply on the physical, or as I prefer to refer to it, the biological appearance. Without showing any other attributes, with no indication of having something unique to offer the world other than the mere fact that it appears to be a human being, a baby is accepted as a person.

It is no small wonder, therefore, that in the first few years of your life, you see yourself as that body. You see your strengths as the strengths of that body and the skills it can express. You want to grow to be tall, fair, agile, muscular or beautiful. With those attributes, you know that you are as valuable as you can be, or at least valuable enough to be accepted by the world. This is the most visible attribute you have. Sometimes it is the only way through which you can identify yourself. If so, you become stuck at this level of development. You may feel powerful as long as the body continues to grow physically strong, shapely and beautiful; as long as you keep it in an environment that considers it attractive; as long as it continues to function well enough for you to display a comely profile. When it begins to weaken—maybe with age, illness, injury, fatigue or stress—or when you have moved to an environment that does not consider your body attractive or your skills useful, then you can become lost. This, sadly, is the case with a lot of people.

Then again, you may have allowed that strength to be enhanced by another visible identity. Sometimes this can reduce the pressures on the body as your sole attribute. Having a respectable heritage, for example, can be the second most visible attribute you can have, next to physical strength and stamina. In fact, it frequently is the identity by which some people describe themselves. That does not have to be a powerful heritage and can simply be your family of origin: the more the family name is respected in your community, the more easily or powerful is that attribute you use to define your identity. Unfortunately, it too can be diluted by age, become less effective in unfamiliar surroundings or become sullied or tarnished by the effects of outside influences. Then, as a result of losing this attribute or by still being defined by it as it becomes inferior or worthless, you can become lost.

The possession of significant material wealth can be an effective source of visible strength. A wealthy person always seems stronger than a poor person. It is not always what that person does with his or her wealth as much as the fact that he or she has it that makes that person appear strong. Perhaps less personal than a heritage, and much less so than your biological body, material possessions can still be attributes that allow you to receive the recognition, acceptance, approval or respect you desire. Again, its power is relative to the situation in which it is used. Great wealth can be unimportant in some circumstances or even insignificant when the demands are too much greater.

If these external attributes are so strong that you do not have to do any more than just exist, believing that your body will always be attractive, strong or agile; that your good name will always be respected; or that your wealth will always be substantial, then you can easily become complacent and allow your personal development to be retarded. If these are your attributes, is it not obvious that you your strength is dependent on something over which you have little control and which is really no part of you? Is it small wonder, then, that so many wars have been started because of people's fears that their bodies may be hurt, their heritage destroyed or their wealth taken away—and with these, their own identities? Fortunately, many people are not endowed with external strengths that are powerful enough to carry them very far. Usually people discover at an early age that these attributes have limited appeal.

It may be because you were born to a situation that demanded more of you than could be satisfied by passive beauty or specialized skills, personal heritage or inherited wealth. This can happen if, for example, your parents were too busy or too drained to give much attention to you. They may have been willing but were ill-equipped, or they may have been neurotically overprotective, denying you the opportunity to be challenged beyond your developed range for fear that it may hurt you. You may have been encouraged to venture out into the world to a more expansive environment—one that was not easily impressed by your basic appearance, one that did not respect you by your heritage or one that was not impressed by the value of your wealth. For example, you may have had to confront a highly competitive or hostile peer group, an educational system that was geared to stretch you to unfair and overzealous levels of performance or a community that was more interested in their own attributes than to give regard to yours. You could have emerged from within a war-torn community, as is so common today. It may have been because you inherited a body that was considered unattractive or limited by some inherited or acquired malfunctions, a name that was not important or well-respected or possessions that were not considered to be of significant value.

If any of the above occurred in your development, you would have had to look deeper for more strength than you obviously had in the attribute you saw as your identity. You would have had to discover that your strengths are not limited to those things that are of value only relative to the time, the situation or the community.

Yet despite the distinct advantage that people can get by having to develop greater attributes than are provided by their visible strengths, it is customary to hear some people bemoaning the fact that they were at a disadvantage because they did not have the attributes with which another person was born. They also do not recognize that the other person frequently had to rely so totally on those attributes that he or she may not have developed any other attributes, only to be caught thoroughly unprepared when these visible attributes are discovered to be fragile.

It is only when you discover that your physical beauty, skill and stamina may no longer be effective as attributes, when the advantage that you may have had with your heritage dies with those who know its background and when your wealth no longer gives you the strength to stun the opposition that you will recognize the limitations inherent in those attributes that are visible. The more visible they are, the more easily they can be destroyed.

It is only then that some people will become motivated to look deeper and discover more personal attributes. This can happen in your early development if you were given the opportunity to expand your personal attributes. It can happen later in life if you had had the privilege of applying your more visible attributes successfully and then seeing them fail. That may never happen, and you may be condemned to be always searching, always hiding your weaknesses or always being lost in your own existential angst.

Insight and Understanding: Your Deeper, More Personal Attributes

When what you appear to be is not good enough to satisfy the world or that part of it to which you are exposed, you have little choice but to find some other attribute that is more personally yours, to provide you with the means to regain that feeling of worth. You look deeply within yourself for strength that is more useful and more applicable than that which has been rejected as insufficient. When you do so, you discover that you have experience in some areas where other people have difficulty managing. Because of your experience, these particular challenges may seem easy for you to understand and manage. That experience may have allowed you to see those areas of your world more clearly than are visible to the casual observer. You will now have discovered that you have insight and understanding.

The insight you have into these challenges and the understanding you have for their management become new attributes that define you more specifically than you were defined by the more visible attributes with which you were first endowed. You now have attributes that are personally yours. You now have something to offer to the world, something that is more than just what you were given. Like the servant described in the parable of the five talents, you are able to display more than you were given. Suddenly you have a unique attribute. You have insight and the understanding which that insight brings, an attribute you can display to impress your world with your prowess.

Sometimes it becomes all that you need to satisfy others' expectations and earn for yourself the affirmation that comes when what you are is good enough to be what you can be. If so, you may still become stuck at this level of development. You may feel powerful as long as what you know, or what you can show that you know, continues to be greater than what is expected of you, as long as you stay in an environment that expects no more of you than that understanding. Sometimes that insight or understanding may be so powerful in a particular area (as, for example, the ability to do a specialized task or excel at a particular sport, to compute a certain level of mathematics or to remember a certain amount of trivia) that you receive full recognition for what you already have and lose incentive to get more. Fortunately, many people are not endowed with such insight that they are able to go very far without improving it. A more skilful player can make the previously successful athlete look unimpressive. A new wave of trivia can make the information possessed by the most widely read person redundant. New discoveries in the field of science can cause any person's limited knowledge to be obsolete. A new twist to an old problem can make the previous solution redundant.

It is a tempting and very frequently used defence to avoid such fall from grace by staying within those situations that do not grow more demanding. Then some people can be allowed the "privilege" of not having a more capable person show them up. They may never be allowed to be exposed to situations where the trivia they know is obsolete. They may be brought up in such protected environments that they are not challenged by any but the most compatible interpersonal relationships. They may always appear successful and powerful. But they will have lost the opportunity to look deeper and to discover attributes that are even stronger than the personal insights and understanding they have acquired at that stage of their development.

If you have had the good fortune to be challenged to the limits of your personal insight and understanding, you will have learned that no matter how strong they are, these attributes have limitations. They are linear, so to speak, in their growth. You may spend the time and energy gathering insight in the field of medicine. You cannot gather insight in the field of literature at the same time. Given the overlap that is inherent in any field, you still will appreciate the limitations that your insight and understanding has.

It is only when your insight and understanding have been challenged beyond the level to which you have developed them that you will get the opportunity to search for deeper attributes. You will discover that every time you find a deeper attribute, it is something unripe, something you have to nurture into a useful talent. You have to develop it.

REASON AND LOGIC: YOUR MOST FLEXIBLE ATTRIBUTES

When the understanding and insight you have is insufficient to satisfy the demands of some part of your world, you again lose the feedback affirmation that what you are is good enough to be what you can be. This is an important realization: What was once good, what once allowed you to feel proud of you, is now no longer sufficient. You are no longer good enough! The need to feel good, to feel fulfilled, is still paramount in you as in everyone else, and if to restore that good feeling, you must have more of that insight and understanding, or at the least, insight that is appropriate to the situation you must manage, then you have little choice but to go to its source. Wherever you acquired it in the first place must be able to supply you with more, or more appropriate knowledge.

This may seem to be a superfluous argument on the surface. You may see insight and understanding as possessions human beings acquire automatically. That may be so; its growth may be generated simply by exposure. I argue against that but include it for the sake of this discussion. If, however, you need something in greater quantity or at a faster rate than is automatically available, it becomes necessary for you to approach the source and influence its supply. With that in mind, you examine the possible sources.

To examine this automatic acquisition, you must consider some possibilities. One possibility is that you may have been born with knowledge that matures naturally as you grow. Another is that you were endowed with genes that predetermined the insight or potential for insight that you have. Please do not dismiss these as unnecessary considerations. The original purpose for IQ tests was to show that children of the upper classes were better endowed with intelligence than were children of the lower classes. A third possibility is that the insight and understanding you have were provided by the teachers and mentors who trained you; if these are true, they will then be the sources you must explore.

However, you know that you were not born with the insight you have now or with what you had at any stage of your development. In fact, you know that you are much more knowledgeable and insightful now than you were yesterday, and even more so than you were as a child. You know that your insight and understanding did not develop automatically with the maturing of your body or the evolution of your genes. If that was the case, you would have acquired as much insight if you were locked up in your parents' attic for your whole youth as you did being as exposed to the world. You also know that it did not come from the food you ate. Consider a simple metaphor: A woman gives birth to a son. She is a caring mother, but she is an insecure and protective person. She therefore provides all the love and food and connection she can give. She does not take the child out or expose him to other people. As he grows, she builds a beautiful apartment in the attic and keeps him there. Every day, three times a day, she brings a well-balanced meal and stays with him as he eats it. She buys a gym set and teaches him to exercise. She buys a sun lamp and stimulates his vitamin D. He grows strong and healthy for 21 years. Then the mother dies. That day, you and a number of neighbours enter the house and see the apartment in the attic. There is a person in the room, about 21 years old, and he is well nourished. Let's face it. The body is an organic machine. It needs organic fuel to stimulate and replace the organic components. It needs exercise to keep the organ systems working. It needs rest to be able to reboot. If you then take this healthy 21-year-old and place him in the community, he will be lost and will not function appropriately. The mind does not seem to be organic, or at least to be developed from organic ingredients. The mind needs a different kind of nutrition, one that will provide its needs.

You do know, however, that your growth in knowledge and awareness had something to do with the training you had, whether it was given by your parents, friends or traditional teachers at school. Yet if you think about it, you will realize that you had about the same training as did the child who sat next to you at classes. What this points out is that these teachers provided only challenges. In some cases, they may have broken down the challenges into smaller, manageable sizes. This is what differentiates a good teacher from a poor one: how he or she can break down the problem for you to solve.

Twenty children in a class who received the same instruction and who were given the same challenges would not develop the same insight and understanding. One factor to be considered is the attention each one paid to the information. Each person will develop insight on what he or she has been considering, whether it is the face of the girl in the next seat or the dream of making a great play in the next football game. What this reveals is that whatever insights you may have acquired are dependent on how you decide to direct your thoughts.

In short, the person who takes the information from the teacher and works on it will develop greater insight into the subject than the person who simply listens in class and does no further studies. Whoever embraces the information, considers the challenge and thinks of the solution will own the insight. It does not come from the teacher—it comes from within. Is it not logical, therefore, that you are the source of your own insight and understanding? Whatever you have, you put it there. You have no one to thank but yourself; you have no one to depend on but yourself. Yes, it is frequently helpful to receive some of another person's understanding of an issue for you to be able to understand it more thoroughly, but even that understanding is not simply transferred from the other person to you. Whatever you understand must be derived from your reason and logic, your ability to create a personal understanding from the information available. Whenever that other person makes a contribution from his or her understanding, it becomes information. It is understanding and insight only within you, after you think on it and create the insight that is personal to the way you see it. You are the source. You are the thought-energy, the source of reason and logic that provides the insight and understanding with which you represent yourself to the world as a person with a contribution that is unique to you and applicable to those parts of the world to which you have been exposed.

Reason and logic are the result of an activity. The activity is the act of thinking, the act of creativity. By using it, you will have created new attributes, those which you did not have before you created them. This, therefore, is no longer a linear attribute; it is completely flexible.

It is not a possession that has limits to its applications. You can think on anything. In fact, unlike your more visible attributes, or even those that you can make visible by choice (e.g., your insight and understanding), creativity is useful when you are challenged by things that are beyond your developed attributes. You now have determined the source, the generator of useable attributes: you, the thought-energy within that body.

Reason is the act of an engine. Every engine needs fuel as much as it needs raw material or a task, so that it can produce a product. So does the engine of thinking. Thus, as that source of thought-energy, you must need two things for you to function to your full potential. One of these is the challenge that stimulates you; the other is the fuel you need to feed that energy.

The first is easy: challenges are available from the world. They are the problems that are beyond your developed attributes. What you do not understand and what is beyond the vision of your developed insight are challenges that stimulate your act of creativity. But creativity does not always function at its peak. There are times when you are more creative than others, and there times when you are unable to be creative.

Also, creativity is not always challenged. Sometimes, as with your other attributes, you may erroneously have been provided with a stable environment, one that does not require that you create any more understanding and insight than you already have acquired. Then you will have lost out on developing the single resource that makes you into a unique person, a competent human being. This is my greatest fear: nothingness, the total lack of stimulation, the state of redundancy that leaves you stagnant.

However, if you have had those challenges, you will have realized that to stimulate that thought-energy, you needed something else, the fuel that energizes it. Again, you need to find a source, but now it is a source of energy that stimulates your creative activity and gives it efficiency.

YOUR MAJOR LIABILITY: THE NEED FOR AFFIRMATION

When you feel good, you can think. When you are depressed and unfulfilled, you cannot think creatively. This is not an axiom; it only is an observation that you can make about yourself. It has less to do with the state of your physical body than it does with your mental state.

35

We have come to the final source, the energy to fuel the generator that gives you more of the attributes that make you into a competent human being. Where do you get it? Do you remember the "feeling-good feeling" that you get when you know that what you are is as good as what you can be? That is the energy, the inner strength that fuels your creativity. You get it from the recognition, acceptance, approval or respect through which the world affirms you as a competent human being.

Figure 1. a   The Affirmation Cycle: the Balance that Allows Us to Function

This presents a dilemma. It seems that the energy you need to allow you to develop the attributes to be strong enough to deal with the challenges of the world comes to you when you are able to satisfy the demands that the world places on you. You seem to be able to get affirmation when you do not need it, and you do not get it when you do need it. This dependence on the world for the affirmation to fuel your creativity is your liability. You have some control over every other attribute you possess, yet the one factor that allows you to build on those attributes, your creativity, seems to be controlled by outside forces, and these forces seem reluctant to give you what you need. Let us look at this schematically.

First I will draw a human being. Just remember that a human being is not a body. Therefore, I can only draw a container, because that is what I see, and its appearance is not important. I have depicted the container as the circle on the left. Outside the container is the world. Inside are the three attributes of creativity, understanding and fulfilment. Then I will depict those expressions of self as arrows curving toward the world, and affirmation as arrows coming from the world to the self. Do you see? It forms a closed loop, a feedback cycle. Yet it can fall apart. You have learned to depend on the world to close that circle.

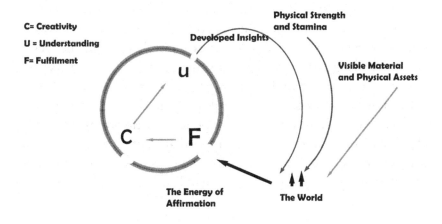

Figure 1b.   The Affirmation Cycle

True, the world may have been willing to give you affirmation when you were a child. Then, when you attempted to do a task, the world may have seemed willing to compliment you on that small part you did well. When, as an adult, you do the same task, the world seems to see only that small part that you may not have done as well as you did the larger part. Just think of how you respond to a child playing soccer, and then how different that response is if the player is an adult, and you will identify with the comparison.

Perhaps we can now use a different metaphor. In this metaphor, you are given a task to paint a wall. Your 8-year-old brother wants to help, so you give him the task. He does a sloppy job, but in one corner he paints so smoothly that it looks almost professional. You will compliment him about the area he did well. Yet if you ask an adult to do it, and he does a great job, but in one small corner it is sloppy, then you will point out the sloppy area and ask what happened there. The point is that we tend to have fewer expectations from a child and are willing to compliment small gains. We expect more from the adult and condemn small errors.

There is one obvious method by which you can overcome that liability, that dependence on feedback that does not often come, and you can get the affirmation while also getting the challenges that will stimulate your creativity. In the world, the way we want to see it, growth occurs in steps. There is a riser, followed by a plateau, followed by another riser. After each challenge, there is, or should be, a period of rest, when you can savour your successes and recharge your energies for the next challenge. Then, by the time you are required to reach deeper to create new insight and understanding for a new problem, you have the fuel with which to do so. You get mileage from the attributes you have acquired to date. In other words, in a perfect system you are allowed to take a challenge, create a solution, apply that solution and savour your success before another challenge arrives. You have a large, flat step before you get to another riser. A child gets that. But you know that in reality, this is not the fate of the adult.

Summary

We see that the human being is a unique life form. We think, but we think as a mind or soul, not as a function of the body. Our ability to think is fuelled by affirmation, the recognition of value given to that which the world cannot see. But the world seems stingy in its allocation of that affirmation, so we need either to get the world to give it or to get it from within ourselves. If only we do not need that affirmation from a world that does not seem to want to give it; if only we can make ourselves so secure that the only thing we seek from the world is what it truly is prepared to give us, new problems for us to solve; then we will be more capable of being effective and efficient as a responsible person.

It is the intent of this work to show you how to secure that affirmation. If you are to be the responsible person you want to continue to be, you will be the person who is expected to give affirmation to the world, not receive it from the world. You therefore must have a source of affirmation that is secure despite the fact that, by virtue of your own progress, you will be faced with expanding problems that dilute the effect of any affirmation you may have received.

Do not be disheartened by the discovery that the more you try to manage your challenges, the more of them there are for you to manage. This is a reality of the world. You who have shown that you can take charge and deal with what is thrown at you will always be challenged by greater problems, even if it is just to know where your limits are.

The capacity of the world is infinite. You do not have infinite physical strength or infinite insight. However, you do have the creativity that will continue to work for you as long as you have the fuel to feed it. For you who have discovered your creativity, your main goal now is to discover how to assure yourself of the fuel you need to be able to use it to its fullest potential.

CHAPTER 3

THE EFFECTS OF MODERN
CHANGE ON CREATIVITY

WE HAVE SEEN THAT the world is rough. We have seen that, as human beings, we have attributes that we must develop before they can be useful to us in dealing with this rough world. We also have seen that our ability to develop those attributes is nurtured by the recognition of those we already have accumulated. In other words, we are rewarded for our resourcefulness through showing what that resourcefulness has allowed us to accomplish.

This may seem to be an unfair arrangement on the surface. Yet you are a human being. As such, you are not just a passive existent. You are a thought-energy. It is natural that any recognition you receive must come from your ability to show that you are such a thought-energy. When you have more attributes than those you were given at the start—attributes that show you to be the individual, the existent that can see the world from a unique perspective and develop similarly unique solutions to offer to the world or some part of it—you will have earned the right to be recognized as a person of value, an important human being. This is because what you have was created by you, and because what you have exceeds by far what you had at the start, it means that your ability to create the energy that is you has value.

THE SECURE REALITY

On the surface, there seems to be a built-in paradox to this feedback system, one that allows you to get the strength you need to be creative only after you already have been creative and can show the effects of that creativity. Yet there is no conflict. You see, you start your life with attributes that are already there for you. They are seed capital, so to speak. It is required only that you add to them. This requisite has been ideally depicted in the parable about the three servants who each were given some money when their master went away, and they were expected to show that they had the resourcefulness to increase their assets. The first, given five talents, invested it and made five more. The second, given two talents, invested it and made two more. The third, given one talent, buried it and offered no more to the master when he returned. Recognition was given only to those who showed that they were able and willing to expand on what they were given.[7] In the parable, the master praised the servant who doubled from two to four no less than he praised the one who doubled from five to ten. It was not the amount that was realized as much as the fact that it was used to advantage that seemed important.

In the same way, you are born with attributes that give you a start. As a human being, you have attributes in your appearance, in your physical strength and stamina and in your heritage. These attributes were given to you; you cannot take credit for having them any more than you can take the blame for inheriting a handicap. Like the servants in the parable, you are not equipped with the same amount of attributes as any other person. You may have more or less. The important comparison, however, is that you have as much capability for improving those attributes as docs the next person. You also live in a system that has been designed to provide you with demands that expand progressively from those that accept your more visible attributes to those which demand more of the personalized attributes you have developed. The successful person does not have less or more of the challenges of life than does the unsuccessful one. Because you need the affirmation of prior success in order to tackle the pervasively evolving new challenges, there always will be the necessity to approach new situations from a secure and expanding home base. You have such a home base: it may be a person who likes you, a place where you can be accepted as you are or a position that is comfortable and familiar. This is your secure reality. When you are with those people, when you go to those places, when you are with familiar

---

7   Bible, King James Version, Matthew 25:14–30

touchstones you may be so relaxed that you know that what you are is good enough to be what you are expected to be in these conditions, and you are fulfilled. In your secure reality, you are a strong and confident person. You become fulfilled, and that fulfilment recharges you with sufficient energy to allow you to go to the next challenge and create the insight to understand, accept and manage it. Then your secure reality will have contributed to your growth and thus will have given itself an expanded base.

If you will look into your past, you will discover that you have enjoyed such expansion. There are many situations, tasks and people that are part of your secure reality now, but that were frightening or uncomfortable at an earlier time. These things did not become different. Riding a bicycle, for example, is no different from the challenge that seemed so formidable when you were young. Now it may be part of your secure reality, but it was not always so. The secure reality you have now is larger than the secure reality you had before.

THE INSECURE REALITY

Just as the things and people you enjoy now were not always a source of comfort or joy to you but have now become so, so too you must realize that there are things and people that challenge or reject you now but that can become part of your secure reality sometime in the future. You need only to create an understanding of them and apply that understanding in your association with them. It is natural to assume, therefore, that under normal conditions the nurturing you receive in a secure reality gives you enough strength to address another segment of territory, conquer it and use your familiarity with it to expand the areas in which you feel secure.

This other segment of your environment does not give you nourishment. The attributes you have do not impress the people in this segment, and neither are they able to conquer the situations. Under these conditions, your position may be uncomfortable, the people may not like you, and the situations may be frightening. Though it may feel that way, you are not lost, lonely or incompetent. You are simply in an insecure reality. If you can accept the changes that are occurring in the minds of the people who are nearest and dearest to you; if you will consider the changes that are occurring even now in the materials that form your most prized possessions; if you can visualize the gradual process of aging that will accumulate to engulf your whole body; then you will recognize that regardless of how large your secure reality may be, you always will be challenged by conditions that are part of a more immense, insecure reality.

In your insecure reality, you are weak and may be afraid. Not only are you not fulfilled, you cannot get fulfilment until you can get out of that insecure reality or conquer it. You may see that there is no such thing as an insecure person, or even a secure person; there only is a person who, under certain conditions, is in a secure reality and, under other conditions, is in an insecure reality.

If, when you feel weak or frightened, you are not just an insecure person but a person who is functioning at that moment in an insecure reality, then when you feel strong and confident, do not be fooled into thinking that you are a strong, confident person. There is never a time when you can drop your guard and be complacent. You must realize that you are a person who at that moment is functioning in a secure reality. Activities are occurring beyond your immediate vision that will bring new situations to you. These new situations have a greater possibility of being part of your insecure reality than they have of being part of your less extensive, secure reality. That strength and confidence will again be challenged, determined less by you than by the depth of understanding you have for that new reality.

An insecure reality, therefore, is something that pervasively afflicts everybody. Everybody is ill at ease in an insecure reality. The strong person is not the one who always seems strong and confident. He or she is the one who starts off with the uncertainty of an insecure reality, is able to assess the conditions, can understand them and can then manage them as though they always were part of a secure reality. It is how you make an insecure reality into a secure one, not how well you enjoy a secure reality that determines your capability.

THE FEEDBACK CYCLE

If as a human being you are expected to be a thought-energy, the two most important prerequisites for you to function competently are the challenges on which you can be creative and the inner strength with which you will fuel your creativity. We have seen that there is no shortage of situations that can challenge your creativity. There also is an adequate supply of situations through which you can obtain the strength to fuel that creativity.

There is a dichotomy, however, because each situation is the antagonist of the other, and they cannot exist simultaneously. That is, you cannot be in both a secure reality and an insecure reality at the same time. Since you need the effects of both of them for you to be successful, there must be a way of storing one to have it when you address the other. The fulfilment you get when you are in a secure reality stays with you long enough for you to use it in a subsequent insecure reality. Similarly, the challenge you have from an insecure reality is still there for you after you return from being restored in your secure reality.

Such a feedback cycle is automatic and inevitable in the evolution of your maturity. You will discover that you work more successfully and efficiently at a difficult task after you have been reassured by your successes in others. When you have done a good and efficient job, it is easier to go to the next task, even if you may be physically tired.

This is the feedback cycle. The feedback you get from the recognition of a past success allows you the strength to approach the next problem with confidence. Obviously, staying in a secure reality may continue to give you the fulfilment you enjoy, but you will not have the stimulation of the challenges from the insecure reality; then, your creativity will be shut down, and you will not give account of yourself as a human being. Life is not just about being, or even being happy—it is about doing. Similarly, staying in an insecure reality will provide you with the challenges, but you will not have the inner strength to fuel your creativity. The net result is that you also will not be able to give account of yourself as a human being. You will begin to fall, or you will become inclined to avoid the challenges or simply hide from your failures.

Therefore you need the balanced input from both. If you cannot get them together, you will have to use them separately and in sequence, one after the other. The act of creativity depletes your fuel reserves when you are attempting to manage conditions in an insecure reality, so you must be able either to return to a secure reality to restore your strength or to make that situation into a secure reality and use it as a new source of fulfilment.

This is the whole purpose of your existence as a human being. You are designed to be able to offer solutions that are unique and specific for each challenge. To do so, you first must create understanding. You may express that understanding in order to manage a situation that you have conquered. But even if you do not express that understanding, you still will have created it. You will have given account of yourself as a human being, an existent that has the ability to offer solutions for challenges that once were beyond you.

THE PREREQUISITE FOR FEEDBACK

When you feel good and when you are fulfilled, that strong, confident feeling, the inner strength, lasts not only while you are in the situation that allows you to be fulfilled but beyond it. When you are challenged by new or unknown conditions in an insecure reality, you use that fulfilment and are able to take with you as the fuel to explore the unknown and understand it. The stored fuel becomes used up.

In the act of exploring and understanding the new situation, you will have used up much of the stored fuel. If you are fortunate to have completed the exploration, and you understand the new situation, then you will have reestablished the conditions that can restore your fulfilment. You will be able to enjoy the satisfaction that is associated with the recognition of your accomplishment. Then you can be strong again to address the next issue and explore the next unknown.

Obviously, this positive growth and progression cannot occur if you are not able to complete the task and enjoy the pleasure of accomplishment. It is necessary that the challenge of the task is such that you can complete your exploration and understanding of it before you use up all of your inner strength. This is the way it must have been devised. You get reinforced, and then you approach an unknown, overcome it and use it as the expanded secure reality to be reinforced again for the next challenge. If things always happened this way, then we would all be successful and fulfilled without needing instructions on how to become so. The prerequisite for this is that each new challenge must be within the range of the inner strength you can receive from your accumulated secure reality. It is comparable to having a bank account: the more money you have saved in the account, the more you have available to spend.

In an extension of the same comparison, you will observe that

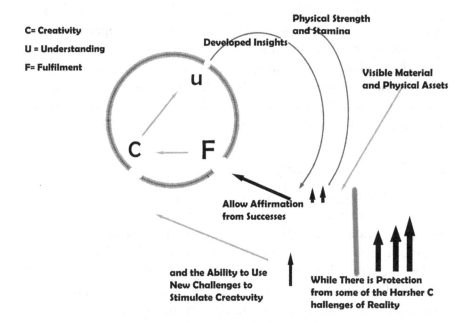

Physical Strength and Stamina

Developed Insights

Visible Material and Physical Assets

U

C — F

Allow Affirmation from Successes

and the Ability to Use New Challenges to Stimulate Creatvvity

While There is Protection from some of the Harsher C hallenges of Reality

Figure 2.   The Feedback Cycle

as your secure reality expands, so too will the fulfilment you receive from the expanded version. In effect, there may be a chance that the fulfilment you can receive may increase exponentially—that is, the more you accomplish, the more areas there are from which you can be replenished and the more strength you get for accomplishing the next challenge. Then, under such circumstances, it will be easy for you to confront challenges that arrive in progressively expanding stages of difficulty. This is the way it was when the world was young. This is the way it was when you were a child. When the world was young, you would have lived in very simple surroundings. The challenges you would have had to face were those challenges that were relevant to your immediate society. What happened a hundred miles away would not have concerned you, did not affect you and might never have been brought to your attention. You would have had the time to savour your successes before you were required to manage another problem. You also were reassured that you did not have to be concerned about certain problems that were presented to you. They were thought to be the specific activities of the deity.

As a child, even in modern times, you would not have been required to solve the type of problems that are imposed on you as an adult. You would have been given the privilege of having challenges that were controlled so that they did not overwhelm you and deplete the inner strength that you had for managing them. Grade 5 is grade 5 and gives you only the work of grade 5 and the challenges of 10-year-olds. You did not have to think of the gas bill or food bill or any of the other things that you as a child would have thought should come naturally.

THE REALITY OF MODERN CHANGE

This ideal progression, however, is not the way life seems to evolve. Under modern conditions, you rarely are able to savour your successes and gather enough strength to tackle the next problem. What seems to happen instead is either that the next challenge is so large that you deplete the strength you were able to gather from your accumulated secure reality before succeeding in managing it, or that new ones come so frequently that you rarely have the opportunity to savour your success and replenish yourself before having to tackle yet another problem.

What I want you to visualize again is that bank account. If what you have is enough to allow you an investment that, when mature, will pay you handsome dividends, then you will be able to put back into the account more money than you withdrew; thus you will have more to invest at the next opportunity. If, however, the demands of the new investment are such that you deplete what you have withdrawn before you can service the investment properly, then you will lose what you have invested, and your account will be deficient when you want to use it next. What this means is that no matter how extensive your attributes, they are limited and can be exhausted by the demands of new or extensive problems. No matter how great your inner strength may be, it is also limited by the size, stability and availability of your secure reality, and it can be depleted by demands that are too persistent or too extensive. Simply stated, you do not have to be inadequate as a person for you to fall victim to the demands that can exhaust you. You can be just as easily overwhelmed if the demands arrive in too rapid a succession or present in too extensive a fashion.

In our modern world, there are very few people whose exposure can be so limited that everything will inundate them. The stresses of our modern world, however, can make the knowledge of the most educated person redundant. Then, just as you will stagnate in barren conditions even if you have all the desire, but there is nothing for you to discover, so too will you stagnate in fertile conditions if the fertility is so demanding that it exhausts the inner strength you need to fuel your creativity. The net result is that you are forced to try to deal with never-ending challenges without the strength that you need for dealing with them.

The problem with modern conditions is that they are fast-paced and extremely demanding. Each new challenge, therefore, has the potential to exhaust the inner strength that you have for dealing with it, and it frequently does exhaust that strength. The only way you can be sure of staying ahead seems to be for you to be infinitely knowledgeable and be 100 percent sure that everything is within your secure reality, or to have an unending supply of inner strength.

No one can be infinitely knowledgeable. In addition, the dichotomy in the feedback system ensures that the supply of inner strength is determined by the strength of a secure reality, which, in turn, is affected by the size of the insecure reality. In a world that changes as rapidly and with such immense parameters as that which you now are experiencing, the size of your insecure reality is infinite. Then, regardless of how well-established your secure reality may be, it still can be insignificant by comparison.

MODERN CHANGE: WHY IT IS SO DEMANDING

Life as we know it has always been affected by the same volatile environment, the same fragility of the organic body and the same unpredictable dynamism of other people's thoughts and actions as they are now. Your insecure reality, then, must not be any greater than it would have been in earlier times. Yet the pressures of change have never been as great then as they are in modern times. If you were to look at change within the parameters in which we described it during the discourse in chapter 1, you will understand that there couldn't be any more activity within the materials that form your physical environment than within those that formed the physical environment of your ancestors. We may have more stable chemical structures forming fabrics that erode more slowly, but we did not get these materials from another universe; they were part of the environment before we used them. Before Marconi sent the first radio waves across the Atlantic Ocean, radio waves were present. Marconi only learned how to influence the activities of an already-existing phenomenon. Before we polluted our oceans with oil spills, oil was already in the earth. we simply relocated it.

Similarly, there could not be any more activity within your body than there was in the body of a human being 1,000 years ago. We have evolved, but our evolution has not been a physical evolution of the makeup of the body. We may have better medicines and more balanced diets than before, but medicines are not generated from nothing; they simply are the restructuring of new chemicals or the purification and concentration of those that have always been here.

Other people's thoughts are not any more diverse or measurable now than they would have been in those times. They may be influenced by things that are more modern and perhaps more clearly defined, or perhaps more diverse than they were back then. But these thoughts are not any more active than were the thoughts of earlier people. We may have languages that are more complex and universal than the simpler dialects from which they evolved. But language still does not represent thought accurately. There are many instances when a person will express an idea using a string of words that accurately describe the idea, only to be misinterpreted by an observer who uses that same string of words to describe a totally different idea just as accurately.

What this all shows is that the activity was always there. Some of it has been brought to you; you have been taken to others. What makes the difference is that even though you are exposed to more of these sources of change than you would have had to face in less volatile times, you need no greater preparation to face any of them now than you would have needed if you had to face them then.

Even though the world is not any more volatile than it ever was, you are exposed to more of the normal amount of change than you ever were, and therefore you are more susceptible to being drained by the greater demands placed on you. What brings this about is the compounded effect of industrialization, urbanization, transportation and communication.

INDUSTRIALIZATION

Mankind has always been one step behind nature and has always been able to see only as far as our instruments allowed us to see. Therefore, when we were able to invent instruments that allowed us to do more than we were able to do before, those new instruments also showed us more things that had to be done.

Just think: were once able to plough an acre of land with a horse-drawn plough, but now with the help of a combine, you will be able to consider ploughing ten acres, and most surely you will attempt it. In more modern terms, you may remember that the computer was introduced to the business world in order to save the time and effort of doing a lot of paperwork. In theory, bookkeepers were expected to be able to finish their chores and have time for more creative ventures. In practice, more paperwork was created by computers, which now gives us the ability to see more deeply into the figures and to calculate them more accurately. Expectations of greater precision and productivity are now the norm. Typists were supposed to be more efficient because they could correct errors without having to retype the whole thing. In practice, what is now seen is the ability to create an even more stylish finish to the letter. More work and higher expectations are all that have been accomplished.

Industrialization has been able to bring more of the changing world to people who, without such instruments, would never have been able to experience many of the demands they are expected to address. In modern times, we are aware of the power we can get with such instruments, and we sometimes let that get in the way of reason and believe that we can solve everything with the use of more powerful instruments—only to be inundated sometime later with the greater problems that these more sophisticated instruments tend to reveal or generate.

URBANIZATION

The limitations that people once experienced allowed the formation of very isolated communities. People segmented themselves into groups based on the areas of the environment that were familiar to them and on the challenges it provided to their particular skills. There evolved a homogeneity among those who shared each isolated area; their learned responses would have been influenced by the limited challenges that were common to their specific areas and the limited thoughts and activities that were developed to address these challenges.

With industrialization, people from varied and distinct communities, attracted to the promises of greater success with the tools of industry, moved to live in newer and larger centres with other people from entirely different communities. This introduced each person to a greater variety of new ideas, personal idiosyncrasies and deeply ingrained beliefs than they could have been prepared to address. The other people with almost irreconcilable differences always existed; urbanization only brought them together. On the whole, urbanization attracted a more sophisticated industrialization, which in turn serves to attract an even more diverse range of people to each urban centre. Modern urbanization, therefore, brings an even greater range of people with an even greater range of backgrounds, ideas and learned behaviours to affect each other.

Look around you now. The people sharing your office, living next door to you or even sharing your home are highly likely to have been brought up under totally different circumstances than you were. They are from different countries, possibly with different languages, religions or social stigmas. The personal skills these other people developed to help them survive the conditions within their specific communities are almost predictably different from the personal skills you needed and developed to deal with the conditions within your specific community. In ancient times, too, a well-defined class structure was established so that even within small communities, the people with whom one related were less diverse. With industrialization came the emergence of the middle class and a greater range of backgrounds, ideas and beliefs; it came not only from the merging of different communities, but also from the merging of different class structures. Urbanization has brought more of the change that always existed to impact each person more immediately, more profoundly and more rapidly than ever before.

TRANSPORTATION

You have fast cars now to take you over a wider expanse of the environment than ever before. Airplanes make the farthest comer of the globe accessible within a very short time frame. In one day, it is possible for you to move from one time zone to another, or from one season to another, being able to experience the full range of environmental activities that people of more ancient times did not have to experience.

There was a time when all you had to worry about were the problems that could arise within a very limited area of the common environment. That did not mean that there were not weather systems destroying crops and threatening lives in other places while your environment was safe. It does not mean that you are exposed to a more volatile environment now. It only means that, with better transportation, your immediate environment is now much more extensive than it ever has been.

Think about it now: The extent of the environment that a person was expected to cover in a day, say, 200 years ago, was much less than you will now expect them to cover in one hour. If you drive to one store to get something that is not available there, you will think nothing of proceeding to another store much further away and expect to be able to purchase it and still return to use it that day. The distances that some people must travel to go to work and still return home to do household chores can be excessive; this may have been considered to be a week's journey in ancient times. The number of different activities you would have expected of yourself then would have been dictated and minimized by the limitation of what you would have been able to reach.

COMMUNICATION

A little more than 50 years ago, say, in the mid-1900s, an important event happening some distance away would not be known for many days. News had to be brought by way of airplane or surface mail, or transmitted electrically through the use of a wire photo, the facsimile taking some minutes or even hours to be reproduced. An event occurring in a distant place might not have affected you then; by the time you might have heard about it, much of it might have been defused. The difficulty with which such news was carried made it impossible to cover too much of the global scene. Many things would have occurred without many people in different parts of the world becoming aware of them.

Now, communication is instant. As I write this, I can use a modem and transmit the material instantly to another computer in another country. The whole world is brought to you in your living room every night as quickly as new events unfold. It is now so easy to transmit news and pictures of such events that more of them are brought to you than would have been considered important 50 years ago. What this means is that in modern times, you are affected by the events that occur in every comer of the globe and by the behaviours of the whole range of people that occupy that enormous environment, even if they are not important. You are required to consider more information from a wider range of sources in one day now than anyone would have had to process in a month in earlier times.

THE EFFECTS OF MODERN CHANGE ON THE ACQUISITION OF FEEDBACK

When you were a child, even in this modern and rapidly changing world, you did not have to worry about the problems that were beyond those you had to address. Even consequences to your actions were diluted by the adults in your world; a spanking intended to discourage you from playing in the streets as a child might have been uncomfortable, yet it would have been a diluted consequence from the more serious possibility of being struck by a car.

You are an adult now. In your rapidly changing world, there are few precedents to guide you through the new problems that arise. There are so few people who are ahead of you, as parents are to a child, that you cannot look to them for guidance in these unpredictable times or for assistance in diluting your consequences. Now that you are an adult, you are responsible for forming your own solutions not only to problems that increase gradually, but also to the sudden presence of sometimes even devastating situations.

The objective is the same: like everyone else in the past, you want to feel fulfilled. The challenge is different, however. You live in a world that has become so immense in the range of its demands that, in order for you to be fulfilled, you must be able to rise above an impossible range of difficult and rapidly evolving problems. It seems that you must prove yourself to such an insatiable world where, no matter what you do, you rarely receive the feedback you need to feel fulfilled and be able to rise above your challenges. The only way to break this vicious cycle is for you to be able to secure fulfilment without having to depend on the feedback from a world that is no longer willing or able to provide it.

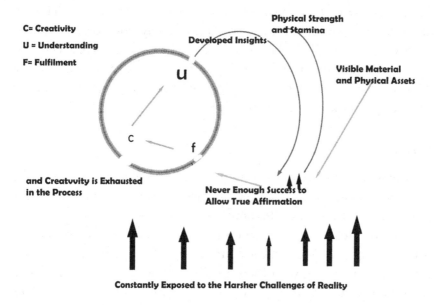

Figure 3. The Reality

Yet no matter how experienced you may be, or how much of this vast environment you already understand, it is natural for you to look for someone ahead of you to guide you, to provide you with a precedent or a tool by which you can measure your success. Frequently you seem forced to measure the value of a new idea not by how well it addresses the issue, but by how well it compares with another idea. Yet it may be one that has been developed for a totally different set of circumstances. Sometimes proving ourselves to be able to equate or apply the ideas of a more recognized authority can give us an incorrect or inappropriate solution for the condition as it appears now. Every situation is so multifaceted that though it may seem to be a repetition of a similar condition on the surface, there are facets that may be quite different from previous situations. Then the solution that once worked may no longer be applicable because the real problem has already evolved.

Only when you realize that the solutions which another person can offer is based on events that occurred at a different time or viewed from a different perspective—and therefore is created for a different set of conditions—can you be better prepared to deal with the evolving events that challenge your creativity in today's environment. Only when you realize that even if that precedent was set by you yesterday, it still is very likely to be irrelevant for the conditions of today, will you be ready to focus on the more important challenge of honing your creativity and using it to address problems from a position of personal strength. Only then will you be ready to devote your attention to securing the inner strength you need to fuel that creativity.

SUMMARY

If you can appreciate the immense and unpredictable range of the changes that constantly occur even in the apparently stable conditions you have to address, you will know that your failures are less due to your own unpreparedness than to the general immensity of the challenge. If you can appreciate the relative limitations of the attributes you have developed for dealing with those infinite problems that can challenge you now, then you will know that you must learn to rely on the flexible resource of creativity more than on any stored knowledge or acquired solutions.

As an extension of what happens in the other areas of change, even while you are formulating an answer to a question I may have asked you, I still am thinking. By the time you offer your response, my thoughts will have carried me beyond the problem I first shared with you. If you can appreciate this, you will be able to accept that the solution you offer, although entirely appropriate for the original question, is inaccurate for the problem the way I see it now; it no longer addresses what is more important to me at the moment. I therefore cannot in good conscience share with you the affirmation you deserve for the correct solution you have given me. Thus you will see that you cannot even depend on your creativity if, to feed it, you need the affirmation from a fickle and stingy world. What you need is to be able to secure another way of obtaining affirmation, another way of measuring yourself, so that you can be affirmed for what you truly are able to be rather than for being able to keep pace with an impossible situation.

As Albert Einstein stated,

> *The belief in an external world independent of the perceiving object is the basis of all natural science. Since, however, sense perception only gives information of this*

external world or of "physical reality" indirectly, we can only grasp the latter by speculative means. It follows from this that our notions of physical reality can never be final. We must always be ready to change these notions—that is to say, the axiomatic structure of physics—in order to do justice to perceived facts in the most logically perfect way.[8]

You can measure yourself differently only if you truly are different from those things you can measure easily. If so, traditional methods will fail to identify you. If, by using traditional methods, you succeed in being able to identify yourself fully, it shows only that you are not truly different. Then you are doomed to tying to give account of yourself by satisfying a world that never can stay still long enough to be satisfied by your attempts to please it.

In order to be able to measure yourself and determine your identity as that distinct existent, you must have at least a working knowledge of the things you can measure, why they can be measured, and, by applying the same rules to yourself, whether you are governed by those parameters. Only then will you be prepared to examine yourself without those diversions and determine an independent means of measuring who you are and what you can be. Only then will you be able to develop an objective that will be more appropriate to your relation to the world as it is rather than trying to adapt the world to be more appropriate to what you believe you should be.

---

8   H. Margenau, "Einstein's Conception of Reality," in *Albert Einstein: Philosopher-Scientist* (Cambridge University Press, 1970) 243–367.

CHAPTER 4

UNDERSTANDING CHANGE AND DETERMINING ITS LIMITATIONS

IF YOU LOOK AROUND in the room you occupy now, you will observe a number of situations that you may accept as the results of natural events. For example, you may turn on a radio and hear voices coming, apparently from nowhere. You know, however, that these sounds are created by the amplification of radio waves that are picked up by the radio antenna. In fact, you do not even think about what causes it, accepting the sound from the radio as a natural event. Similarly, because of the contributions of modern science, you have learned to accept that there are bacteria floating around the room, little squiggly monsters that can invade your body and cause you to become ill. If instead we were sitting in the same space 5,000 years ago, and if I were to make the same comment about those squiggly little monsters or about those waves of energy that carry voices, you might not have stayed too close to me. You might have thought I was crazy—or worse, a consort of the devil.

It is possible that what I am about to discuss with you now may evoke the same fears. What is important here, however, is that you understand that just as there were events that our ancestors did not understand and either dismissed as being unreal or relegated to the supernatural, so too there are events that you do not understand now and, for similar reasons, still either relegate to the supernatural or dismiss as figments of the imagination.

You may believe that you are much more sophisticated than they were and that you have a better understanding of what is real. Yet you too would have reacted just as they did, even to the things you understand now, if you did not have the benefit of insight provided by the explorations of previous generations. What you know from the discoveries that gave you the insight, however, is but a miniscule portion of what still remains to be discovered. It is possible that some of the things you presently dismiss as being unreal or perhaps as being some type of supernatural event can, at some time in the future, be seen to be as natural as you see those other things now.

We may have exhausted our understanding of the unknown as being squiggly little monsters. We may have demonstrated uses for most of the energy sources that can be harnessed. Yet the unknown is still as fearful and as immense today as it was when it also contained things we now have the ability to identify and understand. What is more, much of what we fear as the unknown is brought to us by the process of change in those things we already know and understand. It is important, therefore, to see those events we accept as natural now from the perspective of our less enlightened ancestors in order to assess whether we are doing the same thing, albeit to a different set of events.

A Metaphorical/Historical Observation of Why the Human Being Has Been Slow in Addressing the Issue of Change

Change has always been an enigma to the human being. The fear and discomfort it evokes can threaten our survival or even cause us to question our personal value in the physical or social reality we occupy. We can be so unsure of what we are or what we should be or how we can survive comfortably that we can feel secure only by fixing our individual identities to something stable. We see ourselves as fragile. What we see of the world through the crude instruments that are easily available to us seems stable. We have learned to secure our fragile identities by attaching ourselves to the world as we see it, unaware that those apparently stable states are parts of a constantly moving universe.

Yet we know that the total universe is huge; it extends into a vast unknown so vast that it always has been impossible for us to feel comfortable with the things with which we have chosen to identify, because they seem to be puny and weak sections of the whole. From a crude observation, it seems that we saw three levels of existence: the vast unknown, the stable or apparently stable reality that comprises what we know and our fragile selves. The rest was always seen as the potential enemy, one that had such great authority over the small sections we can know, that we either must avoid it or obtain protection from it. This power appeared to have the ability to take facets of the vast unknown and impose it on the areas we know creating havoc. Therefore, to stay secure in such apparently unstable conditions, we learned to refuse to accept change as an integral part of those things we saw as stable. If something happened to destabilize what we learned to accept as stable, either we were oblivious to the change or we viewed it as an abnormal disruption of a normal state caused by interference from some outside source. Then it was easy to conclude that the change imposed on what we considered stable was caused either by the inconsiderate activity of another person or the manifestation of the power of an entity greater than ourselves. Life must be stable; change was an imposition into that stability. In our ignorance, this was the way we thought. Now, in some circles, it is taught within a religious context that life was stable until sin caused a punishment of instability, but that stability will be restored in the end.

As long as we are satisfied that the change is imposed by an entity over which we have no control, we have shown little desire to explore it further. Instead, in the past we have directed our efforts toward pacifying that more powerful entity and suppressing any exploration that might offend whomever or whatever that entity might be.

Let us simplistically examine the way mankind appeared to have viewed the universe 5,000 years ago. The world was a flat surface on which we lived and had its boundaries beyond which we were not allowed. The rest of the universe, to our imagination, was populated by more powerful entities that had dominance over us. Then it was easy to explain any unnatural change as being the activity of one of these superhuman beings or deities. Limited by the crudeness of the instruments available to us then—namely our five senses—it was easy to force ourselves to remain within the safety of what we could see and touch, and explain any changes as the activities of the deities. We invented gods whose activities disturbed the stability we craved, either intentionally as a control over us or through a recklessness that ignored the effects on us. Many of us progressed to a single God, but our gods seemed to always have the penchant for being punitive and imposing.

Obviously, it would have been dangerous to explore any of those activities because such exploration would constitute insubordination, perhaps punishable by those same gods and perhaps unleashed on a larger group of people. Therefore, it would have been necessary to establish a watchdog group who would function as liaisons between man and the deities. They would also ensure that nobody would do something that would bring down the wrath of the deities beyond that which already was displayed. Such groups were called the priests, and they were even more powerful than the kings of any particular country. The Church was deemed the first estate, the king the second ... and the populace the fifth estate.

Meanwhile, there always were events that were sufficiently removed from our immediate environment and that we could have explored without such explorations being acts of insubordination. One of these was the movements of the stars. Our fears, however, prevented us from exploring that activity simply because they were seen as the movements of the chariots of the gods across the heavens, and therefore they were sacred to those powerful beings. That which we might have been able to explore was also denied us because our fears attached them to forces we feared.

Since any activity that changed our stable world could be explained as the activity of the deities, something we could not dispute and had to accept, and since there was no need to explore the movement of the stars as that activity also was easily explained within the same definitions, there was nothing left to challenge our curiosity. Everything was explained. We became content to accept what was meted out to us, passively accepting our fate as toys for more powerful beings. We were kept in the dark by our basic ignorance, which led to fears that fed the ignorance. I suppose that we would have remained in that ignorance had it not been for the visions of one man and the subsequent attempts of another to expand on that vision. But first, let us examine it in its proper sequence and see how the truth may have evolved.

How the Stagnation Was Broken

About 5,000 years ago, in the very powerful country of Babylon, a young boy named Abraham had a dream. In his dream, he was told that there was only one deity. That deity was invisible and all-powerful, and it had authority over all men. His dream also revealed that man was created in the image and likeness of that God. Wow, what a powerful statement! If God was invisible and powerful and creative, and if man was created in the image and likeness of God, then man must be invisible, powerful and creative. We couldn't see that logic then, but it will unfold as we continue our discussions.

Just think of what might have been happening at that time. Abraham was no fool and knew that Babylon was a powerful city with powerful governors. The governors believed that they achieved their status because they were favoured by the deities, *their* deities. Abraham now knew that he could not reveal such a dream to the authorities of that place. However, he knew that there were many people who came to his father's idol store to buy idols of gods for protection on their journeys in the dark and dangerous desert. They were nomads and goatherds who did not belong to the establishment. They would welcome an invisible deity because it would relieve a number of camels to carry more valuable luggage than idols. He could share his beliefs only with those people who happily welcomed the concept.

Let us face it. As nomads, they were not considered part of the elite of that society, and thus they were not always welcome to participate in the sacrifices. They could do with a deity of their own. As nomads, it was difficult to carry around the requisite statues of the many deities. A deity that was not only single but invisible was easily transportable—a godsend so to speak, for a nomad.

A new explanation for the natural events in our environment was born. Theoretically, it should have allowed scientists to be free to question the activity of the stars, an activity that no longer could be explained as being the chariots of the deities. The new deity was single, all-powerful and invisible, and therefore it did not need chariots. It must be remembered, however, that the people who carried this concept were seen as simple goatherds, not a group who wielded any authority or received any respect in the more sophisticated society. The ignorance persisted. History tells us that Abraham and his ragtag group of followers were forcibly encouraged to leave Ur because their religion conflicted with the polytheism of the Sumerians.

Those who had an interest in exploring the activity of the stars were prevented from doing so by their beliefs in the multi-deity concept. Those who were free to explore it because of their conviction in one deity were too busy establishing their relationship to that private deity that they had neither the time nor the inclination to explore the phenomenon that would have given us our first explanation of the natural activity of change.

Despite this opportunity, we remained in ignorance for another 3,000 years. One part of the world still worshipped many deities and prevented itself from exploring a visible phenomenon. Another part of the world was free to explore a phenomenon that they could not see. What we needed was a way of connecting these two parts together. This was difficult because the fears of each side were so deeply set that anyone who tried to convince the other was immediately seen as a threat to the whole of that society.

Then, about 2,000 ago, someone achieved it. Whether we see that person as a courageous and visionary man, a special messenger from the deity or the human manifestation of God is irrelevant to this argument. What happened could have been predictable. His deep conviction of the nature of the deity and, in the human connection to that deity, evoked the fears of both sides, and they had him killed, a consequence that he did not fear. This instilled a similar conviction in his followers, providing them with the courage to spread the word to other sections of society even though they knew that it would evoke the fears of these people and jeopardize their lives.

The ultimate effect on science of this merging of beliefs was not felt for many years, but the seed was sown. It was inevitable that those who wanted to explore the visibly unstable environment of the stars would be freed from the restrictions imposed by the general fears that they were the personal chariots of the deities. Without those restrictions, the curious, the lay thinkers and the scientists, unfettered by either the dictums of religion or the fears of authorities, proceeded to explore this area of reality.

The first recorded study was done in Alexandria, Egypt, in AD 150 by Ptolemy. He observed the movements of certain stars and designed what he referred to as the intergalactic clock. He referred all these movements to the earth as the central theme in this system. There was one major error in it because he also saw the sun as one of these planets revolving around the earth. The treatise was accepted by the established Church, the authority over science at the time, as being in accordance with the teachings of Genesis in the Bible, and therefore it was not sacrilegious.

One must remember that this body represented the connection between the deity and man, responsible for man's showing of respect to that deity. They had the self-proclaimed authority to condone or ban any act that could jeopardize the relationship between man and God. The unexplained was explained as purposeful sources of light created by God as part of the creation of earth instead of randomly moving chariots, and the matter was laid to rest. People were encouraged to revert to their simple acceptance of our role as mere sheep living in the pasture of earth and governed by not a multitude of gods, but a single, powerful God. The fear of the gods remained; they simply condensed it to one.

It was not until the year 1542 that an astronomer named Nicolaus Copernicus was able to query Ptolemy's theories successfully and suggest that the earth was a rapidly moving body, a movement that people did not sense because they too were moving with the earth at the same speed. He demonstrated what is considered the first explanation of a heliocentric universe and suggested that the earth moved around the sun rather than the sun rising and setting.

The Church could not accept this contradiction to the absolute power of God as interpreted in the book of Genesis, and it placed Copernicus'ss book on the prohibited list, preventing further exploration of the issue. Then in 1632, at the University of Padua (now Italy, but then part of the Holy Roman Empire), another astronomer by the name of Galileo, with the advantage of a new instrument that extended the reach of the crude sense of vision, the telescope, was able to recognize the nature of some of the planets and became further convinced of the accuracy of Copernicus's theories. However, the Church forced Galileo to rescind his theories and abandon the Copernicus system. He was further punished in this decision by the Inquisition, which relieved him of his position and confined him to house arrest.

It was due to these acts of defiance by people who were willing to be condemned for their beliefs that the fears that we were not allowed to explore the universe by the selfishness of powerful gods were laid to rest, and the search for a natural source of change was initiated. The important point to observe from this dissertation is that our pervasive fears of the unknown have always prevented us from understanding what is there for us to understand. Whether we explain the unknown as the activity of a more powerful entity, or whether we simply ignore its presence, are we not also doing on an individual basis what we see now as the ignorant and frightened defensiveness of less enlightened people? Are we not also stifling our further understanding by hiding behind the protection of a different ignorance? Let us face it: Galileo was only exonerated for his beliefs and his "heretical" teachings in 1994, about 300 years after his death.

There are many examples of our subsequent search for the source of natural change. This search does not negate the presence of a powerful deity; instead, it recognizes that a better understanding of what can be measured, even with more sophisticated instruments, will provide a stronger basis for our acceptance of any less visible nature we may share with an visible and all-powerful God.

THE SEARCH FOR THE SOURCE

Following the pioneering work of these early scientists, there emerged a rapid proliferation of experiments and theories on the nature of our material environment and what caused it to change so readily. As new instruments were developed to extend our vision into what was immediately relevant, each layer was peeled back, revealing another problem that had to be solved. In a simplified discourse, we now can say that what instilled the fears in people were the activities of elements that were not obvious to them as being part of the natural environment. Therefore, when it first was discovered that apparently solid objects were not truly solid, but were composed of smaller parts called crystals, some of the activities were explained. The disintegration of what was seen as a stable entity could be explained as the release of the crystalline substructure of the object. Crystalline particles were too small to be seen with the naked eye. With the aid of magnifying instruments like the microscope, however, they were observed to exist freely and, therefore, with the capability of interfering with the crystals that form the solid object, thus changing the visible appearance of that object.

With the discovery of the crystalline state of matter, one source of change was revealed: it did not explain all change. However, it exonerated the deity from being directly involved in the initiation of the change, at least to that level. It also proved that the change was not a purposeful imposition by some greater entity intended as a punitive measure toward the human race.

The human body is an object whose solidity is similar to other forms of matter, so it, too, must be composed of a substructure of a crystalline nature. These crystalline structures have been identified as cells. Cells can exist freely as well as being joined together to form an apparently solid object. Those free cells are not visible to the naked eye; therefore they can move about undetected and interfere with the cells that form the body. The simplest freely mobile cells were called bacteria. Bacterial cells are only cells, similar to the body's cells, but they have adapted to an environment different from that of the body. Their presence in the body only serves to let them compete with the body's cells for survival.

Disease was no longer seen as the wrath of God. We were beginning to see it as the normal activity of a highly mobile object, the body, integrating with similar activity in an extensive universe. When something happens to throw it off its balance, we now see that as something that can be reversed or even prevented, simply by restoring the previous balance.

This discovery came with great difficulty and great pains to the discoverer. It was no less serious than the fate of Galileo, this time not perpetrated by the Church but by the scientific society who should have known better. In 1847, Dr. Semmelweis was a young physician in Budapest, Hungary. He recognized that there was a big problem in obstetric clinics caused by a disorder called puerperal fever. Healthy women would be admitted for childbirth, and a significant number would die within a few days from a fever contracted there; it happened in the rest of the world as well. Dr. Semmelweis observed that the fever occurred more frequently in his hospital than in another hospital run by midwives. He observed that the only difference between the two hospitals was that in his hospital, they also did autopsies. He surmised that doctors were taking something on their hands, something invisible, and transferring it to the women. He suggested that doctors scrub their hands before examining a pregnant woman. Again, that fear of the unknown and the tendency to reject that which we cannot see played havoc. Dr. Semmelweis was rejected by the scientific establishment as wrong and crazy. His fate was that he was lured to a hospital where he was jumped, beaten and admitted as insane, and he died a few weeks later from his injuries. That discovery, however, eventually led to the germ theory of disease and established the cellular composition of the body in parallel to the crystalline composition of inorganic structures.

This discovery, however, did not explain all of what was happening. Surely the disintegration of apparently solid objects was not confined to their breakdown into their crystalline substructure. Also, the presence of other types of activity could not be explained by the free movement of crystals. This search for further explanation into the cause of less detectable activity, without going the easy route of ascribing it to an act of the deity, led to the discovery of molecules as smaller building blocks of which the larger blocks were comprised. With the discovery of molecules, another series of events was explained. The free movement of an even less visible entity could explain some of the activities that caused change. Air movement, wind storms and hurricanes were understood and explained as the free movement of molecules of air because they were rising as a result of heat or rushing to fill a void caused by those effects of heat, cold and humidity. The freer these substructures were seen to be, the more obvious it became that the effects of their activities were the result of random movement, or at least movement caused by their relationship to each other. In short, much of the change was not the result of a purposeful act perpetrated by an angry or mischievous god, but was the result of an activity that permeated every object.

Each time a new substructure was discovered, it explained another activity. It also showed that the apparent disintegration of what we saw as solid objects was not the destruction of the material at all. In fact, it was the release of the object into the smaller particles that formed it. Each succeeding particle was observed to be formed by the integration of a group of even smaller particles and therefore revealed activities that were less visible to the naked eye or to the instruments that were designed to view the previous particle. What became more intriguing, however, was that each time they were able to identify a new substructure, it was observed to be more mobile than the larger particle it formed. Therefore, it explained why so much activity was happening to the objects they thought to be stable. It did not explain what caused each smaller particle to be so active, however.

One thing it showed was that the events that occurred in the world became less likely to be a direct interference by a deity. The search became more intense for the reasons that such activity occurred. Many complex theories were put forward, each respecting the possible effect of such a powerful entity as a deity, but each focused on the activities as being self-perpetuating, even if initiated by such a source. Perhaps the reader may indulge me by letting me summarize what was discovered and why it still is pertinent to this discussion.

Stage 1. We recognized or organized reality into two parts: that which we can see and identify and that which is beyond our reach.

Stage 2. We assumed that the beyond was occupied by powerful beings whose activities there could inadvertently or purposefully affect the part we could identify or measure.

Stage 3. Proof of Stage 2 was that the part we could measure did suffer change that we could not understand or explain.

Stage 4. We started to look deeper into things we could measure when we finally were released by separating science from religion. Then we discovered that what we thought were stable entities were actually composites that were inherently unstable. We discovered that the underlying instability dictated that nothing stayed firm, even if it appeared to be that way to the naked eye.

Stage 5. We discovered that the instability was caused by the fact that every small particle was also composed of even smaller particles. We saw an atom as solid when it is really 99.9 percent space. We discovered that, for the most part, we were and still are unaware of the innumerable and unpredictable possible outcomes of every subatomic interaction, let alone of the more complex interactions as we move to the macro level of our lives and interactions. We discovered that structure and predictability were not as they seemed.

The unfolding of the secrets of the activities of the forces that affect the structures we can identify continued in what I offer as the onion skin effect. Many prominent scientists contributed to that unveiling process. With the discovery of the atom, even more explanations became available. When Lord Rutherford was able to split the atom in 1895, until then thought to be the smallest particle to form the visible contents of the universe, the explanation for yet another activity was available. Lightning could be explained as the activity of free electrons. These were considered to be negatively charged particles that, joined with similar particles, formed the atom and so on to the more solid structures we observe in our environment. Activities that were thought to be distinct from matter were discovered to be part of the whole range of particles that formed matter.

Then newer, more sophisticated instruments were developed. The electron, proton and neutron, particles that could only be differentiated by their behaviour toward each other, were discovered to be formed of smaller particles, which were even freer and thus more active than the electrons. At this point, the term quark was used to designate those smaller particles.

These smaller particles were so active that their activity within any object could be the source of much change within that object, other change being induced by their activity outside that object, affecting it. In order to possess such constant activity, however, it is necessary that these particles have some inherent property whose main effect is to generate activity. If not, we are back to the same stage as we were 5,000 years ago, explaining all change as the imposition of the supernatural on a submissive world, albeit through a more indirect approach. Again we go back to Hawking's summation that God could not have created the earth because it has been conclusively shown to have emerged from the Big Bang. God may have created the Big Bang and so allowed the creation of the earth. This leads us to wonder whether God may be creating change by manipulating the movement of the electrons. We used to think that the crystalline structure of matter, or even the cellular interaction in an organic body, was held together by some sort of cement. This was even taught in science classes in the early 20th century.

What we are attempting to introduce in this discussion, however, is the idea that change is not only inevitable but is the basis of matter. Therefore, we cannot and should not attach our identity to anything that is directly or indirectly dependent on matter, or we will relegate ourselves to being as unstable as matter.

THE RULES GOVERNING THE ACTIVITY OF THE SOURCE

In 1905 Albert Einstein, after observing a simple activity while working as a clerk in the Swiss patent office, suggested that if, as with all other things, light was also a particle (in this case a photon), then the light he observed coming from the clock would have reached his eyes a fraction of a second after it left the clock. What he saw as three o'clock, for instance, was seen a fraction of a second after three. He went on to suggest that if he were to climb onto that particle of light leaving the clock at a particular time, he would always see that time, even many hours later.

This seems to be an obvious statement now. You must realize, however, that it is true only if light behaves like a particle, albeit extremely small. These were followed by more serious observations that suggested quantum particles, those miniscule particles that are the basis of every material object, behaved like particles that were affected by the presence of other similar particles. In fact, the specific law of relativity suggests that every particle existing in space is affected by the presence of every other particle. This is certainly based on these particles having the same property that induces activity. What seemed to be the reason for their behaviour was that each particle possessed a sort of energy charge, perhaps electromagnetic or perhaps some other similar energy. The interesting conclusion is that the electromagnetic force that causes the movement is also the same force that creates the adhesion. It is the "cement" we were looking for. What creates structure is the same force that destroys it. This can be a confusing discovery but also a revealing one.

If that is the case, we then will understand that these particles move in what has been described as a wave, presumably because they respond to the forces from all the other similar particles in all directions. Because the freely moving particles are so small compared to the range of sizes that the composites of other particles in space can have, the forces acting on each of them will be varied and numerous and will come from a vast range of objects, including other freely moving particles.

That revelation means the movements of these free particles can never be straight but will follow a more curved path, the tightness of the curve (or frequency of each wave) probably being influenced by the distribution of the other particles around it. They then will induce different effects on the instruments that we use to measure them. Particles moving at one frequency will, for example, stimulate the rods and cones of the eye and will be termed light. Particles moving at a different frequency will stimulate a photographic plate and may be described as X-rays and so on. In fact, this is the process by which we measure any object. Particles leaving that object affect the instrument we use to measure it. The instrument, in turn, undergoes a change that we observe, allowing us to draw the conclusion that such an object is present. This came out as the general theory of relativity, simply explained as the idea that because an instrument that measures such movement is composed of the same particles, then as the object interferes with the instrument, so does the instrument interfere with the object. By measuring something, we actually change it, requiring us to make a correction to determine what it was before we attempted to measure it.

Perhaps you will be able to visualize it better if you see it in terms of what you consider reality. When you touch something, what happens is that the forces from that object irritate some cells that are located in your skin. These cells, by being irritated, undergo a temporary change, causing them to initiate an electrochemical response. This response is taken by the nerves to the brain, letting you know that there is an object present and also how hard it is. The fact that there are many cells over a small area also allows you to have a comparative idea of the surface, and so you can determine whether it is rough or smooth.

Similarly, you see because light photons reflect off an object and stimulate the rods and cones in your retina. If these particles did not leave the object, you would not see it. What you see is the light from the object. You identify the object by the comparative amounts of light reflected from surrounding objects. You see a particular colour because the full range of vibrating particles does not reach your eyes all the time. Sometimes a certain range of light activity comes, stimulating a section of rods and cones at one stage and another set by a different range, giving you a comparative view of the world, which you interpret as colour. It is said that objects have no colour, however; they have properties that absorb certain parts of the light spectrum, allowing you to see the parts that are reflected. The point is that you measure things because they emit particles that affect the instruments you use to measure them. The more precise the instruments are, the smaller the emission you are able to measure.

SOME PRACTICAL CONCLUSIONS

You now can draw a series of conclusions from this information so that it is more applicable to a less abstract view of the world. The first conclusion you can form is that if something exists as matter, it either exists as a quark particle or some composite of quark particles, being atoms, molecules or larger and more distinct objects. Then it will have a property that allows it to be measured by the way its composite particles affect another object, namely the instrument.

The second conclusion you can form is that because what you can measure is either a single, highly energized particle or a composite of such particles, then what you identify cannot stay that way. It either will be broken down into its composite parts if it is a composite, or it will be drawn to other similar particles and form a composite. In other words, by being able to measure something, you will have determined that such an existent is unstable. It will either be destroyed by being separated into its composite parts or distorted by being drawn into another composite.

The third conclusion you can form is that if you can measure something, it follows that it is composed of such particles that affect other similar particles, and therefore it will fall under the general rule governing such entities. That is, what you measure cannot be the same by the time you have finished measuring it; it exists in a state of constant change.

The last conclusion you can form is that if you cannot measure something that you believe to exist, it either does not truly exist, or it exists as an energy source with different energy from that which has been determined to be possessed by matter, whether you call it electromagnetic, quantum energy or whatever. If you know it exists, then it is not matter. Of course, we can also presume that we do not yet have the instrument that is sensitive enough to measure it at that level. What we do know, however, is that we can measure the fact that the quantum particle has been disturbed. For example, this is the basis on which antimatter is presumed to exist.

THE BEHAVIOURS OF ENTITIES THAT ARE GOVERNED BY THAT SOURCE

I want to discuss this difficult subject in order to show that you cannot do anything about the activities that are happening to the world that you can measure. Nature exists because of this activity. As a result the world, by its very nature, is destined to be in a constant state of change. About 450 BC, a Greek philosopher named Heraclitus figured this out. In his time, he described this as an observation that no man swims the same river twice. If we think about it, we can see the logic. But in his days, Heraclitus was called "Heraclitus the Obscure" because of the apparent obscurity of his ideas.

What you see as matter is only a stage in a continuous transition of those particles. They move so constantly that they always will form some object that, relative to another object, can be determined to have some size, shape, colour or texture. That object, however, lasts only as long as the particles forming it stay within the same relation to each other and to the rest of particles outside of it. This state of instability was actually calculated by a scientist named Heisenberg, whose principle of uncertainty, stated in lay terms, indicates that all particles are in a state of motion that causes it to change at a pace equivalent to the tolerance of the quantum, a constant known as the Planck constant. Simplified, this meant that if everything changes at that pace, nothing stays the same for any longer than a fraction of a second (thought to be 10 to the power of minus 90). But we do not see it because we cannot measure movements at that level.

The movement is so continuous that the object is never that object for more than a miniscule amount of time. But because our instruments are crude, we do not observe the transition until it has progressed beyond a significant stage. It is probably because the instruments are also going through the same transition that we can continue to measure the object as being stable relative to the instrument. This reminds me of a television show where the woman says to her spouse that she was unhappy that she was getting older and less attractive. Her spouse responded that his eyes too were getting old and weak at the same pace; therefore, she still looked as attractive to him as the day they met.

You can visualize this by thinking of yourself as being large enough to view the universe as a whole, from the outside. What you will see is a veritable cauldron of activity. Within the composite of that which is limited to what you know of as matter, there is constant activity. As one section seems to be destroyed, the composite parts separate and move to other sections, distorting what was there and forming what seems to be a new creation, only to continue moving so that the new creation is destroyed as easily as it was formed. This is the consideration of the formation of nebulae, supernovas, brown dwarfs and such. The time, from the destruction of one section and the temporary formation of another as the individual particles continue to move, is measured in light years. Thus it is easy to see why you can be led into the belief that, in the miniscule time frame of a few years, everything seems stable. In a fair comparison, you must view the movements at the stadium in time frames of fractions of a second; then those pictures, either of the flag or of the message, will appear to be stable and permanent.

Even more down-to-earth is the observation of a group of people performing at a stadium during intermission. They each have a specific path to follow, constantly moving. Yet as viewed from above, what you see is the formation of a flag, then a flower and then a message. Just remember that in terms of the universe, the individuals are so miniscule and numerous, and the product so vast in range, that the obvious transition of this observable product occurs over longer time frames.

REALITY VERSUS SYMBOLISM

Imagine a small particle moving in a circular path in space. If that small particle moves so rapidly that we cannot examine it at any single point in its motion, we will no longer see a particle travelling in a circular path; we will see a ring. The faster the particle moves within that circle, the more solid that ring appears to be. Let us continue by making that particle move in a three-dimensional plane. The ring will now take the form of a sphere. As the particle moves so fast, say, at the speed of light, the sphere begins to appear to be more solid. We believe that what we see is a well-defined solid object. What we have, however, is an illusion. We can "prove" that the sphere is solid simply by attempting to force another particle through it. Because the particle is moving so fast, it can appear to be occupying all areas of the sphere's surface at any time. Therefore, the second particle will always be repelled by the "surface" of the sphere, "proving" that it is solid. We can become quite satisfied by the dimensions of the structure of the sphere and do not even consider that it is really an object in motion. If you can see this, you will begin to see what this book is getting at. Structure is only an illusion of motion. Any object, being a composite of atoms, is also in a state of perpetual motion. It is so much easier to dismiss the idea of constant motion in everything that appears solid. Yet we are challenged by it every day; our world does not adapt to our vision of it. So regardless of how much we see structure, we have to learn to deal with the reality of persistent change.

If we can do this experiment, we will also notice something of great significance. The impinging particle will be repelled in unpredictably different directions each time it is directed at the sphere. We know that this is because the sphere is actually a particle moving so rapidly that it is approaching any location from a different angle at any time. Thus the impinging particle will be repelled at a different angle each time it is directed at the sphere. Because the movement is so fast, the angle of reflection is almost impossible to predict. It is highly unlikely, therefore, for two successive impacts to give two exact reflections. When we calculate this on the infinite range of positions the particle can be coming from at the point of impact, we can arrive at an infinite range of responses, none being predictable. When we further consider that even the object reflected is also a particle in motion, the unpredictability of response is further compounded.

Now, when we consider that we typically deal with structures that are complex composites of even these complex spheres, we can see that predictability in its true sense is an impossible objective. What saves us is that we measure in crude terms. We do not, for example, examine a quantum of light being reflected off a proton; instead, we contemplate the response of a ray of light reflected off a surface. Of course, that ray of light is a complex composite of quantum particles. The surface is a very complex composite of these illusionary spheres. Therefore, the reflection of the light is in highly varying and unpredictable directions. We know that the total effect is a composite of each unpredictably varying response, so we must acknowledge that it, too, is truly unpredictably varying, but within a coarsely acceptable range. Nonetheless, we focus only on the crude response of the major part of that ray. We dismiss the subtle nuances of reflective responses and consider only the total or average effect. Yet these variations can accumulate, allowing the total effect to become perceptibly changed in the long term. Thus although we may have learned to expect or even predict the general outcome of an encounter in the short term, we inevitably will discover that in the long term, our predictions and expectations will be flawed. The Newtonian law of equal response has been redefined by quantum physics.

A conclusion we also can draw from this is that matter is not reality. Reality is the particle, or perhaps energy source, that gives rise to the forces that allow the particles to form what we can observe as matter. The object we observe is only that object as long as the tiny subatomic particles continue to interrelate in the same way they did to form the object. As soon as they are arranged differently, the object disappears. To illustrate this, think of a fist. A fist is a fist as long as you close your fingers tightly together. The fingers are real; the fist is a perception and exists only because the fingers are together. If you separate your fingers, the fist no longer exists; what you have is an open palm. Similarly, your body is your body as long as those proteins, minerals and carbohydrates are in the relation they need to be in order to form what you recognize as your body. There will come a time when those same building blocks will be reorganized to form daisies, for example.

What exists, then, is interrelationship. The object you can identify exists only while the particles that form it continue to be in the same interrelationship as they were when they first were joined together to form that object. If you can restructure those particles, the original object will cease to exist, and something else will exist in its place. Again, we can conclude that matter is not reality. Rather, the energy source that allows the formation of matter is reality. The thing that you cannot measure, the quantum particle, is more real than the thing you can measure, the object. When you can measure something, therefore, you are measuring only the aggregation of the base energy, the transitional stage in the activity of a reality.

Look around you. According to this logic, the chair you are sitting on is not real. It feels real because you are perceiving it through an instrument, your body, which responds to the same forces that are aggregated to form the chair. There are so many "kazillions" of those particles that even though many of them have proceeded onward, no longer part of the chair, the transitional structure of the chair will appear to remain intact for some time. This may seem to be such a long time of transition that you possibly can accept it as stable. Just remember, however, that what to you is a long time is only a miniscule stage in the transition of those particles from the position of the whole universe.

In addition, you can destroy that chair by burning it. What you will have accomplished is a destruction only of the way the particles interrelated to form the chair. The freed particles can restructure themselves to form something else somewhere else; they cannot be destroyed. They may not be accessible to the instruments with which you can measure them, but they still exist, even freely dispersed in a wider area of the universe.

It can be assumed that measurement is possible only because some sensory input in your body has been stimulated by some activity that we now know to indicate energy in transition. Regardless of how sophisticated your instruments may be, they only magnify the instruments with which you were born. Therefore, any instrument that you can operate using any of your five senses is an instrument that can measure only the activity of matter as an activity of quantum particles. When you become aware of something, that thing must therefore be matter because you are aware of it through your five senses, directly or indirectly.

If we see matter as the objects that can be observed, we will see that matter really is something that can be measured. It exists only as an interrelation of what is real. It can be "destroyed," but what is destroyed is the interrelationship, not the reality that forms that relationship. Seen in this way, matter can be created simply by restructuring the interrelationship of the energy particles of which all matter is formed. Of course, if we define matter as the source particle, then the rules will change. The object will not be matter; it will only be the configuration of matter. We see that matter, as represented by the composite, can be measured. That which can be measured can be destroyed.

If an energy source exists but can be neither measured nor restructured, it also cannot be destroyed. It is not made up of interrelating parts; it is not matter. It must have properties that are different from the property that makes quantum particles attract each other, whether this is the electromagnetic property or some other undefined energy force.

A Hypothesis on the Nature of That Which Cannot Be Measured

Many theories have been put forward to explain the extent of the universe. Many of these theories are offered while considering only what we know as space using what we know as instruments. They do not always consider that space can also be what does not contain matter. If you will think about the enormity of our galaxy and the other galaxies we can observe, and if you try to extrapolate that to the possible extent of the universe, then you will become so lost that you will be confused. You also will recognize how insignificant are the things we fight over in our little section of the world and how insignificant you are as a measurable entity. The discovery almost begs that you not be such a measurable entity. Yet how can you know whether there is such an energy source that is not confined by the properties of matter? The fact is that you cannot know that for sure. What you *can* study, however, is whether an energy source that is not matter can exist, what possible properties such an energy source can have and how such a source of energy can relate to the material universe without being matter. Yet if you will consider the properties that govern what we can measure and identify, you will realize that particles endowed with that type of energy must be contained within their own self-imposed space. Within that space, which must be large enough to contain all the numerous particles so energized, there will be enormous forces created by greater aggregates of these particles, concentrated within some central core. This will create its own self-imposed boundary. Nothing can be measured beyond that boundary because nothing that can measure the properties of matter can be taken outside that boundary. We must realize that we cannot be so conceited to presume that just because we can measure one type of energy force, no other type exists. If any other type exists, such an

79

energy force will not be defined within the limitations of matter. That energy force, then, will not have size because this is a property that is relative to the instrument measuring it. It cannot have colour because colour is only the ability of an object to reflect light, an energy force related to matter. It can have neither shape nor location because these are properties that are relative to the parts that form the object, or parts that are adjacent to it.

If such an energy force exists, it will be powerful and indestructible. Something is destructible when it is a composite of smaller subparts in the first place. An energy force that does not have the attractive-repulsive properties of matter cannot be so composed, and it is thus a self-contained entity, immune to the instabilities inherent in matter. It cannot be destroyed, distorted or created. Such an energy source also does not have to have any direct impact on the activity of matter for matter to be any more unstable than it already is.

It also is possible that many such energy forces can exist, perhaps as independent forces with the same nature, or perhaps as different forces, extending through a whole range of possibilities. If such energy forces do exist, they will coexist without interfering with each other as material forces do, because their properties do not include those attractive-repulsive forces that are common to matter.

SUMMARY

As a human being, you have learned to define your identity by attaching it to something stable. You now see that everything you can identify is so unstable that what you have learned to measure of them is determined by their instability. You have realized that what may seem stable because you cannot see the deterioration is so unstable that it actually weakens you rather than gives strength, whereas you do not always recognize or admire what is strong. On the other hand, you may not always recognize the instabilities immediately. You know, however, that people frequently are surprised or disappointed when they are rejected by, separated from or have no accessibility to those things they believe to be able to give them stability.

You can see that such unpreparedness is unwarranted. The fears of losing what they are destined to lose, the discomfort of being left naked or alone when the inevitable separation occurs, the stress of trying to reach something that will always be inaccessible—all these experiences are unnecessary if you only will recognize how unstable what we view as stable can be. If you can appreciate this, you will realize that you have only two choices in deciding how you relate to such a changing environment. The first is to approach it with fatalism. The second is to approach it with detachment.

Fatalism suggests that if you are going to be destroyed by the unstable environment in any case, you should enjoy what you can for as long as it is available to you. You also will be prepared, like the grunion[9] described in Jacob Bronowski's book *The Ascent of Man*, to fit in with the environment, or as sheep totally dependent on the caring of the shepherd, existing as long as the environment lets you exist, experiencing as much comfort as the environment lets you experience.

Detachment suggests that you examine yourself to see how you may be different from the energy type that responds to the laws governing the behaviour of matter. You may discover that you do not need to attach yourself to anything in order to achieve some stability. You may be able to stand alone. You also may discover that in order to be able to stand alone, you may have to do something more than passive existence allows you to do. If such is the case, at least you will have an objective and the information you need for making your choice, fatalism or detachment.

---

9   Jacob Bronowski, *The Ascent of Man* (British Broadcasting Corporation, 1973), 14.

CHAPTER 5

DEVELOPING A SECURE IDENTITY

I WAS SPEAKING TO a colleague about the young daughter of a mutual friend. This girl had recently run away from home, stating that she needed to find herself. My friend commented that he could not understand the impetuousness of youth. He suggested that this girl's father should take her to the nearest mirror and show her herself; she then would be free to address more important pursuits.

Regardless of how chagrined you may feel by such a show of autocracy, it is important to use it to discover whether you feel the same way about who or what the human being is—and if not, whether you have an acceptable alternative for your definition of the person. Many people do what we have seen our ancestors do: accept the presence of something by relegating it to some area of the world that they do not understand. By association, this undefined existent is accepted as part of that complex area. For example, you accept that you think with your brain, yet you do not usually question how this happens. The act of thinking is boxed in with the unknown function of the brain.

You, as any other human being, do not always want to accept that you are just what you observe as a deteriorating body supporting a mind that magically does not deteriorate with the body. You want to be an existent that can function through that sophisticated body, even if you also must be attached to it. You do not always want to be some unknown physical existent, wandering through this life with no measurable objective yet being required to fulfil an obligation to some intangible part of yourself that you are not even sure exists.

Therefore, if the purpose of this work is to help you discover an identity that is immune to the effects of a world that, by its own structure, cannot be stable, then you must have a definition of who or what you are, one that is more tangible than the definition you can get from blind faith or a reflective mirror. The search for the person makes sense only if you can accept that the person cannot be what you can see and measure within the body. That does not necessarily have to be a religious experience, even though religion is dedicated to the recognition of an existent that is beyond the measurable universe. Religion does not have to be right. We may discover that the person can exist without having to be subservient to an existent that is greater than the measurable universe. However, religion is not necessarily wrong. If we discover that such an entity greater than the measurable universe exists, we will have to admit that such an entity has all right to our respect and subservience.

This treatise is intended to deal with you as an entity. If you, as that entity, can be seen to be detached from the things that define the measurable universe, then you will be able to function independent of the things that are known to be unstable. You are free to interpret how you assess yourself then, maybe as a stable entity, maybe as one with a different type of instability. If you wish, you can accept and respect the existence of something greater than you and as much a detached entity as you are. If you wish, you still may pursue an independent goal as that entity if you interpret that there is no greater power beyond your own existence that you must accept or respect.

Regardless of how you define the person, you must concede that mankind has always been intrigued by the presence of feelings, understanding and reason as properties that human beings possess, which makes us into the unique entities we consider ourselves to be. The continuous frustration, however, is that it has always been difficult to locate these properties. You think, and if you can clear your mind of presumptions, you will find that it is difficult to locate where in the recognizable body this function takes place. Feelings, however, seem to be more localized. Despite this, no one has ever been able to locate feelings, either. This may not be because they are not measurable. We now have greater insight into some of those things that have always been inaccessible to our less sophisticated instruments. We know that such inaccessibility does not necessarily indicate that the entity is immeasurable; we know that it may have been the result of an activity that was inaccessible only to our available instruments. It is therefore possible that with the advantage of hindsight, we can observe how we have evolved into our present presumptions about the location of the human psyche, and perhaps we can determine whether such presumption is accurate.

SEARCH FOR THE INTELLECT

The assumption that is most common in our modern world is that the brain, as the central coordinator of the whole body, is also host to the mind. It is believed that though occurs through specific functions of the brain. The source of these functions has never been isolated, however. This assumption has not always been accepted, either. A widely accepted philosophy is that published by Rene Descartes in 1642 that held that the human being is a dual entity, consisting of a material body controlled by an immaterial mind. This philosophy so influenced people's acceptance of the nature of the human person as an immaterial entity that behavioural disorders were long considered to be the result of that person being possessed by the devil.

It was not until the emergence of Sigmund Freud, who saw abnormal behaviour as the result of both environmental and genetic factors, that many people escaped the rigours of repeated exorcism, or rejection by society as evil forces. This may not have been the intent of Descartes, but it was the interpretation that survived at the time. The general conclusion he stated as "Cogito Ergo Sum," translated as "I think, therefore I am."[10] To me, this line and the arguments he postulated in his writings spoke more to my understanding of monism. But in 1642 the ability to understand invisible forces as entities was limited. "I think" refers to me, the mind or soul. I think. Again, to me, it was an exceptionally intelligent argument about the existence of the "I am" as an entity that exists and cannot be seen. Its existence had to be deduced. It was not the body—he knew the body existed. He was stating that the mind was not just a function, nor was it just a possession, but it is the "I am."

In our more enlightened era, we have accepted that a person's

---

10   Rene Descartes, *Discourse on Method* (Penguin Books, 1968).

behaviour emanates from the brain, and subsequently it originates there. From that, we have dismissed Descartes's idea as foolish because what he thought to be a separate and distinct entity was now "proven" to reside in that complex area of the body called the brain. Real proof, however, has never been forthcoming. We cannot and have never been able to measure thought; thus we have never been able to locate the mind, the source of thought.

But we cannot simply dismiss Descartes—he may still be right. I propose and will elaborate later that we are not a dual entity. There are enough facts to support the evolution or natural selection theory on man as a sophisticated body. We still accept the existence of the mind or soul, so how can we not be dualistic? We do it simply by being the mind or soul using the body. The body is not us but is our instrument of perception and expression. This is like the driver and the car: They are not a dual entity; each is functioning independent of the other. Yet each needs the other to perform. The man can always leave the car and still exist.

So great is the fear that any other interpretation will again leave us vulnerable to the possibility that a person's behaviour is controlled by an inaccessible force such as an immaterial mind, that we are afraid to question the validity of the conclusion that the brain is the source not just of the stimulations that activate the body but of thought itself. We already have grown past some of the other possibilities like the heart when we decided on the brain as the central core of the person. That may have been a wise move because recent trends in surgical procedures have included complete heart transplants, proving that the person neither dies with the heart nor is exchanged for the person whose heart subsequently occupies the body. There also is no other area of the body that can be suggested to house the functions of the mind because with modern surgical techniques, people have been observed to have many of these areas removed while still retaining total mental functions.

You do know, however, that it is impossible for us to gain access to you if your brain is removed. This is obviously a possibility if you, the person, are the brain or some vital part of it. It also can happen if the brain is only the medium through which you can stimulate the body to reveal yourself to us. If it is the latter, its removal only prevents you from revealing yourself; it does not mean that you are no longer alive any more than being asleep means that you are dead. If the person is generated by the brain or any part of it, then it must be shown that the person (as determined by the presence of reason, understanding and emotion) will die if that part dies and will be accessible if that part remains intact.

LOCATING THE INTELLECT

There is one thing of which we can be sure in our present era, and this is that we have the capacity to measure anything that can be measured, or at least some activity that indicates its presence. We no longer have to rely on what once was thought to be the absolute indication of the existence of something, its tangible presence. We know that even an electron is an existent though we cannot see, touch or measure it. Instead, we measure it by its effects. The fact that it moves so rapidly and can only be measured by its activity does not preclude its presence, even if that is so for a miniscule amount of time.

Therefore we have the capacity to locate the mind or soul. All we need are the readings of those instruments that measure each level of presence or activity. If the mind is a physical entity, then rather than presuming its nature, we will be able to determine it. If the mind is not a physical entity, we will fail in that attempt regardless of how precise our instruments are. With that as a hypothesis, we can start with a crude examination of the brain and proceed through more and more sophisticated measurements until we find an entity or a function that, if stimulated, will cause our reason, understanding or emotions to become more intense—and if reduced, will cause the opposite effect.

We also must be willing to make logical deductions from those findings. The first logical deduction that is necessary is to conclude that if the mind is the result of the function of the whole brain, we will lose part of those three mental functions if even a part of the brain has been damaged. Without any special instruments, we know that this is not so. People have been known to have full mental function after having surgery removing part of their brain. We also can know that there is no separate segment of the brain that is devoted to the functions of thinking, understanding or reason. Neuroanatomists have dissected the brain and discovered that it is divided into distinct lobes; each lobe has been followed through its nerve fibres to the spinal cord and found to be specific for some function of the body. For, example, there is the speech centre, vision area, motor area and so on.

Do not be fooled by the differentiation of the brain cells into the cortex and medulla. That differentiation only recognizes that the cortex is the aggregate of neurons or brain cells, while the medulla is an aggregate of nerve fibres connecting different parts of the cortex to each other and to the rest of the body. Therefore, when I refer to the brain being divided into lobes, I am referring to the cerebral cortex. This division has allowed a common misconception that we think with only 10 percent of the brain. First, we have not ever located where we think. And yes, the cortex accounts for only 10 percent of the brain. That does not mean that we think with 10 percent, or that if we ever learn to use more than 10 percent, we will be superhuman. Remember, the other 90 percent is formed of fibres connecting the cells of the 10 percent to each other.

The only parts of the brain that are not so connected with a specific function of the body are the frontal lobes. Instead of being connected with the body, the fibres from these lobes seem to connect only to the other parts of the cortex. This led researchers to suggest that the frontal lobes act as the controller to the rest of the brain as much as the rest of the brain is the controller of the body.

Many years and many frontal lobotomies later, researchers rejected the idea of the frontal lobes being the source of intuition or conscious thought. What is known, however, is that their removal does not allow either the reversal of behavioural abnormalities or the correction of emotional pain. The true function of the frontal lobes still remains unknown. What also is known is that after a total lobotomy, a person still has the understanding he had before surgery, still can reason on new problems and still can respond with appropriate emotions.[11] In other words, the removal of the frontal lobes does not remove the mental function of the person. The lobes of the brain are made up of special cells called neurons, the source of a person's outward expression. A neuron can initiate activity from the brain; however, it cannot initiate thought. A simple experiment will illustrate this.

Listen carefully to the sounds around you. You will hear sounds

---

11   W. F. Freeman and J. Watts, *Psychosurgery in the Treatment of Mental Disorders and Intractable Pain* (Thomas, 1950).

that you were not hearing a short time ago while you were engrossed in reading this material. Now you can return to focusing your attention on reading, and again you can gradually dismiss those sounds. The point is that you can dismiss them even though they are there. Between the origin of the sound and your perception of them, it is not possible for such qualification. Sound is a vibration of the molecules of the medium through which it passes—air, in this case. It continues to exist as long as the vibrations exist. Your ear, passive receptors of this vibration, cannot but respond to it and transmit that vibration through some small bones to the cochlea. Here, a fluid takes up the vibration, transmitting it to some tiny fibres hanging in it and causing some cells to be sufficiently irritated to start an electrical current in the hearing nerve. This happens whenever there is sound reaching your ear. Your brain cells cannot but be stimulated by the activity of the nerve bringing the perception to it. (By the way, this is a similar process for any sense, from touch to vision.) Since these nerve impulses cannot but respond to all of the sounds reaching them, it follows that your brain cells, or those associated with hearing, cannot but be stimulated by all the sounds reaching your ears. If your mental function was a result of the activation of those cells, you cannot but be made aware of all the sounds reaching your ear, or by default the most prominent ones.

This is not the case, as you know. You can divert your attention to the most interesting sound or the most threatening one, even if that sound was the softest one reaching your ear. You can turn off your attention while someone is speaking to you, even though that person's voice still activates the cells of the hearing centre of your brain. What is more is that such information is not stored unconsciously for you to retrieve when you are ready to pay attention to it. Conscious activity, therefore, must occur beyond the level of the cells of the brain. As we have discovered, the next logical level should be the molecular level, that of the chemicals of the brain. The brain cells produce many chemicals that are unique to the brain. Some of these chemicals have been identified; others still remain elusive. If your mental activities, including feelings, are the result of the activity of such chemicals (as is a popular perception in some circles), then it is logical to presume that the manipulation of those chemicals can affect your mental function. It also will be logical to presume that any condition that reduces the concentration of those chemicals also will reduce your mental function. As mentioned earlier, many of these chemicals have not been identified. The frustration that medical science experiences in trying to manipulate these chemicals, and so treat emotional disturbances, does not prove that mental function is not related to chemicals. It proves only that it is not related to those chemicals that have been identified and used. Those that appear to work also do not prove that mental function is a result of those chemicals; they simply can be shown to affect the medium through which information can be transmitted to your brain cells or from those cells. As we manipulate the medium, we change the perception, and perhaps vice versa.

In the late '70s, a startling discovery made this even more relevant. John Lorber, a professor of paediatrics at the University of Sheffield, decided to use the new technique of CT scans in 1976 to examine about 500 patients over 20 years of age. Some were patients with treated hydrocephalus and some were never diagnosed with the disease. These included people who had already started functioning at high levels of job responsibilities: nurses, university graduates and members of executive councils. The scans revealed that some of the patients had such enormous dilated ventricles that there was hardly any brain left above the tentorium. The systematic CT showed very thin residual brain in some of these subjects. Yet "they had no physical defects and functioned with IQs above the bright normal range."[12]

Hydrocephalus is a condition that exists when the overflow drainage of excess fluids from the brain through a natural opening to the spinal cord has been blocked. Fluid accumulates in the ventricles and pushes the brain out. In babies, this causes the head to swell to large proportions. In adults whose skulls are more rigid, no changes are obvious on the outside, but the accumulation of fluid on the inside pushes the brain against the skull, causing it to atrophy from the pressure. It is fair to observe that regardless of the type of chemicals that might have been produced by the brain, such chemicals would either have been stored in excessively large quantities in the ventricular fluid or produced in extremely reduced quantities as a result of the compression.

There are no special elements common to the brain that may suggest

---

12   John Lorber, "Is Your Brain Really Necessary?" *Nursing Mirror* 152 (18): 29–30.

mentation at the atomic level. That is, in Mendeleev's table of elements, there is no special element that can be associated with thinking. However as with any other nervous tissue, the brain carries electrical impulses. If the electrical activity within the brain is the process of thinking, a hypothesis upheld in some circles, we will expect that the manipulation of that electrical activity will affect emotional states, thinking or understanding. We also will expect that any reduction or diversion of such activity will reduce those three functions.

It has been observed that if there is interference with the electrical activity of the brain, as happens in shock therapy or stroke, our capacity to express ourselves coherently is reduced. After the acute situation has passed, however, we will regain the full ability to reason, emote and understand. The loss of expression during the acute stage can easily be explained as damage to your capacity to express your thoughts, but not necessarily to formulate them. The return to full function after such injury suggests that thought could not be the result of electrical activity because the chronic effects of such an injury, such as a stroke, will continue to reduce or divert normal electrical activity and so will definitely reduce your capacity to think—that is, if thinking is a result of electrical activity.

This leaves us with the smallest particle known to man, the quantum particle. We have the ability to measure quantum activity. If conscious thought results from the quantum activity of the brain, then we should discover that its activity will fluctuate with fluctuations of emotions, thinking or insight. If such an association cannot be demonstrated, it will mean that the mind is neither quantum activity nor any function that can affect quantum activity.

In 1979, A. S. Gevins and others did a study using 23 participants. They attached electrodes to the skull to measure brain wave changes and, while maintaining constancy in visible external conditions, placed them through a variety of mental challenges. Their findings that "EEG correlates were distinguishable, repeatable and relatively invariant across the subjects," and that "it is unclear whether EEG patterns found to distinguish complex behaviours were related to the cognitive components of tasks or to sensory-motor related factors"[13] suggested that there was no EEG change that was associated specifically with cognitive function. Any changes could be explained by the differences in physical performance. These findings suggest that it is not possible to measure the existence of the person by measuring the physical extremes of the body or activities of the brain. The person, the conscious activity with which everyone identifies, can only be said to exist as an entity that is not measurable as matter.

THE REALITY OF CONSCIOUS ENERGY

From the information discussed in the previous chapter, we know that the discovery that the human mind does not have properties associated with matter does not necessarily relegate the mind to being some ethereal substance, but it suggests that as an entity, it must exist outside of the limitations of matter. Again, Walker concluded that "although the level of the brain's activity is less during sleep, the brain wave pattern does not disappear as consciousness seems to do."[14] This means that as a mind, we must be an energy source that is not matter. It does not function with the brain—it functions distinct to the brain. This argument is intended only to determine the property of the mind from an observation of what it is not. We know that it cannot be a composite of smaller units as this will require that there be some form of attraction-repulsion effect of smaller units on each other, a property that will allow it to be measured. With regard to matter, the true entity must be the quark particle or the quantum energy that activates it, not any of the composite forms. Matter can only be destroyed or distorted to the level of this basic entity. By no longer being a composite of smaller parts, such an entity cannot be destroyed. Only the relationship between adjacent entities can be destroyed or distorted. Matter as identified by the basic component cannot be destroyed; matter identified as the composite can deteriorate into the components and thus be destroyed, at least at that level.

---

13   A. S. Grevins, "EEG Patterns During 'Cognitive' Tasks. 1. Methodology and Analysis of Complex Behaviours," *Electroencephalography and Clinical Neurophysiology* 47 (1979): 693–703.

14   Evan Harris Walker, "The Nature of Consciousness," *Mathematical Biosciences* 7 (1970): 157.

With regard to the human being, the true entity may be described as conscious energy. It is a basic entity—that is, one that is not a composite of subparts; thus it is a complete existent. By not being measurable, it shows itself as not affecting or being affected by an instrument, a sensitive object that shows its reaction to the electromagnetic forces of another physical object. Therefore, like the basic entity of matter, it also cannot be destroyed. For the same reason, it cannot form itself into a different shape, because shape is both a property of measurable matter and the display of how the components interact at that time. It cannot occupy space because space is relative to other physical matter—again a property of matter. Thus, it also cannot be assumed that conscious energy can be distorted by the presence of another conscious energy to form a different entity or build into a larger mass. As such an entity—the mind, person, soul, consciousness or whatever name you give it—cannot have colour because colour is the behaviour of light particles reflected from an object, an event that requires the attractive-repulsive forces associated with matter. Consciousness also cannot have size or position because size and position are measures of existence relative to the location of other units or a composite of such units.

Another significant observation that the human mind is such an immaterial entity is that you can expand your mind, and even if you use the insight of another person to acquire the information necessary to do so, that other person will not be depleted of what he or she may have shared. In fact, the other person can also grow by the act of sharing. On the other hand, a material object can be enlarged, but to do so, you must deplete some other area of the material you have used.

An Uncomplicated Objective

Now that we have succeeded in questioning whatever beliefs you may have had about your identity, it is time for you to take a look at yourself as conscious energy and understand what it means to be such. One thing you do know is that as such an existent, your basic need—one that is common to anything that exists—is the need to be respected as what you are, sufficient to be allowed to be that entity without prejudice or provocation.

Every entity has that need. Go back to chapter 3, when we looked at identity. A thing has an identity as that thing as long as it remains that thing. It has value as that thing only if it is used and respected for being that thing. The longer it stays as that thing, the more valuable it is as that thing compared to another thing that changes or breaks down at the slightest stress. As we have seen in the previous chapter, the natural tendency for any composite form is to disintegrate into its subparticles. Value can be described as the ability to resist the natural tendency to disintegrate.

As conscious energy, as a true entity that is not a transitional composite of smaller particles, its existence is stable. You do not have to fight to maintain your existence as conscious energy. You do not wake up in the morning wondering who you are. You know you are you, and that is a given state. You do not look in the mirror to see if you are the same person as you were yesterday. In fact, if you look into the mirror and see a distorted image, you do not conclude that you are not you but are someone else; you simply wonder what happened to your face last night. Even as the body deteriorates, you exist as a continuum of what you were. Your value cannot be determined by how well you can survive. You will survive—that is, until you die. As Shakespeare said, "It seems to me most strange that men should fear, seeing that death, a necessary end, will come when it will come."[15] But the human being, born with a body that is fully formed, starts life as a mind that needs to be birthed. The only thing anyone has ever gained in life is knowledge, no matter what we have striven to get or achieve, and we get only as much as we have endeavoured to get. While we exert ourselves to get it, we grow; if we do not, we stagnate. The natural tendency of the human mind is to stagnate. Therefore, the value of the human mind is to oppose stagnation. You know that you are significant as an existent when you can contribute of yourself—something that is yours, created by you or earned by you. When you reach that stage, you enjoy the contentment that what you are is as good as or better that what you started off being. You are fulfilled.

If as conscious energy, the product of your activity is insight, you become more significant the more insight you can create. If the rate of creation of such insight is dependent on the momentum of conscious energy, then you become more significant the greater your momentum as a conscious energy. The more you use that energy to create insight,

---

15   William Shakespeare, *Julius Caesar*, Act 2, Scene 2.

the more insight there is to allow you greater significance, and then the more fulfilled you will be. Your objective has to be to develop a momentum of creativity, one that will allow you as much insight as you can need at any time. How can you determine if it is true that your significance can be tied to your ability to create insight? You can determine this simply by examining yourself and observing what you are now that allows you to be of any greater significance than you were when you were born.

Concentrate on yourself for a moment and check the improvements you have made since you were born. You may start from any objective. You may examine many areas that you believe have been improved— yet if you examine them closely, you will observe that any apparent improvement in external attributes is relative to some arbitrary value.

Material wealth is so relative to the desire of others to obtain it that it cannot be considered a dependable asset. For example, owning a large acreage in Antarctica is not a dependable asset. Your body may have become stronger in muscular size, but it is a gain over which you have so little control that a tiny virus can destroy it. Its strength cannot be considered to be a dependable an asset because illness can destroy that strength regardless of your most valiant efforts. What is more is that as you grow old (a process that starts at birth), the cells are less supple than they were as a baby. They are reduced in vigour.

There is only one asset in which you have had any true improvement, and that is your insight. You have a greater understanding of the world and of yourself today than you had when you were born, or even yesterday. You also know that all of that insight was developed by the activity of your conscious energy, your creativity. You created the insight. The greater the momentum of that creativity, the greater is the development of your insight. It stands to reason that to develop yourself to your greatest potential, you need to stimulate your creativity; the more effort you direct at it, the more efficient its development will be.

When you think of it, however, it seems so strange that people spend so much time trying to reach many other less stable objectives that neither add to their identity nor make it more secure, while the only gain they really ever make is that of the development of their conscious energy. It seems strange that they will expend so much effort presuming that the gains they make in these supportive areas are true gains, when those areas actually change independent of their efforts, sometimes in direction they choose and sometimes in the opposite direction. Then their gains must really be only irrelevant gains, their losses irrelevant losses. There are many people who have devoted their energies to securing physical survival by rigidly balancing their diets and avoiding all responsibility that leads to stress, still having to face an untimely death, either from the very problems they were trying to avoid or from some unassociated condition. You must be careful not to conclude that just because you have done what you understand to be correct and have survived, your success is the result of your focus on surviving any more than you can blame failures on your inability to take all possible precautions.

There once was a story told of a man who stood at a corner in Times Square in New York, clapping every 15 minutes on the quarter hour. When an observer questioned the strangeness of his actions, he explained that he was doing it to keep away the elephants. The observer assured him that there were no elephants in New York City. The man then turned to the observer and confirmed, "See? It is working."

Another man, at a different corner, may be stomping his feet at similar intervals for the same reason. Neither will want to stop and consider the other's solution, because each one believes that it is his action that brings on the desired objective, and therefore it cannot be discontinued or even paused.

It is easy to see the stupidity in such an action. Yet, you do it daily; I do it daily. In fact it is the action of everyone in this world. We spend our time trying to survive, a feat over which we have no control. While we are surviving, we believe that it is due to our specific efforts. That is why every single person believes that he or she has the correct approach to life, simply because he or she is surviving. And that is why, despite the fact that your only gain has been conscious development, you still are inclined to devote your time toward securing survival—a feat over which you have no control. It is time for you to do the sensible thing and give more attention to acquiring what you can acquire and less on the wasted effort of securing what you cannot secure. If, as that conscious energy, the only achievement you have made or can make is to grow, is it not obvious that your objective is just that, to grow?

You are born as a
force of conscious energy with
only the potential for creativity

Your creativity grows as you use it.
You attain a momentum of growth that is unique to you.

Figure 4.   Your Development as a Conscious Energy

You start life as a miniscule, conscious energy with the potential to grow. You have the opportunity to grow into someone who can contribute the unique contents of your conscious energy. Is it not obvious that your objective in attempting to grow is to develop momentum in that conscious energy as efficiently as you can? You cannot be efficient if, by focusing on what you cannot achieve, you attain only the minimum gains on what you truly can achieve, but only as the fallout from those other endeavours. On the other hand, you will recognize that any greater use of creativity will lead to a corresponding growth in insight—and as a result the opportunity for a similar growth in fulfilment, depending on the efficiency with which you measure yourself. When you realize this, you will have accomplished that which you have the ability to accomplish, a greater momentum of conscious energy.

A LOOK AT AN ULTIMATE OBJECTIVE

You will see that there is a good incentive to know yourself as more than a mere physical body and to focus on developing the momentum of conscious energy as your main objective. It is not necessary, however, for you to embrace religion or to accept any of our foregoing arguments in order to decide that, as an objective, growth is your only realistic option. If religion or our prior arguments have already convinced you, you will have reached the stage of insight that will take you deeper into knowing and accepting yourself. You can reach your own conclusion simply by examining the alternatives.

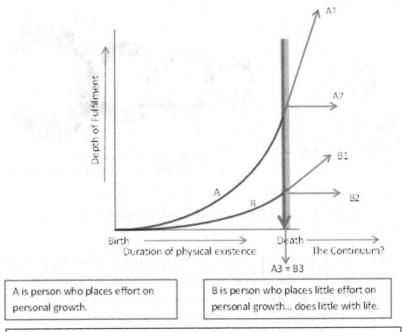

A is person who places effort on personal growth.

B is person who places little effort on personal growth... does little with life.

Each choice has one of three possible mathematical outcomes:

Outcome 1. (A1, B1) Projected into a continuum at the pace developed

Outcome 2 (A2, B2) Projected into the continuum at the level we have achieved

Outcome 3 (A3, B3) No projection; life is only physical existence

Except for outcome 3, A has superior advantage in the continuum. But in option 3, there is no continuum but A also has advantage during physical existence.

Conclusion: There is no advantage to complacency!

Figure 5. PURPOSE TO GROW

Look at Figure 5. From the perspective of our foregoing logic, you may accept that you are conscious energy that can develop momentum through the activity of addressing change (A1, B1). Second, from a religious perspective, you can accept that you are a spiritual existent that will enjoy fulfilment to the level you have achieved from your own endeavours (A2, B2). Thirdly, from a pragmatic perspective, you can reject all theories about that which you cannot measure and accept that you are only a physical body and that conscious energy will disintegrate with the body in some way (A3, B3).

If you will examine each of these alternatives, you will realize that regardless of the perspective you have chosen, there is no argument that will justify any objective other than development of momentum. If you accept continued momentum as your ultimate purpose, an objective of improved creative momentum is the only way to achieve it. If you accept personal achievement as your purpose, an objective of improved creative momentum is the only way of reaching your highest personal achievement.

If you accept that there is no purpose beyond material survival, it does not matter what happens after the body ceases to exist (A3, B3). There is, however, the necessity to enjoy contentment during the period of that material existence. Such a purpose cannot be satisfied without you growing to meet the demands of the material world as it continues to change and challenge you beyond your developed abilities to manage them. An objective of improved creative momentum, even just for immediate survival, is necessary. So you see, it does not matter whether your ultimate purpose is defined; your immediate objective cannot but be growth. There is no argument for complacency.

I wish to reassure those readers who may object to this argument as being a concerted effort to deny the existence of a deity by advocating independent growth. If you will examine it carefully, you will see that it only gives a non-religious argument toward the recognition of purpose as existential growth. It neither uses God nor denies God's existence. The common belief that the human being is an existent created in the same nature of the deity suggests that we must pay respect to that deity for our existence, and such an objective is not necessarily disputed. That is, God will want us to grow to be like Him. There are many people who may be considered highly spiritual but who have no religious affiliation. Some confirmed atheists stimulate themselves as forces of reason and so are growing to be greater conscious forces while denying the existence of God. Conversely, there are many religious people who will not take up the mantle of responsibility, content to bask in the supposition that their acceptance of God excuses them from doing or growing. They stagnate and thus cannot grow to be like that infinite force of reason.

Accepting this commonly held belief that the human being is created in the image and likeness of God, it may be argued that such a deity will also be the epitome of the human being. We are like God and therefore God is like us. If God is invisible, we are invisible, so we cannot be the human form, or God must be a human form. Therefore, if God exists, He must have what we can determine to be the properties of the human being, only developed to an infinite intensity. Since it can be argued that each human being is an individual—that is, not a composition of parts nor a component in parts—each person can grow to an individually determined level of creativity, insight and fulfilment. You and I and many other entities like us can exist to every conceivable stage of development without ever interfering with each other; each is capable of growing from the assistance of the other without the other ever being depleted by that process of giving what he or she can use. There can be a virtual string of individual entities with progressively greater levels of development. At the head of this line, there can possibly be a conscious force that has evolved to such infinite growth or development that it will have infinite creativity, infinite wisdom and infinite fulfilment or love. If such a conscious energy exists, or even if it is not infinite but so far ahead of any of us that it can be deemed to be infinite, we have a picture of a powerful, knowing, loving entity. If you wish to refer to that entity as a deity or God, you will not have defined the deity in any lesser manner than has been taught. The only difference will be that you will have arrived at your conclusion from a direction of logic rather than faith.

In short, you may have accepted that the deity existed because of what has been reported as divine revelations, and because of the awe in which the apparent power that deity seemed to hold in the measurable universe, and from that conclusion that the human being had some special status with that deity. Now, you can conclude that the deity must exist because we know of the special nature of the human being as conscious energy, and that it is possible for conscious energy to exist at infinite intensity without affecting or being affected by the spatial limitations observed of the material world. If such a deity exists as the fullest intensity of conscious energy, then any attempt you make to increase the momentum of the conscious energy that is you will translate as a desire to be closer to that deity. Therefore, we can grow because we want to be closer to God, or we can be closer to God because we have grown. Thus if your desire to be closer to that deity causes you to grow, or if your aspiration to growth leads to greater closeness to that deity, it really does not make a great deal of difference that is more correct; either one will lead to the accomplishment of the other.

Perhaps I can illustrate this with a simple visualization. You are in a race where the only apparent objective is a brass ring that is just out of your reach. Gaining the ring becomes the ultimate challenge. You run hard and are able to get close to it. Yet as soon as you do, something or someone pulls it away, and you have to strive to reach it again. This continues for some time: striving to reach it, almost reaching it and having it pulled away, until you became frustrated by your efforts. You sit down to rest, exhausted. Then you realize something that was not apparent to you while your intent was so firmly fixed on the single objective you thought you had to meet. You learn that in your attempts to strive for the brass ring, you have been gaining distance—you are much further ahead than you would have been had you succeeded in reaching the ring. As it was, you always had something to motivate you to go forward. Maybe it was that you really were required to accomplish the forward movement, or perhaps it was that you were goaded into developing the strength to be more capable of using the brass ring when you acquire it.

We may never know if your objective is to use your capacity to grow in order to reach the fulfilment of being close to the deity, or if the desire to be close to such a deity causes you to develop the strength to deal with a greater challenge beyond your material vision. Does it really matter? Each human being is challenged with the same amount of change and disruption as is anyone else. Each human being has the capacity to contribute as much as or more than can any other. It is the individual contribution of wisdom with which none of us was born that differentiates and determines the value of each person.

THE NATURE OF GOD

We see that consciousness has three properties, each feeding into the other, and therefore each equal in importance. The three properties are those of creativity or reason, knowledge or wisdom and fulfilment or love. Let us temporarily replace the three we have understood and now accepted with the three we have just made equivalent to them. The three properties will be reason, wisdom and love. We have indicated that man was stated to have been created in the image and likeness of God. Thus God will have three properties of reason, wisdom and love, but to infinite levels: infinite reason, infinite wisdom and infinite love. Is this what Thomas Aquinas meant when he confirmed the trinity of God? The manifestation of creativity and reason, or the dominant one, may be the father. The manifestation of wisdom, the word, is the son. Finally the manifestation of love is the spirit. That will make sense because if man is truly created in the image and likeness of God, and if God is a trinity, then man must perforce be a trinity, and God's trinity is also man's trinity. Then God cannot be angry if God is infinite strength. Anger is an emotion of weakness, a defence against hurt. God's relationship to man, then, would be that of a force that does not need us but wants to share the happiness of knowledge. Thus, it is an invitation to grow and join Him. It cannot be that of punishment for wrongdoing. Then the idea of sin must be that of its Latin meaning—that is, without. Sin is the existence without God. Here again is the invitation to grow, to be not *without*.

INGREDIENTS FOR GROWTH

We do know that if we wish to grow efficiently, we require two major ingredients. One is the challenge of something that requires us to create an understanding of it, something that challenges us beyond your developed understanding. The second is the fulfilment to fuel our creativity to increase its momentum and expand that understanding. The first ingredient is already available in unlimited quantities, or at least in quantities that are far greater than we ever can exhaust. It is the near infinite challenge from the constantly changing environment. No matter how much we know, no matter how activated our momentum of creativity is, we can be assured that there always will be more new challenges for us to face, far more than the tiny surface we have already scratched.

The other ingredient is less available. It is the assurance of knowing that we have the respect for our contribution that can allow us to tackle the challenge independently, creatively and purposefully. We have to know that and believe it implicitly. Wow, that's a tall order! We have seen how we can establish a way to get it from how we apply yourself to the world. We have also seen how fickle that feedback can be. Now, we are looking at how we can get that by measuring ourselves using a different definition of our identity and objective or purpose. This definition relies on our ability to see ourselves as primarily a thinking mind with a purpose to grow, not a body with a need to survive.

We will examine how you can do it yourself so that you always have access to it and so that you get it realistically and appropriately. That is, though you give it to yourself, you do not do so cheaply. This requires you to be accountable for yourself in a world that will make your best efforts seem inadequate. This contentment or reassurance comes only when you have been able to satisfy the measures you use to define yourself. Since we are now referring to you as a conscious energy, you will have to show that you have used your conscious energy for what it has been intended: to create new insight. Assurance confirms your value as a conscious energy and gives you the fuel to continue increasing your momentum. The only way you really can be sure of receiving this affirmation if you truly deserve it, therefore, is to have yourself judged for accomplishing what you truly can accomplish, growth of insight and understanding, an assessment that only you can make. You must be accountable to yourself as well as for yourself.

Being Self-Affirmed

If, as conscious energy, you cannot be measured with the instruments of the material world, it also is logical to presume that your momentum of activity and any growth in such momentum also cannot be measured by the world. Yet as you know, the activity of conscious energy creates insight and understanding, greater activity allowing for greater insight. It is possible to assess growth of momentum by growth of insight. You must allow new insight to be judged against past insight. If instead you follow the usual way to accomplish this by judging it against either a task or the opinion of other people, then you will encounter some problems. There are three problems with this arrangement.

The first is that real growth in momentum is a factor of previous momentum. If previous momentum cannot be revealed, such a comparison cannot be made, and you are judged only on the performance you have revealed. This may not allow appropriate recognition of the momentum you truly have developed. Let me give you an example.

103

When I first learned to play golf, I progressed quite quickly from an absolute novice to a somewhat okay player. I joined a group who did not know my past skills. My first three shots were poor, and I flubbed the last one. My partners showed disapproval and judged me poorly for my skills—yet I had played almost 100 percent better than I did before. They did not know that I was just starting and had progressed well to that point. My judgment of myself was approving for my progress. Their judgment of me was disapproving for my performance.

The second problem is that an expressed insight differs from a true insight according to the efficiency with which you can express it. When your body, that instrument through which you communicate with the world, is functioning perfectly, you are able to express yourself at your best. The greater part of this problem, however, is that the body is rarely at peak efficiency. Constant change within that structure, and the need to train any form of expression, precludes any possibility that what comes out will be anything but a small fraction of what is meant to come out. Performers and athletes know this: They know what to do and have practised and reached a peak of performance. Yet on the crucial day, the body does not respond as well for reasons they cannot identify at that time. They appear to know less than they really do. Students taking an exam, or a young man meeting a girl, also can allude to this experience.

The third problem is that expressed insight is judged, either from how it applies to a task or how an observer assesses its applicability. As you know, the conditions that define a particular task change constantly. The insight, expressed to the task as it originally presented, may be inadequate for the new conditions that affect the task by the time the insight has been revealed. When the assessor is another person, you also must remember that the other person may see the situation that activates your creativity from a different perspective. He or she then judges your expression by comparing it not with your previous insight (a factor that may not be available to that person) but with his or her own insight—that is, his or her way of seeing the problem. It is considered right, and you effective, if your expressed insight is similar to or more extensive than that person's. Conversely, it may be considered wrong, and you ineffective, if your correct solution does not equate what they see as right. Added to this is the reality that neither the person nor the task can accurately judge true insight, making such attempts to measure your momentum of conscious energy a predictable failure.

The only way such judgment of growth can be accurate is if you judge present insight against past insight, parameters that are accessible only to you. In addition, as conscious energy similar that which defines every other person, you are as capable of making an assessment as well as those others. In addition, your assessment is more appropriately associated with the level to which you have developed yourself. I have had to use this logic many times to encourage a young person to grow up past their dependence on a parent's approval or fear of their disapproval. I had to show them that they are at the level their parents were when their parents had authority over them. What they also have is access to their personal capabilities, knowledge of personal progress and a view of the issue that is more pertinent to their present assessment than it is to an assessment of it from the past.

If you will accept that you have full capacity to measure yourself by your growth, and if in doing so you discover that you possessed an inadequate understanding at a previous exposure to a situation, then you also must have the maturity to realize that such discovery is a confirmation of growth. Simply stated, if you look back and discover that you were stupid yesterday, does it not also tell you that you are smarter today than you were yesterday? What you knew yesterday was as well-developed as you were able to have then. At that time you did not see that what you were doing was insufficient; in fact, you may have believed it was great. Today, you may look back and realize the inadequacy of yesterday. Therefore, today's insight must be greater than yesterday's. Between the two, there must have been further growth. Instead of being ashamed of your past inadequacy, you can congratulate yourself on being wiser today than you were yesterday. Of course you will also realize that if you have continued to grow, you will discover tomorrow that today's insight is also inadequate—for tomorrow, that is.

This is the advantage of self-affirmation, assessing yourself on the value of what you truly are doing, expanding yourself as conscious energy. The more developed that energy is, the more valuable you are. The fuel for that growth is affirmation. The only way you can be assured of the affirmation you need is to have a source that gives it for the most efficient measure of you that is possible. You have to be self-affirmed.

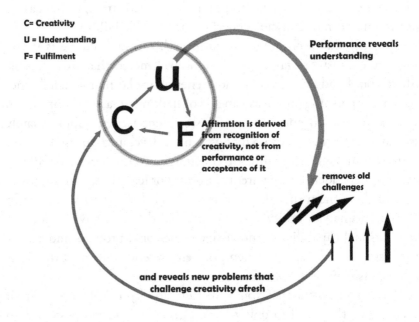

Figure 6.   Affirmation Through Self-Recognition of Creativity

Regardless of how fulfilled you are, however, you are not using it efficiently if you do not divert it into fuelling your conscious energy. This means that that good feeling is not just for you to savour—you must invest it. You must be creative, and for that you need to be challenged. Just as you can stagnate and so lose significance as conscious energy if you do not get the fuel of fulfilment, so too will you stagnate if you have the fuel of fulfilment but do not use it to generate more momentum. You need both. The world has one in abundance: challenges. To grow to your fullest potential, you need both in abundance: challenges and affirmation. You need the other, affirmation, in just as much abundance. Do not also expect it to be given you by the world. It is impossible for the world to be able to do it without having one offset the other. It is unfair to expect the world to provide each to you in alternate sets. This is done for the child. When you have grown up, you must take up your own cause; become a doer to the world instead of a receiver from it.

THE ADVANTAGES OF BEING SELF-AFFIRMED

You are affirmed only when you use your creativity, an activity that is stimulated by new challenges and stagnated in stability, and so you will have the best opportunity to be fulfilled in an unstable world, a world of perpetual, new challenges. Therefore, even though you will draw your fulfilment from yourself, you still will be humble, finding it necessary to keep looking for more challenges, for the opinions of more people (especially if these take the form of constructive criticism), so as to keep expanding your momentum in order to continue receiving affirmation. You will be better able to deal with the realities of the world, seeing new problems as opportunities to develop your mind, not challenges to prove yourself. Your performances will be true revelations of your ideas, not investments to procure affection or recognition. You will be able to accomplish because you feel good about yourself instead of seeking to feel good about yourself because of what you have accomplished—an attitude that lends itself to even greater accomplishments.

You will be more mature, a source of respect and consideration rather than a needy dependent who constantly drains those around you and chases away that for which you have developed a need. You will be able to reveal yourself without fearing that you will show your inadequacies, because you will see inadequacies as revelations of where you can improve yourself next. You will see criticism as the consideration of the other person in reflecting your expression and so giving you the opportunity to improve it. You will be nurtured by what the world is willing to give you (change and uncertainty), not by what it has so little to give (recognition and affirmation). You will be able to receive as much pleasure simply from sharing as much as you do from being challenged, because the act of true sharing forces you to create more insight to be shared, seeking more challenges to feed that creativity. Hence the more you give, the more fulfilled you will be, and the more able you will be to satisfy your purpose of activating and expanding your conscious energy. When you can use what the world is prepared to give you (the continuous presence of more work) as the opportunity for obtaining fulfilment, you will have reached the peak of efficiency.

SUMMARY

If you will examine all the things you see as strong and try to determine what gives them strength, you will discover that strength does not really lie in physical power or size as much as it lies in invincibility. The object that cannot be destroyed is stronger than the one that can be destroyed, regardless of how powerful it may appear. The object that gains its strength from the weapons with which you try to destroy it gets stronger every time you attack.

When, as a self-affirmed person, you learn to use the challenges the world can throw at you, you too will be invincible. You will be unafraid of being destroyed because the weapons they use to try to destroy you are the ingredients you need to give you more strength. Just think: when you are promoted, you really are placed in a position of greater pressure. If you do not have the energy to conquer the new challenges, the promotion will show your inadequacies. If you have the inner strength to use the new challenges as inputs to your creative talents, you will become more capable than you were before the promotion; you will be strong. When you accept that the unknowns the world uses to manipulate you are only new challenges to stimulate your creativity, you will be immune to manipulation.

If you will examine the things that are weak, on the other hand, and try to determine what makes them weak, you will discover that the world can only weaken something that is vulnerable in the first place. In the case of the person, a true entity, that vulnerability comes only when we leave ourselves open for the affirmation we seek from the world—and therefore the rejections it will also give us. When the world withdraws what it was giving, it leaves only what was there. The world does not weaken you; it can only leave you to your own level of weakness.

If, when that affirmation is withdrawn, you are left without any energy or inner strength, it is because you were without it in the first place. An empty glass filled with borrowed substance remains empty when that substance is withdrawn. Yet we see the glass was made empty by the withdrawal. We must learn to see that the withdrawal leaves only what was there in the first place. Getting affirmation from the world is not wrong and can be a pleasant experience. Needing affirmation from the world is wrong because it places you at a disadvantage and raises the world to your master.

As a self-affirmed person, you will be less affected by the withdrawal of affirmation. Because you are fulfilled from a source that rewards your creativity, you are less expectant of acceptance or recognition from others. There will be times when you will receive affirmation from the world; appreciate it and let it be icing on the cake. But you have the cake, so when the icing is taken away, you will feel little loss. Then you truly are invincible. As a self-affirmed person, you will be accountable, independent, capable and a true contributor to our common environment.

The intent here is to use scientific arguments to prove the existence of the mind or soul as a distinct and real entity, not simply a function of the body. Of course such proof is difficult because we are using physical constructs to measure or determine a nonphysical existent. The best we can do is to prove that it does not exist as a physical entity. The argument leaves it to the reader to conclude that because it does not exist as a physical entity, it either does not exist at all or does exist, determined only by the knowledge that he or she exists. Then, since God is of the same nature, the reader can also determine the existence of God using the same arguments. The ultimate objective is to construct a sense of personal purpose in a world of continuous change and instability.

CHAPTER 6

ORGANIZING YOUR MANAGEMENT SKILLS

Now THAT YOU KNOW how to be a self-affirmed person, you will have a different perspective on your relation to the world. Of course, you may not be there yet. You still have to ruminate on the ideas discussed and let them grow in you. When you understand them, they will be yours. You are not learning and applying a technique. You are stimulating your creativity and letting it grow as you think differently. The end result will come on surreptitiously. Regardless of whether the opposition is formed by the material surroundings, the people to whom you relate or your own biological health, you will begin to see them less as potential contributors (or conversely, as agents provocateur to your desired peace of mind) and more as recipients of your organizational skills and administration. You will begin to see that what you do cannot be measured by the world as much as it is needed by it.

When those aspects of your environment are not managed by what you can do, you will see their response less as an indication that your contribution is inadequate, and more as recognition that you have the capacity to give more than you have been able to give so far. Any rejection of your management skills from any part of the world can be seen to be a request for more contribution from you rather than a rejection of what you have already done. You will see this as a compliment. If what you did was not good enough, why would the world ask for more? Remember, the world is not ready to give affirmation to an adult. The world shows its approval not by giving it but by assuming you already know it; you are simply asked for more. A great artist gets three curtain calls not just to give approval but to ask for more.

The world is big, however, and its demands can go on forever. Therefore, no matter how capable you are, you must know that you cannot always give to the world all that it will demand of you. But the world does not know your limits. It therefore will come at you continuously, until those limits are reached or exceeded; then you may be discarded. It is in being discarded—that is, being given a reprieve—that says you are no longer useful, at least at this time. This does not mean that you are expected to do all that is thrown at you or die trying. It means only that you are given the opportunity to function to the level of your own personal limit or reach. In other words, your objective is not to form or shape the world but to be formed and shaped by its persistent demands.

The only way you can satisfy your personal objective of developing your conscious insight and fulfilment is by using your creativity; that means discovering your limits and challenging yourself beyond them. The way you can do that effectively is to use your personally unique management skills if only to determine their limits. In other words, you must have the humility of knowing that whatever you have, no matter how great they may be, can function only within some recognizable limits. Humility gives you the incentive to keep expanding those limits. Knowing those limits means knowing how and where to extend them.

You must know, too, that even after you define your limits, and even if you function beyond them, your contribution will be offered to a world that sees only your presentations (limited as they may be), not the assets that drive them. You will not receive support or encouragement from the world for something it cannot see. Therefore, you must be able to get that encouragement from yourself. Again, I must reiterate, you must be self-affirmed. As a self-affirmed person, you will have learned that affirmation can only be guaranteed when it is based on creativity, your ability to formulate new insight beyond what you already have developed. And you need new challenges to allow that. Your management skills can then either be a way for you to make a contribution from your more developed insight or a way of removing the now redundant problem in order to reveal the next problem that will challenge your creativity anew. In other words, you do in order to show what you know or to get past what you have already conquered in order to be challenged at the next level, not to get approval.

The first requirement for your management skills is that you have something to offer from a unique perspective, or one that has improved beyond your previous perspective. The second is that you must be prepared to use your creativity to analyze and understand the new problem that you will have unearthed.

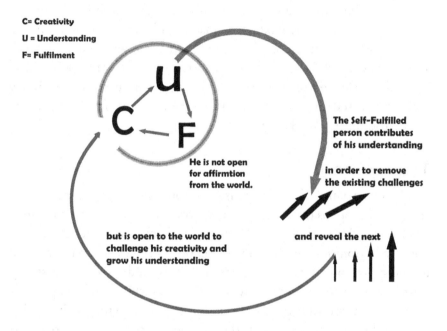

C= Creativity

U = Understanding

F= Fulfilment

The Self-Fulfilled person contributes of his understanding

in order to remove the existing challenges

He is not open for affirmtion from the world.

but is open to the world to challenge his creativity and grow his understanding

and reveal the next

Figure 7.   The Mature Person—the contributor

Both of these requirements ask something of you. They demand that you be independently commissioned to the performance of your duties. You now are recognized as having grown up; you are no longer a waif to be nurtured and groomed into a useful contributor, because you now have reached the maturity of your development. You can take your position as a member of the team. You now are expected to be able and willing to take charge of your own growth, further development and degree of contribution. You are now the helper of the less enlightened. You are the manager, not the managed. In return, you will be given all the ingredients you need to reach your fullest development. As a child, you had at best half of the possible challenges, because space had to be left for the fuel of affirmation, the other half of the necessary ingredients. Now, you can have control over one of the ingredients, affirmation, getting as much of it as you can allow yourself. In addition, you can have as much of the second ingredient you want, the challenges, taking from the infinite quantity available.

The only prerequisite is that you take advantage of that opportunity to be emancipated. You now are your own leader. You must be able to plan your own path and organize your own responsibilities. You must be able to examine the challenges made available to you and choose how extensively you will explore them, when you will take a breather and where you will fix the limit for that particular area of responsibility. You will do this to the satisfaction of your primary objective of always making yourself into a more capable person tomorrow than you are today. You must take charge.

TAKING CHARGE

A person who takes charge is a person who is strong enough to consider the opposition, regardless of how wrong the opposition may seem to be. We indicated in the previous chapter that strength comes not simply from how powerful you are, but from how immune you are to being overcome by the opposition. We also indicated that a strong existent is one that can not only withstand the attacks from the opposition but also use those attacks as nutrition for its own growth. It is invincible because the more you attack it, the stronger it gets. I am sure that you have been exposed to science fiction stories where the invader from outer space is seen as a formidable opponent, even if it does not attack us, simply because it is invincible to the attacks from our weapons, and because it thrives on the energy from nuclear blasts. This is the ultimate example of true strength. This is a state that is fully available to you as a human being. The weapons the opponent uses are the changes that make your familiar conditions uncomfortable and that challenge the upward limits of your higher reason. They are the untimely erosion of a favourite object, the aging or injury to one of your body's organ systems or the unexpected hostility from a previously friendly person. The invincibility you have is your capacity to understand the challenge by growing as a result of its threat. Your only vulnerability is your need for affirmation, the reassurance that you are good enough to do what you are meant to do.

Therefore the first requirement for you to be able to take charge and manage the events that challenge your management skills is to immunize the source of your affirmation from the forces of the world. In other words, you must not wear your heart on your sleeve. The world can only withhold from you what you have allowed it to provide to you in the first place. You must not only learn to be the most dependable source of affirmation to yourself, but you must be prepared to be the only acceptable source. If, as a self-affirmed person, you receive affirmation from the world, then it is icing on the cake—but for goodness sake, have the cake first. The important thing to remember is that it is okay to get affirmation from the world. It is *not* okay to need it, because such dependency places you at the disposition of the world in an area where you are most vulnerable.

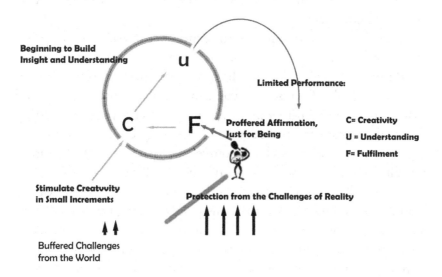

Figure 8. How the Child (or Immature Adult) Relates to the World

SELF-AFFIRMATION

You learned in the previous chapter that you can assure yourself of that affirmation simply by tying your fulfilment to the recognition of your activity as a conscious energy. All you have to do is to look at what you understand and compare it with what you understood prior to taking on that responsibility. Even if you still do not understand the problem as fully as it is presented to you, the important measure can be satisfied if you understand a little more of it than you did before.

If, however, there is no enlightenment to allow you to feel good about your creative capacity, it may be because the problem is too different from the background information you have. This is comparable to a farmer trying to feel good about his ability to use a new deep-sea fishing process. In such a case, you may benefit from doing a strategic retreat and reexamining a smaller part of the problem, perhaps from a different perspective. You may also find that the acquisition of information from a more experienced source can provide you with the necessary foundation to progress at a faster pace. You can ask for help. Remember that other people are only too willing to express their perception of a problem to a person who seems to need it. Such an opportunity provides them with the reassurance that they may have greater wisdom than you, or that what they know has value.

Because you are self-affirmed, the experience of asking for help and exposing your relative lack of insight for that problem does not embarrass you. Rather, it allows you to get the other ingredient, the challenge, in a more manageable form so that you can stimulate your creativity and be fulfilled from its infused momentum. It prevents you from getting affirmation from an unreliable source while giving you all the ingredients for getting it from a truly reliable source and for a truly reliable reason. Humility is the greatest strength anyone can have. It is not that of putting oneself down; it is the strength of immunity and of not caring if another person thinks you are foolish, only seeking the information. Take as an example two of us in the same room with different ideas. Your humility lets you listen to mine and learn from my perspective. My pride lets me feel superior and even condescending of you, because you allowed me to look smarter. At the conclusion, you leave more informed, knowing what you know plus what I know. I leave knowing only when I came in with.

If, on the other hand, you already are in a position where you have drained whatever fuel you have so that you still cannot work on the newly acquired information, then rather than go to the world to have it recharge you with unearned recognition, you still can be fulfilled from the only dependable source: yourself. You must remember that the world

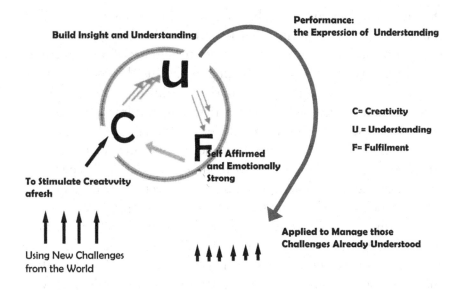

Figure 9.   How the Responsible Adult Relates to the World

prefers to have you as a source of organization and administration, not as the recipient of its good graces. The world resents having to stop to give you even a small recharge. If you wish to understand this a little better, think of yourself as the rest of the world to someone else for a moment. You, just as anyone else, prefer to associate with people who have a lot to give than with those who are seeking something from you. You may feel that way even if those other people rarely request your consideration. It may simply be that they approached you at the wrong time; they may not know that you may have been more considerate at a different time. They only receive the message that you resent having to stop to provide for their needs. Yet you may be one of the few people who are willing to stop and help the other person. This does not matter. What I am trying to get you to understand is not what should be, but what is available to you, as the recipient.

The way you can work on recharging yourself, then, is through looking back at your past accomplishments. First you have to make a strategic retreat from the oppressing situation—take a break. Then you must look at what you understand now, not necessarily of the presenting problem but of something over which you were able to preside, even as it presented as a challenge at first. I frequently tell people that whenever they feel that they are incapable of conquering a new problem, they should think of the first time they learned to ride a bicycle. The idea is to feel affirmed for your ability to be creative, to rise above something that once was above you. By looking at the insight you have been able to create for something that once was difficult, you can respect that conscious energy again and experience the fulfilment you need to energize yourself into working on the new information.

This is the whole idea of prayer: not the penance of repeating a string of words or the attempt to reach a God who will relieve you of your stresses, but the opportunity to reflect on what you have accomplished—even if, to do so, you must be able to perceive that it has been affirmed by some powerful but invisible entity. Therefore, one form of prayer is meditation. The objective is to disconnect yourself from the distractions of the physical reality and get you to appreciate yourself as that conscious or spiritual life force. Then you can truly look at what you have accomplished within the scope of your inner properties of creativity, understanding and fulfilment. You may visualize an invisible God and attempt to associate with that conscious or spiritual energy. You may recite mantras or a repetitive prayer, like the rosary familiar to Catholics. The end result is the same: to disconnect from the physical world and allow the progressive ability to function without distractions in the spiritual world.

The opportunity for you to be recharged does not just lie in your constant accomplishment in a thoroughly unstable situation; neither is it only available when you are forced to make a strategic retreat from an oppressing situation. Instead, you can incorporate it as a disciplined part of your day. As you become more used to doing it, you will be able to fall back on it automatically as a useful source of reassurance. I wonder if this is the undisclosed purpose of evening prayers.

PURPOSE

Another prerequisite for being able to take charge is to have a firm sense of purpose. You will have to become the only person to whom you can look for guidance and direction; therefore you must know what your objective is and why you are going there. One of the determinants we have uncovered in our quest for the nature of conscious energy is that such an entity cannot be destroyed; it cannot waste its opportunities at trying to secure survival, a foregone conclusion, but it must have as its objective the determination to expand itself into realizing its full potential. Your ultimate objective, therefore, must be determined by that need to grow more creative, more insightful and more fulfilled—the need to learn. Your immediate objective must be determined by your need to use the opportunities that are available to grow, and to procure the ingredients that will allow that growth to proceed most efficiently.

The temptation is to reach a stage of development that will provide you with the conditions to guarantee you peace of mind without further effort. However, as a rational being you will be able to use the information provided in the foregoing chapters to conclude that no such conditions are possible. As a rational being, you must take the time to assess this and accept the objective of the maturity of your existence as a conscious energy, not just to win an immediate goal but to make personal growth your major and ultimate objective. Only then will you be capable of taking charge of your own relationship with the world.

The final prerequisite is that you must be prepared to use the opportunities constructively. You are going to be challenged whatever you do. If you do nothing, the old problem stays to haunt you. If you get down to it and solve the old problem, a new one replaces it. I sometimes tell my clients to visualize being in grade 5. If you do well, they place you in grade 6 with harder work. If you fail, they make you repeat grade 5, where the postponed work is just as difficult as it was when you postponed doing it. Therefore, be hungry not for the pleasure of the conquest or the peace of mind but for the new problems. The only way you can do that and enjoy it is by seeing the new challenges as ingredients to the realization of both your fully visualized purpose and your search for fulfilment. Your purpose is to develop your conscious energy, to grow. As a self-accountable person, the fuel for achieving that fulfilment comes from your recognition of its activity. Together they allow you to need only one further ingredient: the challenges to stimulate that activity. You must want those challenges for your own personal development.

This may seem to be a selfish undertaking, one that is directed only at your own personal growth. Yet we all are selfish. The human being is a self-propelled individual; we cannot experience the insight, creativity or fulfilment of another, and neither can we share what we have. We only can share what we can reveal, and we can reveal only as much as we understand. In fact, we cannot but reveal what we understand. Just by the act of applying our insight to a problem, we will have revealed whatever we understand of that problem, even if that application is made only with the intent of surviving the problem.

I am sure that you will admit that much of what you have learned from other people may have occurred without that other person knowing that you were learning from his or her actions or words. Therefore, it cannot be selfish to try to improve that understanding if by improving it you have more to offer the world. If instead you focus on your performance, you will discover that no matter how hard you try, you never can show more of yourself than that which you have been showing repeatedly. However, the harder you try, the less that revelation will be, or the less it will be appreciated by those who already witnessed it.

Performance must be a passive flow from you to the world. The acquisition of the insight that allows the performance is the active pursuit. Performance then becomes a simple revelation of your burgeoning insight, a gift you share with the world—not an offering by which you measure yourself. By being self-affirmed, you can give selflessly because giving does not reduce you; it is only the overflow from an already-fulfilled person.

If you can take charge of that objective of constantly learning, whatever you do will be a true gift, a true representation of a dynamically expanding and fully dependable resource. You know that your association with a challenge is to extract from it what you do not know, so your discovery that a new task will reveal an inadequate performance will not threaten you. Instead, it will stimulate you not to prove yourself, but to improve yourself and then share of that improvement. The world does not teach or coddle you; if the world wants more, it simply shows you that what you gave is insufficient. Someone may even tell you that you are wrong. What that person is really saying is that he or she has an opinion he or she wishes to share, even to get your approval. That person wants to give you something, a unique insight, but does not say that. He or she tells you that you are inadequate. As a self-assured person, you are fulfilled and are not looking for affirmation, but you want more information, so you will use that comment as an invitation to get more information. Thus, you will simply ask for the opinion and listen without feeling compromised. You want information and are getting it. You do not want affirmation and are not getting it.

Establishing Objectivity

You have learned to immunize yourself from the negative feedback of the world simply by recognizing that what appears to be negative feedback is really a challenge to your capability to be more creative and to manage more of the task with greater insight. You have strengthened that immunity by accepting that feedback as the ingredient you need to stimulate your creativity, a momentum you desire. You have learned to be the source of your own affirmation from within to allow you to fuel your creativity and make full use of those challenges. Yet despite emancipating yourself from the inconsistent assessment from the world, you still must emancipate yourself from you.

You must separate yourself as the creative entity from what you recognize as your ideas, the insight, which is the product of that creativity. If you will recall one of the rules that govern modern society, you will see how such objectivity does not conflict with traditional beliefs. You must remember that modern Western society has evolved in great part from the teachings of Christianity, imposing conditions on you even if you are not partial to religion. Part of the Christian teaching is based on an admonition to love God with our whole hearts and to love our neighbours as ourselves. Whatever you do, the acceptability of your performance is affected by how different people interpret this commandment. The important consideration here is the definition of love: It is an expression, not just an experience. To love is to respect, appreciate and honour the existence of an entity not as something else, but as that entity is meant to be. Thus you will consider the unique qualities inherent to that entity and appreciate it with those qualities intact. Let me explain in metaphorical terms. I have an expensive pen. I appreciate it, but that appreciation is only real if I appreciate it as a pen and use it as a pen. If instead I appreciate it only as an ornament, I cannot have love for that inanimate thing. If I disrespect it by using it as a lock pick, am I not also disrespecting it and thus not loving it as the entity it is? The point is that even if you consider or respect the entity simply to be able to benefit from its unique qualities, the same goal will be attained. You use it appropriately because you respect it, and you respect it when you use it appropriately. On the other hand, any attempt to change it into something else as a prerequisite for that consideration not only cheats that entity from being what it is, it cheats you from benefiting from what that entity can contribute to your growth.

Let us see how this can be applied to the three entities to which you are expected to give consideration: God, your neighbour and yourself. From our preceding discussions, you will remember that we have considered the human being to be a conscious energy functioning within a body. Our purpose possibly is to evolve into a useful contributor to the world and to our own peace of mind. As a result, we have suggested that what we believe to be the deity may be a similar conscious energy, but one that has evolved to a stage of usefulness and fulfilment that supersedes all others. If so, it is easy to give consideration to each of these entities without having to take from one in order to give to the other. You can give consideration to any conscious energy by respecting the product of that conscious act. As creative entities, we create insight; we share that insight either as opinions or expressive acts. The acts of the other people are their opinions that are expressed as their personal solutions for some common problem. Your acts are the opinions you form on the perceptions you have of those common issues. The acts of the deity, then, must be those unexpected changes that are visited on us by nature as a natural consequence of its existence.

This presents us with a dilemma. How can we give consideration to an entity whose acts are in conflict with ours? Are we not then required to choose one over the other? This is the dilemma that you have to face daily. You frequently solve it by making either a rigid choice, or by indulging in inconsistency, giving consideration to one now and then another at a later time. Some people choose to consider themselves, but that is as a physical presence. They see the unwanted changes in life as burdens that hinder their comforts. If they are religious, they may resort to prayer, asking for help to remove those problems. If they are not religious, they may use other means to be relieved of them. They may see the different opinions of other people as unnecessary issues that burden them and interfere with their peace of mind, frequently putting down these other people in order to elevate the value of their own opinions.

Some people choose to show blind consideration to the deity. They may accept every problem and every change as impositions they must face to show their undying devotion. They may do this at the expense of their own personal growth and development. They may impose their interpretation onto other people or neglect their consideration of them in order to place all their efforts at pleasing God, believing that they are accumulating "brownie points" as compensation for their total disregard for themselves.

Some people choose to show consideration for other people, placing the opinions of other people ahead even of their own. They suppress their own opinions as long as there are other possible alternatives available. They act to help other people not with their own solutions, but as instruments for the satisfaction of the expressed needs of those others. They allow this interpretation to supersede their responsibility to nature (the acts of God). They please people at the cost of themselves and their responsibilities.

Look at these three considerations: There is a common thread in that we focus on survival. We relate to God as a protector or correctional

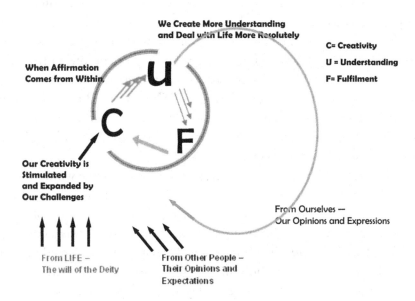

Figure 10. How to Show Consideration for all Three Entities (and GROW)

authority. We consider ourselves with respect to our comfort or physical survival. We relate to others either to respect their feelings or to follow their opinions as facts that supersede ours. Any one conflicts with the others, so we cannot do justice to all at the same time.

Yet it truly is possible to be able to accomplish all three without resorting to inconsistency. Let us return to the definition of the human being as conscious energy. Then you are not just your opinion; you are an entity that can create opinions. Can you see the power in this? First, if you create opinions, then your strength lies in what you can do and not what you have done. Simply relying on what you have done in the past stifles what you are now, even though you created it. But by respecting yourself for being creative, you already know that your last opinion is not you; it is only your product. Any new challenge is an invitation for you to display yourself and your creativity.

We also cannot see or know the creative force of the deity, so showing consideration for the deity must be directed at the product of what we consider the acts of God, the changes and unwanted problems imposed by nature. Then every imposition and disaster is an opportunity for further growth. Prayer, if you are so disposed, will more appropriately be conducted as a request for more challenges, the opportunity both to grow and to prove to God that you are a good soldier, servant or worker, whatever name you choose. Somehow it can be seen as being chosen for a tough task; it is a privilege and consideration. I often tell people that we tend to use prayer to ask God to take away a stress. Isn't that asking Him to stop considering us? What we need to do is really to use prayer to give thanks for being chosen to do the tough task. When life is too easy, it is time to pray, to wake up God and ask if we are not worth His attention.

On the other hand, showing respect for other people would mean considering their opinions, especially when they provide you with a different perspective, not just accepting those whose opinions are compatible with yours. I remember a play I once saw. It was a comedy called *I Love You. You Are Perfect. Now Change.* But the consideration must be genuine, and showing consideration for yourself means respecting your opinions of yesterday as good products of yourself as a creative entity, even though they may be different from those of other people or inappropriate for the challenges of today. Then you can be the true creative entity, always being able to grow because you can give full consideration for the existence of the deity, the equal importance of other people and that of yourself, all as creative entities, their acts and opinions being only the products of their true existence as conscious energy.

Making a Commitment

If you can see that your primary objective is the development of yourself as conscious energy, you will be able to see that it really does not matter what you have to experience in order to get the opportunity to create a new insight. In fact, it is less the particular experience that is important than it is the fact that you are experiencing something that you do not already know. That is the important thing: to be challenged beyond what you already know, not to be challenged to do the same repetitive task as a performance of what you know. This latter may benefit a series of observers or recipients. It is of no benefit to you.

As an example, if you leave a job because the work is too demanding, it may either be because there are too many new challenges that strain your capacities, or because there is too much repetition of the same performance that stresses your physical stamina and stagnates your mental capacities. In the first case, running away cheats you of the invitation to expand yourself; in the second case, it gives you the opportunity to be exposed to more challenging tasks. In short, what is important is less what you do and more why you do it.

I have been able to use this logic when advising people in marital situations that are distressing. A woman who leaves a marriage because of an abusive husband, for example, may actually be allowing herself to be exposed to more problems in the outside world, but her creativity may be stimulated more consistently. Staying in the marriage may offer her a lot of challenges but provide her only with repetitive demands that may do nothing for her conscious development. If, on the other hand, she wants to leave the marriage because of expectations that she prefers not to bear, or because there is a promise of a less demanding life with someone else, she may be cheating herself of the possible creative stimulation these challenges can give her.

Another way of looking at this is to state that you must be selfish— that is, selfish for the things that will stimulate your growth. The only thing that, as a self-affirmed person, you need from the world is the challenge that stimulates your creativity, and so you can only be selfish for the challenge. As this type of selfish person, you will be the one to get up to do the dishes after a meal because such activity keeps your conscious energy strong and alert. As this type of selfish person, you will be the one to volunteer to do a difficult or dangerous task because you want the stimulation that the task will give you. It is also the tendency to stop and listen to the other person's opinion first before offering your own. Do you not see that this actually gives you more information and thus places you at a more intelligent position, knowing what you know plus what the other person knows? This type of selfishness is the commitment that shows courage and builds intelligence.

You must have ahead of you at all times the realization that you are here to benefit by using the problems that are beyond you as invitations to grow stronger as a conscious energy. What is important is the problem that will stimulate your creativity; it does not matter what type of problem presents itself. It may come from the material environment. It may arise from the social environment. It may be part of the biological environment. By being responsible for your own growth, you are responsible for whatever of these that emerges, not just for the challenges you want.

Your commitment, then, is to accept responsibility for your contribution toward all three parts of your total environment. Within yourself, you must be able to justify that total commitment, not just what is obvious to some partial observer. You are responsible for your own personal health, your material surroundings and your social associates. It is easy to believe that you are totally committed when you are focusing 100 percent of your efforts on one-third of the whole responsibility, but that is a fool's errand.

Full and singular commitment to your physical task, for example, may appear to the biased observers who need your contribution to be the performance of a thoroughly dedicated person. The boss may commend you for your interest and dedication. Such dedication, however, can be accomplished only at the expense of similar commitment to the other aspects of your total responsibilities. In fact, it also may be accomplished at the expense of other material tasks, such as tasks that arise at home. You will be cheating yourself of the opportunities you can have from these other situations. Workaholics are known to neglect their own biological needs or the needs of their families while being commended for their contribution to that one third of life. These other challenges can offer variety to your creative prowess, perhaps providing you with more growth than can be obtained using the same efforts to eke out the last drops from the end of an exhausted, singular challenge. Remember that 100 percent of one-third is still one third.

You may choose instead to be totally altruistic, a people person. As a people person, however, you may expend all your efforts on the challenges presented by other people. You may receive quite a large amount of stimulation from this. You even may benefit from the experiences of all of those other people. However, you will cheat yourself of the opportunity to have the variety that truly stimulates your creativity. To your friends, you may be a true 100 percenter; you are a man (or woman) of the people. Remember, however, the other person cannot experience your pains, discomforts or stresses; the other person does not know about the tasks you may have left undone. You may be given full praise for your dedication to people. Still, it is only 100 percent of one-third.

You may choose to be a health fanatic. As a health fanatic, you may pay particular attention to your body's nutritional requirements, its pains and discomforts and its health. You may feel that your body will live forever, will never grow old or will never experience stress. You may succeed at achieving one of these wishes for a short time. You will give little consideration to material tasks or social development. As a result, you will lose these opportunities to stimulate your creativity. The challenges you can get from focusing on your biological health— the pains, discomforts or stresses that are present to stimulate your creativity—are multifold. They are sufficient to occupy your attention for your whole life. Just think: if you focus on the messages from your lower back as you sit reading this material, you may be amazed at the amount of information there is for you to discover and analyze. Yet they were already there while you were focused on reading this material, previously oblivious to their calls. You do not have to be so focused on them that you will neglect the other opportunities there are for stimulating your creativity—yet some people do. They spend much of their time worrying about things that are inevitable parts of living, moving and aging. These, too, can provide enough challenges to occupy you if you want to grow only from the changes that occur within your own body, but they are at best 100 percent of one-third.

The point is that there are many challenges available to you. Your commitment is not to be totally dedicated to only one range of them. It is to the total dedication to the growth you can derive from your exposure to the whole range of them, the greater the jump from where you are to where the challenge takes you the more you benefit from it. The whole idea is that you must be committed to yourself as soul, your own growth as a conscious energy. To yourself be true.

On your death bed, you answer not to your boss, your friends or your aging body. You answer to yourself. If you can answer that you have used all the opportunities you were offered to your best advantage, then whatever you have gained is as much as you could have gained. You will have done the job you needed to do in order to satisfy your higher purpose. If you have missed out on the variety of opportunities that you were given only because you were intent on being the specialist in one and then seeing that one drift away in the end because it never really belonged to you, you may discover that you will have missed the boat.

ORGANIZING YOUR TIME

Now that you are willing to make a commitment to all three areas of your changing environment, you can easily become inundated if you try to take all the challenges from all the areas whence they arise. Remember that there is sufficient change in each area to occupy you fully for your whole lifetime. You are the one in charge of reaching your objective, and you know you can do that most efficiently by being aware of all the opportunities that come at you. You can end up accomplishing very little, however, if you simply place yourself at the disposal of whatever comes at you. You must manage your commitment and your time. Let's face it: Although each of these three categories of challenges can be seen to be distinct entities, so different from each other that what we do with one should not interfere with how we relate to the other, we may find that they are more ubiquitously related than such interpretation allows. What I mean by a ubiquitous relationship is that each of these three areas of activity will affect and be dependent on the efficient function of the others for any of its challenges to reach us. Let us see how this happens.

As a conscious energy, the challenges of the material world are brought to you by the efficient functioning of your body. The body, however, can only bring to you those challenges that are close enough to stimulate its senses. Other people, on the other hand, can experience challenges that are far from your body's senses.

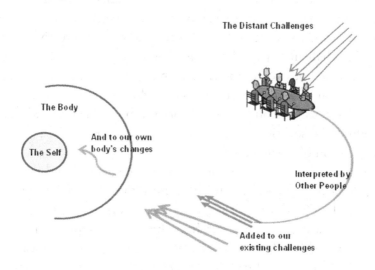

Figure 11.   The Ubiquitous Challenges

Therefore, people are needed to bring distant challenges to your immediate vicinity, either through the sharing of perceptions or through their activity in your immediate surroundings. Your body is needed to bring these immediate challenges to you.

Therefore, if you wish to benefit from as many of the opportunities to use your creativity as is available, you must recognize that whatever information reaches you flows to you in a sequential pattern. Each section requires the adequate function of the previous sections in order that the maximum information can reach you. In any sequential transfer (e.g., in the links of a chain), the strength of the whole is only as great as any single section or link. You must be able to use each section effectively. You must be able to take charge and consider your responsibility for the independent functioning of each area. You are the coordinator. The areas exist independently of the others, yet though they are independently functioning, they will always affect and be affected by the others.

USING YOUR BODY EFFECTIVELY

First, you must take care of the body if only to ensure that it is capable of bringing to you as much of the available stimulation that reaches it as is possible. The more efficiently it functions, the more useful information that will be transported to you for your creative growth. Whatever challenges you, they must reach you through your body. If you allow the body to get too tired or burned out, the senses also will get tired; then what reaches you will be a reduced representation of what has been offered to you. If you distort the body through exhaustion or chemical absorption, what reaches you may even be a distorted representation of what actually exists.

I like to draw an analogy of you being the general and your body being the army. The senses are the communication media that allow the general to be informed of enemy formations and through which he reveals his battle plans. The front line troops report a particular observation. This information is sent to headquarters by means of a two-way radio, which also transmits new orders (the senses). Somehow, the radio transmitter has been abused causing its decoder to function improperly. A new piece of information sent to the general becomes distorted, giving a wrong translation. The general creates new orders based on the wrong information he receives, though they are accurate for that wrong information. These are sent back and again become distorted by the decoder. The solution that arrives at the front line seems so inappropriate for the problem that the general is thought to be incompetent. If applied, the solution may bring disastrous results.

In terms of the body, you must realize that abusing it will cause you to have inadequate information on which you can work. Your poorly devised solutions will cause your contribution to appear confused, perhaps leading to disastrous consequences. Thus it is easy to see that a person can actually be thought of as mad or incompetent when all that is happening is that the transmission of information is distorted, not the capacity of the person to create an appropriate opinion. On the other hand, you may do the opposite and keep the body away from those challenges that can strain it. Then you will have little to stimulate your creativity. You must remember that it is only those challenges that are beyond your developed understanding that can stimulate your creativity.

It is foolhardy to abuse the body—but it is also foolish to not use it effectively. The solution is to balance its use and its rest. You must be willing to insert planned breaks, even if there is so much pressure from other areas of responsibility that it seems foolhardy to take that break. You must also be willing to use your body as much as it will allow, even if there is the desire to stay in a position of rest. If you do not insert planned breaks, your body will fail and an unplanned break will result, perhaps at the most inopportune time. If you do not use your body, those unused areas will degenerate or atrophy.

Many people who are addicted to cigarettes, coffee or alcohol are people who also will admit to not having true planned breaks. These people will rarely if ever be found resting at their desks for the short period of five minutes, yet they will stop to smoke, a task that requires a few minutes, sometimes 10 times per day. They may stop for a drink. Then they learn to associate that message from the body that a break is indicated as a desire for a cigarette or a desire for a drink. In other words, the planned break is instilled, but with the benefit of a distraction.

THE BREAKS PROVIDED BY CIGARETTES, COFFEE AND ALCOHOL

If you drink, smoke or even drink coffee, think back on the times when you experience the feeling for a cigarette, for a coffee or for a drink. These feelings come at a time when you want to enjoy a break. You either have learned to associate the taking of a break with some act that excuses the break, or you have learned to associate the enjoyment of the break with some act that enhances such enjoyment. In the first case, what you will have demonstrated is that you have not accepted that breaks are necessary parts of working efficiently, but you will use them if there is an obvious excuse. In the second case, you will have revealed that you have not learned how to enjoy the simple pleasures of pure relaxation but need to enhance it artificially.

If you indulge in any of these relaxation-enhancing habits, do not be fooled into believing that you have no control over your desire for them. These are associated with a natural need. As long as you suppress that natural need your body has for a break, or as long as you do not know how to enjoy that break when you provide it, you will not be able to take that control. You cannot just stop smoking or drinking without also giving consideration to that natural need. It is impossible, or at least impossible to maintain. Relapse is frequent when you attempt to manage a habit through unbalanced restraint. Sometimes what is observed to be an addictive behaviour has nothing to do with the substance or activity; the activity is only the red herring. The real need is for a natural break, and it is not an addiction—it is neglect coming home to roost. On the other hand, just managing the body with consideration can allow you to discontinue a habit, sometimes without even having to manage it.

WHEN TO TAKE A NATURAL BREAK

Pay attention to your body; it communicates with you and only with you. It cannot talk, but it communicates by feelings. Those feelings are so personal and hidden that they have never been universally identified. The way I perceive those feelings may be absolutely different from the way those feelings are brought out in your body. You will know them. If you smoke, they will be associated with the sensation of what the cigarette will do for you. If you do not have an addiction, they may be associated with irritability, tiredness, lack of concentration or some other experience that cannot be described but that is uncomfortable or worrisome. From these discoveries, you will learn that your need for a break can be affected by many external factors, including the pressures of the work, health, level of insight or state of nutrition. It can also be manifested in a great variety of forms so that a true description is not really possible. Each of these forms is so personally variable that only you can determine when a break is most needed and when it can be delayed. Each of the factors, which can precipitate an exhaustion or distortion in one or more system of the body, can be so personally determined that no single area can be designated the culprit. Every variable is singularly and personally actualized. Once you have determined the frequency with which a break is needed, and you have allowed flexibility for different situations, you will know when to insert regular breaks to reduce the degree of internal strain that determines when the body will indicate the need for a break. In some conditions, you will insert breaks more often than in others. In some conditions, you may insert no breaks, waiting for the expected conclusion to signal the need for the break. In some conditions, you will insert breaks that may seem unnaturally long to an outside observer but that are appropriate for your existing needs.

Then your breaks will be natural, inserted not because your body desperately needs them but because you have organized one of the things that is necessary for you to function efficiently—your instrument, your body. You will have been able to do this because you will have your ultimate purpose paramount in your mind, a purpose of creating and nurturing your conscious growth and development. You will insert breaks not to be unproductive and lazy, but to be able to use your body more efficiently and develop yourself to your highest potential. The insertion of breaks will be a discipline that pays heed to the deeper discomforts while ignoring those that are less severe. It will be a discipline that allows you to continue to function fully by disregarding a discomfort you know to be associated with some chronic change that will not be reversed or reduced with rest, especially if it is less detrimental to your total well-being than the consequences that will arise from inaction. It will be a discipline you easily can accept because you know that you will give consideration to your body without requiring a total shutdown to remind you of that consideration.

Sometimes, however, it is necessary to work for long periods without a break. Your body has the capacity to rebound from that as long as it is an occasional occurrence. Letting it happen too often can lead to severe burnout.

How to Take a Natural Break

Take charge. The factors that determine the need for a break are so variable and personal, so it usually is unlikely that any observer will be able to understand why you may need a break at a certain time. That observer also may have a different method of taking a break. I am sure that you will be able to identify with this when you think back on one smoker telling another that he does not understand that person's need for a cigarette at this time. Similarly, a smoker who takes 20 breaks daily may think you lazy if he sees you just doing apparently nothing for five minutes. You must know your objective and know that an efficient approach to that objective is more beneficial to you than an inefficient one influenced by the comments of an observer who cannot know what you need at that time in order to be competent and efficient in your overall responsibility.

Be aware. A natural break is necessary in order to allow you greater efficiency. A natural break therefore cannot be justified if, by taking it, you will have neglected to deal with an urgent situation that proceeds to a disaster because of your untimely and inconsiderate withdrawal. Such a break will be followed by a greater problem that must be addressed with more effort than was required for the initial problem.

HOW TO USE A NATURAL BREAK

A natural break is designed to allow you to temporarily free your body from the external pressures that strain it. On the one side, these pressures arise from the external environment; on the other side, they come from you (that is, the activation of the senses and muscles of expression by you, the conscious energy). In fact, more often than not the strain arises from your attempts, those of the conscious energy, to gather information, express insight or seek affirmation from the world. Since you are the main culprit, you can reduce that strain by removing the need to be aware of your relationship to the world. This means removing yourself temporarily from the external pressures that stimulate and challenge you.

One way of achieving this is to keep your focus totally within yourself. During the period you allot for your break, you may focus on a memory, a pleasant thought or a repetitious idea, as is done in some forms of meditation. Perhaps the most useful way, however, is to train yourself to be aware of the other less prominent messages you are getting from the body—messages that send out feelings that can be interpreted as pleasurable. For example, you may train yourself to appreciate the taste of your saliva, a useful tactic if you want to stop smoking. Your saliva can begin to taste like cool spring water as it becomes less affected by the presence of tobacco and its associated compounds. You may learn to appreciate the pleasant feel of air as you breathe. In other words, you can learn to indulge in very simple pleasures. This is an activity that cannot satisfy you for long periods of time, yet it can ease you repeatedly over different periods of time. That is the intent: to give yourself a simple distraction that will not usurp too much of your time and reduce your total interest in the task at hand.

This is not a technique for managing stress—in fact, it is a preventive technique. By training yourself to do it, you will allow less problems to accumulate and be stronger to do those that are immediately important. Then you will reduce the incidence of stress-related problems in two ways. First, you will insert regular breaks that will delay the onset of strain. Second, you will more effectively stop or reverse the progress of strain that has already been initiated. These insertions of regular breaks will allow you to be more effective over longer periods, accomplishing more and being able to solve more problems.

NURTURING THE BODY

You know that if you own a delicate instrument, you will be required to use it, rest it and take care of it, providing it with the proper ingredients for nurturing its strength. You cannot appreciate something as useful as an instrument if you simply place it on a shelf. You must use it. You cannot appreciate it if you use it so constantly that it breaks down. You also must balance its use with rest. You cannot expect it to function efficiently even if you do both of those things in proper balance, if you do not also provide it with the proper nutrition to maintain its strength.

If your instrument is made of wood or leather, you may polish it to let the oils strengthen its fibres. If your instrument is a more delicate life form such as your body, you will take care of it by providing a balanced input of the nutrition that it needs to function efficiently. Your body may be a sophisticated instrument, yet it depends on the logic from you, the conscious energy for it to be nurtured properly. If you put the necessary proteins in your mouth, the body will absorb it. If you put cyanide in your mouth, the body will absorb it. Your body is a passive recipient of your management skills. It will function for you as well as you have nurtured it to function for you. True, there are many things that can affect the function of your body over which you have little control. Yet you have control over how you place it within the environment in which these activities occur. Therefore, you have indirect control over many of these things that will affect your body.

With regard to nutrition, it is important that you provide your body with a proper balance of the necessary building blocks of protein, carbohydrate, fats and water. Many times we feed our bodies purely by reaction, not by taking charge and providing for its needs as the more capable decision maker. You may eat on the run, eating only to stop the incessant demands from an empty stomach. You may eat while watching television or conducting a meeting. You may believe that these activities save time or increase efficiency, yet they are costly in the long run in ill health, obesity from too much unbalanced foods, tiredness or injury. It disturbs me to know that many people will eat poorly and treat the subsequent weight gain with diets that provide a different type of imbalance. It is important for you to know that your body needs to replace, with new protein, the protein that must be removed daily from dying cells. It needs carbohydrates as the fuel to effect that rebuilding. It needs fat for a great number of reasons. One reason is to be able to absorb some foods and vitamins from the intestine. Another is as concentrated storage of carbohydrates. Yet another is as padding in crucial areas—for example, the bursa under the scapula that softens its movement against the ribs. Yet people will eliminate fat from their diets entirely and wonder why they are not absorbing the vitamins they take by the fistful. They will eliminate protein from their diet and stay in ignorance as the body breaks down good tissue in order to get the protein it needs to replace the cells that have reached obsolescence. They may believe that they have lost stored fat when any apparent weight loss is due to the unhealthy loss of necessary protein. Then the body will function so inefficiently that their total management skills will have all but been lost.

It is important to labour on this area of your responsibility because, unlike any of the others, you are the only one who can care for it. You must decide what type of balance it needs in the type of nutrition you are able to give it. From this, you must establish a pattern that is specific for your body's needs, working with the sources of nutrition that are available to you. You also must not believe that you are nurturing it well just because you balance your meals if you do not consider the act of eating as any one of your main responsibilities and plan it into your day.

Over-feeding your body in the mistaken assumption that you are treating it well is as bad a management approach as are the attempts to feed it only on demand. Eating is a pleasurable activity; people do not only eat to feed themselves. Sometimes you will eat excessively, just to enjoy the pleasure of eating. Sometimes you indulge in the pleasure in order to counteract an unpleasant experience, usually one associated with rejection or lack of affirmation, an emotional discomfort, a behaviour called emotional eating or comfort foods. Then the ideal management is not a diet. It is the development of immunity from the hurts from the world—the main theme of this book.

Yet you must know that your body cannot use all the nutrition that you feed it above its needs. It must store whatever excess you feed it as fuel. It cannot store protein, but it can transform excess protein into carbohydrate and fat. When it next needs protein, it still must have fresh protein. Therefore, whatever excess you may have fed it cannot now be useful to you any more than excess fat may be useful. Your body needs protein. Its needs for protein are determined by how quickly the old protein is used and broken down. This in turn is determined by how vigorously the body may be breaking down, as in recovery from an illness, the healing of an injury or the overexertion needed for intense physical activity. In other words, you also must be willing to be flexible in your management of the food intake. Sometimes, when you are using the body vigorously, you may need to provide it with more protein, even if you are attempting to lose weight. Sometimes when you are less active, you may determine that you need very little. You may achieve this by varying the proportions of protein, fat and carbohydrate and by varying the amount of non-absorbable fibre content of the total food intake.

Lastly, you must not knowingly poison your body. This is a strong accusation, yet if you smoke, you are introducing carbon monoxide, nicotine and tar, among other things. None of these is a useful ingredient to your body's nutritional needs. They accumulate to poison it. If you drink alcohol, you are introducing compounds that can be metabolized and used by the body only to a limited extent; beyond that level, you are poisoning the body. Remember that without an efficiently functioning body, you never will be able to benefit from those other ubiquitously related challenges the world can throw at you.

Communicate with your body: listen to it and consider its needs purposefully. No one can consider it for you. No one can know its needs. Your body can give its messages only to you. Therefore, no one else can deny it appropriately. Train it personally and free it from the expectations of others. They cannot experience its limitations. Only you can know how far you can push it today. Only you can know what specific discipline it needs today in order to function efficiently for you tomorrow. Determine those areas and train your body to be more responsive where you need it. You cannot train it to do everything. You must therefore train it in the areas that are pertinent to your needs, not someone else's. As a silly example, if you live in the desert, training your body for mountain climbing at the expense of training it to survive the desert, just to satisfy a critic or indulge in a fantasy, may be detrimental to your more immediate needs.

USING THE IMMEDIATE CHALLENGES EFFECTIVELY

Just as you have learned to manage the body so that you can benefit most efficiently from the challenges you receive through your use of it, so too you must learn to assess and manage the material things that comprise those challenges so that the changes in these also will occur in a way that will allow the most efficient transfer of new information to you. You know that whatever challenges you get will come to you because of the changes that have occurred in the material that forms the immediately relevant tasks. For example, you will not need to clean the house if dust and dirt had not gathered in it. You will not need to mow the lawn if the grass did not grow too tall. You will not need to balance your budget if nothing is taken out and nothing put in. In fact, you know that there never will be any job for you to do if change never occurred in the structure of the materials that affect you for you to have to restore these materials, or for you to have to strengthen them against unwanted change.

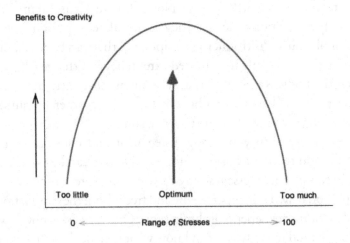

Figure 12. An Efficiency Model

Again, it must be emphasized that as conscious energy, you have an ultimate objective to stimulate your creativity to its highest potential. If a task can allow you to stimulate that creativity, you will owe it to yourself to accept that task and use it as a means of realizing your personal growth and development. If, however, that task becomes so great that your creativity is overwhelmed, the benefits you receive are as reduced as though you had no challenge from it. You must know when to use the task, when to dismiss it and when to take care of the objects that influence it.

USING THE TASK (FACING CHANGE)

It is universally recognized that whenever a task is not addressed, it remains to be done even as other changes continue to evolve beneath the surface of that task. These new changes may burst out and make the original task more difficult than it was. They may remain hidden until you deal with the original task, becoming manifest only after that has been managed successfully. What this means is that there always will be a problem to challenge you, whether it is the original one or the one that replaces it. If you fail to address the original problem, it stays to haunt you; its degree of difficulty may increase, but the benefit you get from addressing it does not. If you address the original problem, the next one that emerges can be more difficult. The difficulty inherent in any new problem ensures that your creativity will be stimulated to the extent that it is difficult. In short, you will never have fewer problems as a result of procrastination. You will only have old problems with more work but with no more benefit than was associated with the original problem. With industriousness, you never will eliminate the work; you only will have more stimulating challenges waiting for you whenever you are ready to tackle them.

There are some tasks, however, that no longer challenge you. They once may have stimulated your creativity but now have changed so completely within your range of insight for them that you can do well without having to address them. You know these tasks; they are the humdrum, routine tasks that you can do with your eyes closed. It may be argued that since these tasks do not stimulate you enough to allow you to reach your ultimate objective of personal growth efficiently, they are better left undone or perhaps given to another person to do.

Of course this passing down can only be fair if it is new enough to be a stimulant to the other person, and not one he or she considers to be similarly humdrum or routine.

You must remember that by applying yourself to a task, you are able to manage the rate by which that task changes and evolves into some other problem. Leaving such tasks undone can cause you to have to attend to unnecessary work later because it will change. If it changes in a direction that does not benefit you, its presentation may offer unnecessary work for you to do. In other words, although the encouragement to keep your personal objective in the forefront may be interpreted as permission to forego responsibility for things that do not benefit you, it also can be seen that such a selfish interpretation can cause you to be inundated with unexpected work more often than it will give you freedom to do other things. The main objective of personal development can only be achieved through forming an intelligent approach to managing the immediate tasks. Procrastination and indolence can hurt only you.

RESTING THE TASK (ACCEPTING CHANGE)

Things are going to change. You know that even if you manage a task perfectly, there still will be an area that will be beyond your understanding. You also know that you cannot manage everything. Some things, therefore, will have to undergo unpleasant change, and you will not be able to do anything about it. Instead, you must learn to adapt to the new situation and live with it.

Surely, you will reap great personal benefit from attending to tasks that can challenge your creativity. On the other hand, you also will achieve greater personal benefit from a wider range of issues if you know when to stop your management of a particular task and go on to other responsibilities. Even though you may expect such a task to become more difficult if left unattended, you sometimes may find it necessary to offer what may be considered to be an incomplete management of it as your total effort; only then will you be free to attend to other issues. Let us see this practically. The common statement that a person is such a fastidious householder that one can literally eat off the floor has one major fallacy. That which one cannot see (e.g., bacteria) still exists and still accumulates. One can clean and then clean again and yet always find a small amount of dirt that was missed. The effort expended is never equal to the benefit. On the other hand, doing it to a personally acceptable level, knowing that it is not and never will be perfect, will leave you time to tackle other more meaningful and useful pursuits.

You have learned that you must contribute of your unique insight to all sections of the common responsibility, and in as many areas of each as you honestly can. It is easy to conclude that you must be able to free yourself from some things and direct your attention to others even before you manage those things satisfactorily. You have learned that everything is in a constant state of change; therefore you know that whatever solution you may formulate for an existing problem cannot remove all traces of the problem. It serves only to reveal the next problem.

PERFECTIONISM

As a result, you cannot be any better organized by trying to complete everything to an absolute degree of perfection. The responsibility for tasks that appear from the material world can be compared to an impossible mathematical problem: no matter how much you remove from what exists, you still are left with all that was there before. You never can finish any task completely.

There is a story about Michelangelo that is purported to have occurred before the creation of *David*. According to the story, Michelangelo was possessed with the need to create the perfect statue. No matter how he tried, some part would be out of proportion. He was very disappointed until one day he completed a statue of a male model. For the first time, he was satisfied with the proportions, and he felt he had made the perfect statue. While he was admiring it, a thought struck him that something as perfectly human as this must be able to speak. He commanded the statue to speak, which of course it was unable to do. He became so upset that he threw his mallet at it and destroyed its knee, making it flawed and imperfect. This may not be a true story, but it represents an important lesson. Perfection is a state that cannot be achieved. This is simply because what you may see as perfect at any moment is only the probable solution to whatever part of the problem you can see to that moment. As Heisenberg's uncertainty principle suggests, change will occur within the tolerance of the quantum, at least in areas we can't see naturally, so perfection is only a manifestation of the limitations of the observer. Conversely, the mature observer or performer can accept the outcome without wanting it or assuming that perfection has been reached.

OVERPREPAREDNESS

You also must resist the temptation to extend your understanding of a problem so fully that you believe you can manage all of its ramifications at the same time. You must remember that, regardless of how detailed your solution may be, it is only at best 100 percent of that little part you can see. It is also so rapidly changing that whenever you apply your solution, the relevant aspects of the problem will already have transmuted far beyond what you were able to see as the original problem.

Perhaps an example is necessary. Suppose you have an exam or a presentation tomorrow morning. You may prepare yourself overnight by examining the problem as you see it in such extreme detail that it takes up an inordinate amount of your time. Then, at the time you are ready to present your solution, a new and unexpected twist is introduced into the problem. It may be a question from an observer who sees a different perspective of the problem. It may be that your solution can be applied so effectively that a new aspect is revealed, so closely tied to the original problem that the effect of your solution is dimmed. When this happens, you are left wanting; you are too worn out to consider the new challenge. At the same time, you are seen as not having addressed the complete picture that is now more obvious to all observers. Although your presentation may have been prepared with great consideration for all the detail that was obvious to you, it is seen as an incomplete solution for what is now the immediate problem. Yet, having exhausted yourself in preparation, you do not have the strength to reassess the new problem adequately and create a more appropriate solution for it.

Therefore the only way for you to know how far to go in addressing a particular task is to have unswerving belief in your creativity. Examine what you can see now and create a solution. Reexamine it when you have to it apply the solution, being prepared to recreate a new solution for the new problem and to do so on the fly. It is easy to do a task to the limits imposed by another person. When you are doing it to your level of accountability, it is only when you have educated yourself about more than is readily obvious, and when you are prepared to consider some of the natural change or the repercussions that may arise out of your interference, that you can decide when you have managed it as well as it can be managed, and therefore, when you have done enough.

Nurturing the Task (Influencing Change)

Problems do not arise out of nothing; they come about because of the inherent changes that occur within the structure of the areas that form the task. Some objects or tasks undergo change more rapidly than others, creating new problems faster than you have the time to deal with them. Yet you can nurture those objects so that the rate of change that occurs within them can be made slower, or even faster than ordinarily will happen. Remember that whatever these tasks are, you share them with everything and everybody else. You are not the only force that can affect them. Some forces may be the elements; others are the actions of other people. If you do not allot some time toward protecting these objects, perhaps strengthening them to withstand more use than is immediately apparent, then the next time you attempt to manage them, they may be so distorted from what they were that they become an unnecessarily large problem to you.

Using People-Challenges Effectively

Lastly, you must take care of how you relate to the people who affect you either at home or at work. People do not only represent challenges that are different from those you can perceive; they represent experiences that can stimulate you beyond the reaches of your limited senses. You must remember that your creativity is stimulated by the perception of a problem that challenges you beyond your developed understanding. Such perceptions can be evoked directly through the activity of a current problem. We have seen that they can be evoked from the activation of the senses even if no true problem exists. For example, this happens when your senses are distorted (drugs, alcohol, tiredness). Such perceptions can also be evoked indirectly, from the experiences of other people. If you believe that you can grow to your fullest potential through your exposure only to those problems that confront you directly, you will be left wanting. You do not have the time to experience everything. You never will reach your objective of total self-growth efficiently without also benefitting from the perceptions and perhaps the shortcuts to understanding their intricacies that are available from the experiences of other people.

Obviously, you can get carried away and spend all of your time learning only from the experiences of other people. People want to reveal their opinions to you. In fact, they may even force their opinions on you. This is because people, especially those who are not self-affirmed, want to receive consideration for their opinions. Therefore, what is available to you can be an oppressive amount of repetitive experiences, a much-too-detailed view of a singular experience or a variety of new and exciting challenges. It is up to you to manage this source of information so that what you get from it will be useful to you and to your future contributions to the world.

You cannot dismiss anything that may be useful to you without considering what is offered, yet you cannot allow yourself to be inundated by all of the possible opportunities that can come from these other people's experiences. You must learn from the wise, but you must also be able to educate yourself, even from the fool.

USING OTHER PEOPLE'S PERCEPTIONS EFFECTIVELY

We cannot emphasize too much that the world is multifaceted and vast. What is available to you is the whole range of activities that can stimulate your creativity. Yet you are not able to experience all of them, simply because of the limitations of your reach. Even within an apparently simple situation, there are so many facets that 100 people examining it at the same time, in the same room, will have 100 different perceptions of it. You can take, as an example, the act of sitting in a room with three other people. You may be examining the same piece of paper, but it is impossible for all of you to see it from exactly the same angle. Each person's perception will also be influenced by the presence of the other two people, a situation that is definitely different for everyone. More so, each person's perception is influenced by that person's past experience. How much you can see in a problem is related to how much insight you already have on that or a similar problem. Each person, however, believes that what he or she sees of a problem is all there is to see, because he or she cannot see any more into the problem than that.

To each person, therefore, the other conflicting perspectives are wrong. If you do that, you will lose the benefit of the information that you can get immediately but which you will have to extract from your own experiences at a later time anyway. If you behave immaturely, you will reveal your perceptions and become satisfied that you can overwhelm the opposition. It is so easy to come out of a confrontation having expressed (or been allowed to express) your opinion and feeling that you have shown intellectual superiority over the other person. What you do not realize is that the other person has left the confrontation knowing what you know plus what he knows (totally withheld from you because of your arrogance). Who, then, is truly wiser?

If you behave maturely, however, you will recognize that you must educate yourself on more of the problem than is obvious to you before you can make a qualified decision on your management of it. You will consider the other person's perspective not as a competing opinion, but as one that may add to your perception of the problem. You then will have more information on which to base your decision. The roles will then be reversed. The other person may leave with the feeling that he or she has made a point, but without also considering yours, he or she will leave in no better position for managing the problem than before. You, however, will be the one who will leave the confrontation stronger than you were when you entered it.

RESTING OTHER PEOPLE'S PERCEPTIONS

Notwithstanding the fact that you need other people's input in order to stimulate your creativity and increase your capabilities, sometimes it is necessary to ignore what someone else is doing or has said. You must realize that you cannot learn from every aspect of every issue, and neither can you remove all consequences. You know that every problem is multifaceted, and as a result there always will be other aspects readily exposed or easily aroused. You know also that these new aspects may have little bearing on the task as it pertains to the conditions that are immediately relevant. Just as in your management of the task, you have to know when enough is enough; there is a point in your relation with other people when you also must shut off their further contribution and be satisfied with the information you have acquired so far. Sometimes you must put a halt to the input even if you know that the other person truly has more information to share with you.

Just as it is inadvisable to be a workaholic or a self-indulgent person, so too it is unwise to focus all your energies in pleasing other people by completely giving your consideration to their opinions. Therefore, you must be able to stop further input, even if you are pressured by the private needs the other person has for your consideration. You may be accused of being inconsiderate. You, however, have two other responsibilities that you also must consider: your task and yourself. Your job is to try always to be more aware and more informed on the widest possible range of conditions in order to make your best contribution of yourself.

NURTURING OTHER PEOPLE AS SOURCES OF DIFFERENT PERCEPTIONS

People do not always share their perceptions honestly. Sometimes they will withhold their opinions in order to give consideration to yours, and sometimes they will express false opinions, distorting the immediate challenges and making them more difficult for you to manage. They may do it from fear that they will reveal an inadequacy. They may do it in defence against your perceived displeasure. They may do it just so that they will not be challenged by you or give competitive information to you. Yet you need these different perceptions that the other person can share with you so that you can stimulate your creativity and increase your vision of the common problem. You therefore must be able to nurture other people as sources of useful information, knowing when and how to draw out that information so that you can use it efficiently and effectively.

Feed their ego. Like you, other people are non-material, conscious energies. What they need for nourishment is the feedback affirmation that what they are is good enough to be acceptable to the world. They need to know that their opinions are important. You cannot get much from a scared or defensive person if you send the message that what they will reveal to you will be treated with disdain. You must be honestly interested in the differences they will reveal, willing to consider those that seem way out, even if it means expressing an honest interest in exploring them further.

Sometimes people are not willing to reveal an opinion that they believe may be upsetting to you. Shake the tree; if the lion comes down, it was up there in the first place. It is better to know the dangers that lie in wait for you when you are alert to them than to have them creep upon you when you are least capable of defusing them. If you first immunize yourself by being self-affirmed and being prepared for a new challenge, then your early exposure of a new problem will always serve to stimulate your creativity.

Lastly, whatever you do, you may not be able to obtain any information from the other people. Respect their right to privacy and place yourself in their position. You may be self-affirmed, but they may not be. They may in fact be functioning in an insecure reality of vast dimensions, so vast and varied that they will not be able to ascertain what may be threatening them at the moment.

Summary

We have discussed your role as a person who should be accountable to yourself, not just with the goal of physical survival (an objective that is destined to defeat itself) but to nurture your own growth and development always into a more capable and useful existent. This is not a new philosophy of what should be; rather, it is a realization of what is, and an exhortation to be efficient through respecting what is, and fitting yourself (the more flexible and expandable existent) into it. There is much talk in business circles of the right fit. In social circles, although the reference is not made to the phrase, the concept also influences our actions. Getting the right fit in its common interpretation, however, means that the task or the people can be managed most competently if they are compatible with the skills and understanding of the person who is responsible for managing or relating to them.

In this dissertation, we have attempted to show that such a right fit is impossible not because of the inadequacies of the manager, but because of the constant change that takes place independently in all three areas: the task, the other people and in the manager's expressive and perceptive skills. The idea is not to destroy the hopes of the many people who look toward the realization of such a right fit either in their jobs or in their social and family relationships. Rather, it is to proffer the suggestion that there is an alternative. Instead of trying to force the impossible or pretend that such a state does exist, you now are expected to be able to develop an awareness of what truly is happening and use that awareness to your greater advantage. You must be flexible to the variety of challenges that come at you so that you can enjoy those with which you fit and expand yourself to fit with those that are new and even daunting. This realization exhorts you to free yourself from being judged so that you can prepare yourself most efficiently to manage the problems that challenge you—problems that may not be apparent to other observers. Now, you also must learn that you cannot judge other people. You do not know what priorities those other people have to consider, and they may not be apparent to you. You must therefore be able to function in your world and let the other people function in theirs. You must be able to relate to them without requiring that they should follow your priorities or you theirs. Judgment can only be performed when you can see all aspects of a problem and all solutions. You have to be omnipotent and omniscient to be able to judge. Those qualities we can never have.

CHAPTER 7

PERFORMANCE MANAGEMENT

A CAPABLE PERSON IS only as useful as that person can reveal his or her capabilities. A person, however, is a self-driven force, and you are no exception. Your capabilities are as dependent on you as their usefulness is dependent on your ability to reveal them. We have discussed how to develop the management skills you need to let you manage the problems that challenge your capabilities. We have discussed how you must organize those skills to take charge of what you have to do and do it. Now, we must discuss how to express those skills accountably. You must be responsible for the way you express yourself in your attempts to manage the task, not only for taking the initiative in managing it.

Too often you are led to believe that in order to be accountable, you must manage those issues that are apparent to any observer in a way that is acceptable to that observer. To be accountable under this presumption, therefore, requires that your performance be not a revelation of the way you see the issue but an expression that satisfies the way it is viewed by another person or other people. This can be dangerous. The other person's view of the issue that you must manage may not be an accurate perception of what the issue truly is or how it affects you. The other person may offer a subjective opinion, one that is influenced by that person's personal need, not by the pure needs of the issue. This makes your management of the task an irresponsible act, even if you presumed that you acted in good faith. Similarly, if you apply your accountability to the satisfaction of an established standard or representative of such standard and not to your own judgment, you still will be inefficient in all you do. This is not true accountability. Let us examine why.

First of all, you are a self-driven force, and what you do is an expression of the way you see things—and things do change. If you must suppress your perception or the opinions derived from that perception so that your performance will satisfy an established standard, such performance will not be an efficient representation of anything. Your opinion, made for the problem the way it presents at the time, will be suppressed wholly or partially. The standard, made for the problem as it presented at a different time, will not be accurate for the problem as it presents at this time. Your performance will then be irresponsible because what you do is a false representation of how you see the issue. You will have misrepresented your responsibility for managing the issue. You cannot then be accountable.

Second, you have a mandate to grow and to become a source of insight. You cannot allow yourself to be no more than an instrument— the arms, legs and torso for the expression of opinions that are not yours. You must remember that your management skills are the tools you need to make you into a more capable person, one who has something useful to contribute to this world. They allow you to express what you are capable of doing so that you can go on to the next challenge and use it to make you even more capable. Just being the instrument for some other source of opinions, like those of a boss or some other authority figure, cheats you of the advantages you can get from addressing or managing that aspect of the problem that you see. You cannot then be accountable.

Third, you may see a standard or expectation that places too great a pressure on you to perform as being inappropriate for the issue as it presents now. This can cause you to disregard the importance of those standards or expectations. You may then express an opinion that was formed only from the way you see the issue or, rather than be considered incompetent in your performance, you will reserve judgment and suppress your opinion. Then you not only will be inefficient, but you will be misrepresenting your responsibility to consider the opinions of those other people. You cannot be accountable this way.

To be accountable can only mean being able to be objective at all times, considering the needs of the issue and the needs of the people affected by the issue and by your management of the issue. It means having the courage of your convictions because you believe in you. To achieve this, the issue (and your management of it) must affect you only as a creative consciousness, being the ingredients for your continued growth and development. To be accountable means being always willing to increase your vision so that you, as a judge of what you do, can be not just the most appropriate assessor of your performance, but the one that considers more of the factors that are pertinent to the issue—and does so objectively.

BEING SELF-ACCOUNTABLE

Standards and regulations are necessary for leading those who are not self-accountable, and for guiding those who are. The child who is told not to cross the street has to follow a regulation. It is necessary for the child to be responsible to that standard because he does not have the vision to understand the reasons for its presence. The standard at that time is higher than the wisdom or experience of the child. A young adult who still follows that regulation is irresponsible because he has the ability to do more while still using it to guide him in the way he manages the greater issues that challenge him beyond those regulations.

Being accountable to yourself does not mean being unaccountable for the way your actions are influenced by the experiences of other people. Rather, it means being more than accountable to these other people's experiences. It means being able to use their experiences as a jumping board to propel you into having a wider vision of the issues so that you can apply your decisions objectively and appropriately.

For example, your parents may have had good reason to make decisions the way they did for the circumstances as they presented at the time and for the information available to them at the time. Many young people, respecting the successes their parents may have had in addressing those issues, attempt to apply those solutions blindly. Yet you must know that an apparently similar situation may have significant differences that can cause those solutions to be inappropriate for you now. You also will have grown to the same age now as your parents were when they made that decision, but with even greater experience—or at least experience that is more appropriate for the situation as it presents now. A new solution, even one that is directly opposed to the one they may have used successfully, will be more ideal for the situation as it presents to you now than your parents' solutions can be. This logic is true for any issue.

The blind allegiance to ceremony as opposed to doctrine among many religious laypeople, for example, does not take into consideration those two factors—namely, the limitations of the teacher's exposure and the presentation of the challenge at the time. Ceremony and standards pertain to the meat of the problem and can be applied successfully by those who are not experienced enough to be self-accountable. When you need to address the issue more accurately, you have to be able to grow past the limitations of ceremony and standards. Restraining yourself to stay within the boundaries of rules set out at a different era just to show an allegiance to the exact requirements of a deity can be a dishonour to you, and then it is also a dishonour to a deity who has invited you to grow to be with Him. Remember, in the Judaeo-Christian faith, at the end of his life, Jesus was purported to have said that instead of the ten rigid commandments, he would give two. These two have included all the admonitions of the ten, but they also give flexibility to interpret them according to the demands of the time.

Sometimes your determination to be accountable to opinions or rules that have been formed for you is not always caused by your own feelings of personal insecurity. Frequently it is caused by a need for relief from taking responsibility for your actions. It is easier to face the unknown with the instructions from a recognized source than to have to go through the exercise of examining it carefully. Then, if you fail, you still will have been accountable to a recognized measure. If you succeed, your accountability will have been exonerated, at least from your perspective.

As a self-accountable person, however, you are required to take full responsibility for how your actions relate to the issue and how they affect other people while you are attempting to manage the issue. You therefore must have the maturity to make a decision considering as much of the information as is available, the awareness to express your opinion knowing that it cannot address all aspects of the issue that are visible to all observers and the courage to accept and deal with consequences not as measures of you but as new problems to be addressed. To be accountable to a more experienced person, however, is neither wrong nor self-deprecating. It shows respect for the greater vision of that other person. To be accountable to that person while suppressing your own experience, just to prove loyalty, is not only wrong but is self-deprecating and dishonest. This does not mean that you will be exonerated from accusations of irresponsibility or from the consequences that those accusations may evoke. You must know, however, that the fall from grace that accompanies accusations of irresponsibility cannot be as reprehensible to your true self as the real irresponsibility you will demonstrate by choosing to appear accountable to external measures while being unaccountable to the more appropriate vision you may have of the issue.

There are a number of requirements that the self-accountable person must satisfy, and there are an equal number of benefits. The greatest benefit to self-accountability is the freedom from having to perform to a measure that you cannot honestly satisfy. This is because the most frequent cause of stress and its companions (failure, burnout and the tendency to resort to chemicals to stifle, hide or hide from failure) is your belief, as a self-driven force, that you are required to perform to a measure that is different from the way you see the issue you are managing.

If you succeed in satisfying the accepted standard of accountability, you still will have failed to apply a solution to the way you see the problem. If you succeed in managing the problem the way you see it, you will be seen as having failed as measured by the externally observed standard of accountability. Because you have not succeeded in managing the issue acceptably either way, the pressures of the unfinished task will still remain to haunt you. As a self-accountable person, therefore, the freedom from this unnecessary pressure can be the best gift you can give to yourself in addition to the gains you will have made in your conscious development.

The requirements for self-accountability are that you have the flexibility to adapt your performance as the situation demands it, and the ability to accept criticism of your performance or failure to discharge the issue completely from another observer's perspective, as mirrors that show you how your performance appears. This allows you to judge the adequacy of your presentation compared to your intent. Only then can you use it to be even more accountable to your own deeper purpose. It is no good having the sagacity to assess a changing situation and create new insights as it changes, if you do not also have the similar flexibility to adapt your performance to address the newly changed issue. It is no good having the accountability to yourself if you do not take the feedback from the observers as mirrors allowing you to observe your performance as accurately as any other external observer.

Be alert. Everything has a new presentation every time you are exposed to it. Be inventive. Yesterday's solutions are appropriate only for yesterday's problems. Be wise. The appropriate solution for any problem is no more than is necessary to nullify the immediately relevant presentations. The overkill is as dangerous as the underkill. Be considerate. If your performance creates a greater problem for the other person, the effects may be disastrous for the other person, and the consequences to you may be more than you have the resources to manage.

Knowing these methods of managing yourself in a changing environment does not mean that you never will be wrong. It only means that whenever you are wrong, you will be able to accept it as a natural part of life, and that you will have the belief in yourself to have the creativity and wisdom to correct it.

ESTABLISHING FLEXIBLE PRIORITIES

In the spring of 1987, a tragic accident took place in Europe. It was reported that a ferry taking passengers across the English Channel hit a sandbar and overturned, killing many of the people aboard. The initial explanation was that a door to one of the holds could not be closed. A more detailed explanation was offered later. According to the international press, the events that led to the disaster were multifold and were compounded by bad weather on the day of the accident. In order to understand this and the lesson that can be learned from it, you first must be made aware of how a ferry functions. You must recognize that this event is recalled with the benefit of hindsight and of course without the pressure of having to make a decision under duress. Therefore, there is no intent to make an accusation; it is offered as an opportunity to assess the benefits of being ready to establish flexible priorities.

It is common knowledge that ferries take vehicles and people across large bodies of water. What is not common knowledge are the problems that must be addressed for the apparently simple management of that responsibility. A ferry floats on water. Cars must be driven from land onto the deck of the ferry, a movement from a relatively stable base to an obviously unstable one. Naturally, a ramp makes this better accessible. The sea level, and thus the angle of the ramp, varies considerably from one port to the next and from one weather system to the next. In addition, the weight of cars as they are loaded causes the deck level of the ferry to vary, again affecting the angle of the ramp. These variables are countered by having holds in the ferry that take in water, allowing the bridge (the administrative centre) to compensate for these fluctuations with adjustments to the floating weight of the ferry. When it is empty, more water is taken into the hold to sink the ferry to dock level. When the tide is high, it also is necessary to take even more water into the hold so that the deck level is lowered and maintained at a reasonable equivalent to the level of the land. Usually a ferry will stay in port after loading in order to flush the holds and return to a proper water line. This is not always necessary; under relatively calm conditions, it is possible to pump the hold while leaving port and close the doors before reaching open water. Apparently, because of austerity measures adopted to make the ferry runs economical driven by the impending opening of the Chunnel, this was the method used in the months prior to the accident.

This leads us to the whole concept of flexibility. On the day of the accident, conditions were not normal. There was some irregularity with tidal conditions, making the water level four feet higher than usual. This required that a lot more water be taken into the hold to allow the ferry to be loaded. Obviously with such unstable weather conditions, there also might have been other changes in areas that are less visible, like sandbars or other underwater conditions. With that in mind, it would have been advisable to reassess priorities and stay in port a little longer so that at least some of the additional water could be pumped out.

You may know what happened. The boat left the dock on schedule, requiring that the hold be pumped out as the ferry steamed to open water in accordance with the general edicts of the company. It sailed so deeply to waterline that it encountered an unexpected sandbar. The captain then did what was the most appropriate manoeuvre: he turned sharply. This caused the excess water in the hold to rush to one side and cause the boat to roll. Frantic attempts to close the door and force the water out were in vain because too much water still was in the hold. As a result, the boat overturned and a number of people drowned.

The human being is perhaps the most flexible source of solutions there is. No computer can read as many variables, have as great an accumulative insight or create a solution as quickly as the experienced person. Even if a computer can do it nearly as well, it will be because it has been programmed to consider as many variables and store as many perceptions as the programmer or group of programmers can think of loading into it. As a human being, therefore, you should never degrade yourself by allowing yourself to become only the tool for the computer or for the decisions of people who are not as familiar with the new variables that pertain to the issue as you may be. You must be able to visualize and consider the new demands of the task, consider the conflicting opinion from the other person and consider the experience you already have accumulated in order to make the most appropriate decision for the problem as you see it. Then you must have the maturity to accept the consequences with the dignity of someone who has done what he had to do as well as he can do it. This is not always respected by the observer.

Let us reenact the event of the ferry disaster. This time, the captain will have the foresight to reassess his priorities and be accountable to himself in his management of the task. He would have observed the boat lying deeper to water line than was safe. He would have surmised that such weather conditions would have had unseen dangers that might more easily be precipitated on the boat in such an unstable condition. Then he would have made the decision to defy orders of company edicts, and to wait until a significant amount of water had been pumped out, letting the boat sit more stably in the water. Because of his added precautions, he would have missed the sandbar, and no disaster would have occurred. He would not have been honoured by the passengers who would not have known that a potential disaster was averted. In fact, he might have been fired for defying orders.

In other words, there would have been a consequence, whatever his action. Now, tell me: Would it have been easier to face the consequence of appearing accountable (to his bosses) while being unaccountable to himself, even if the disaster had not happened? Or, would it have been better to be punished for defying orders while, within himself, he could proudly know that he did what was most appropriate? In the first case, in the absence of a disaster, no one would have known that he just did his job. In the second case, no one would have known that he did his job well, with accountability. The rewards will lie within his self-respect.

As a self-accountable person, you will realize that your responsibility lies in your ability to relate to all areas of the world that affect you, or which you can affect. Some of these, like the feedback from your body, are privy only to you. Your actions must be taken with consideration for all pertinent areas. It makes no sense to be so concerned about acquiring experience that you run your body to the ground and so lose any further opportunity to acquire any more experience.

I indicated in the previous chapter that you receive experience in a ubiquitous fashion, explaining that this quality places you in a position where you cannot gain by paying more heed to one aspect and neglecting another. Each one will affect the other at all times, even if only covertly. Your total capacity is as efficient as any one of those three areas of responsibility can be. Therefore, sometimes it is necessary for a self-accountable person to do less of a common responsibility if there also is an important problem in another less visible area.

Perhaps a simple example will serve to illustrate this need for flexibility, not just in the obvious task but in the management of the whole range of responsibilities. If you have to make an important presentation but are struck with a severe migraine headache, you may have a compound problem. You may assess that the presentation is important and must be made on time, even at the expense of its accuracy, or you may decide that the headache is so severe that you will be unable to make a proper presentation while being so distracted. In the former, you will establish a priority that allows you to continue as planned. No apparent change will be observed except in the accuracy of your presentation. In the second, you will have rearranged your priorities to make your physical well-being important in the planned sequence. You know that you will be able to discharge the problem better when the headache has subsided.

Regardless of which decision has been made, even if you already have changed the planned sequence, you still keep assessing all three areas: the task, your body and the needs and actions of other people. At the final time for the presentation, you may discover that you cannot make the presentation with the headache even after a grand attempt. You may discover that the headache subsided earlier than usual, allowing you to reconsider making the presentation as has been planned or anticipated.

With flexibility, you are in charge. No one will know why you have made such apparently strange rearrangements of priorities, and no one needs to know. It is your responsibility to manage all that is presented at you. You are responsible for yourself and for how you do your tasks. As Maynard Keynes is reputed to have said, "When the facts change, I change my mind; what do you do, sir?"

Begging off because of a headache does not allow the observer to make the decision for you or exonerate you from the consequences. That person only accepts that for whatever reason, you have decided to give priority to something else. You still are held responsible for your decision, regardless of how much information you offer the observer so that he or she can exonerate you. Asking another person to endorse a decision with information gained indirectly from you is no more appropriate than asking that person to endorse the decision without information. Information so subjective that it cannot be verified is not really usable for making an accurate decision; such an action only removes from you the dignity of being truly accountable. Also, asking another person to create a decision based on information available only to you may provide you with a decision that does not consider the real importance of the source of information to you or the severity of its interference on you. You may be forced into a position where you definitely will be seen to be unaccountable if you then change your priorities.

Remember that no other person sees anything the same way you do. No one else has the same vision of consequences as you do. No one has the same effect from those consequences as you will. No one, then, can establish the priorities that are important to the greater efficiency of your overall contribution than you can.

USING FAILURE TO ADVANTAGE

You may assess a task perfectly and make a decision that is ideal for the level at which you can observe the task. You can express that decision efficiently. Yet when you do, you still are unable to discharge the task as well as you believed it should be managed. Your best effort was inadequate; you failed. This does not mean that you are inadequate. There are two considerations you may not have entertained. The first is that everything is in a constant state of change, causing much of your well-prepared solution to be redundant by the time you are able to express it. The second is that everything is so multifaceted that you cannot see all aspects of any task, regardless of how experienced you may be or how carefully you may have examined it.

Without those considerations, you cannot have assessed your apparent failure with true objectivity. First, if you approach a task with the objective of sharing what you know—that is, expressing your opinions in order to manage the immediate aspect of the problem, disclosing the parts that are not yet visible and influencing its continued change—you will have been prepared to accept that there always will be something else that needs to be done. You will have been able to realize that a new problem is not always a new problem. It may also be the problem that you did not intend to address in the first place while effectively managing the problem you chose to address. The first consideration in recognizing failure is to assess whether the failure is real or whether it is the appearance of success from a different angle.

If you succeeded in managing the immediate aspects of the problem, all your apparent failure will have done is to allow that part you never intended to address to become more visible. You will decide whether this increased visibility has given it new prominence, and then you will determine what you will do. Your apparent failure becomes a complete success applied to the original situation, the way you intended it to be in the first place as a person who is accountable to your own greater sense of responsibility.

If you succeeded in exposing the hidden aspects of the task, you can use your apparent failure to allow you to assess the new problem, decide whether it is necessary for you to continue its management at that time and do what you determine to be necessary. Your apparent failure will have given you the opportunity to have more information to feed your expanding consciousness. If you succeeded in influencing the further change that the task has been destined to undergo, your success will have been complete. You know that such change has been addressed and that any more will be a fraction of the problems that may have evolved from the unattended task. You will have influenced and managed its direction.

Obviously, even if you have a realistic objective, you still could have failed because your actions may have had the opposite effect to what they were intended to have. Instead of dealing with the immediate problem and revealing the underside or influencing its change positively, your actions may have disturbed the existing problem, making it more visible or introducing consequences that made further change less controlled. Thus you may not have considered as many factors that influence the problem as you may have thought you did in your formation of your solution. Your solution was insufficient. This is not a condemnation of you as much as it is an invitation for you to hone your observation skills, increase your respect for those other sources of influence and reassess the approach you took to formulating your solution. You must accept that you were not born perfect, that you were not provided with perfection. You only are a human being with an opportunity to learn. Through this, you develop your intelligence to whatever ultimate purpose your logic or faith allows you to accept, as was discussed in the previous chapter.

These tasks are not tests of your development; they are opportunities for you to determine your level. I tell students who panic for exams that they must realize that the examination is not set in order to see how stupid they are. It is information for them as much as it is for their teachers. The examination shows them where their level is. It is for them what a spike is to a mountaineer: a method of fixing their position, a point from which they can plot their further progress.

Failure is a necessary input for you to make any improvement in yourself. It is only from failure that you learn. If you do not fail, whether your failure is apparent failure or true failure, you cannot grow, and growing is the only realistic objective there is to life. Failure, then, is a source of inspiration. Real failure is not the inability to discharge a task acceptably; instead, it is the unwillingness to use the new information to improve yourself. It is the revelation that you neither respect yourself enough to use the feedback to grow nor respect others to know that your lack of accountability leaves them with a greater burden. Real failure is failure to be self-accountable. Under these conditions, other people must manage not only the responsibilities that you will not bear, but the consequences that will be revealed when your performance serves to worsen the existing problem, irritate hidden areas that you are not prepared to manage and unleash further change rather than influence it.

If, on the other hand, you will accept failure as an invitation that is given only to those who are seen as having the capacity to be more capable today than they were yesterday, you will see failure as a compliment to you, recognition that you have more areas that you can develop. A truly successful person always fails. Like Edison, that person can recognize that the thousandth failure is the ability to know a thousand solutions that will not work for that problem.

USING CRITICISM TO ADVANTAGE

Your performance is your action, as a self-driven entity, to express your opinion or impose them on your environment. There are two variables that can affect this. The first is your perception. You cannot see everything that pertains to a common issue; therefore the opinion you create cannot be appropriate for every possible aspect of that issue. The second is your expression. Your performance is an attempt to express your opinion; expression is a function of your value systems, your learned language or behaviour and your developed skills. It is obvious, then, that what comes out is not always an accurate representation of what you want to reveal, and frequently it's even less representative of what the issue demands.

You need criticism. Criticism, properly taken, can save you from the extremely severe consequences that sometimes can be evoked if a performance is too inappropriate for dealing with the issue. This is objective criticism, the attempt to provide you with honest information on your performance so that you can adjust it to be more appropriate to the issue. You need objective criticism from an observer because when you see your performance from your perspective, you always see it with the benefit of knowing its true intent—an awareness that can give you inaccurate information about what really comes out.

Not all criticism is objective, however. People can be so subjective that the main thrust of their criticism is directed either to get you to stop doing something that can disturb their comfort, or to condemn you for not being accountable to the same standards as those to which they adhere. It is important that you are able to accept all criticism and get from it whatever you can use constructively. Subjective criticism is computed on how your performance is observed to address the issue. However, it is directed not at your performance, but at you. Subjective criticism can be as useful to you as objective criticism. It is up to you to be able to interpret it objectively and make it objective and useful to you—you cannot depend on the observer to make that adjustment.

For example, I can tell you that your management of a particular issue fails to consider an aspect that I believe to be important. I can tell you that you managed that particular issue stupidly. The first comment is objective criticism and is tailor made for you. You have the information that can allow you to improve your perception, and so your performance. The second comment is subjective criticism, yet it is based on a similar observation and assessment of your performance.

You can handle this in two ways. First, you can expect me to be intelligent enough to know that I can comment only on your performance, not on your ability to understand the issue. However, this is an unfair burden not only on me but on you, because it places you at the mercy of every other person, giving them control over the benefits you can receive from the criticisms they can give. Second, you can attempt to transform that subjective criticism into objective criticism. Probe into my reasons and find out why I believe that you managed it stupidly. This may be an invitation for me to destroy you more. Yet how much more can I destroy you? I already have expressed my opinion.

If I continue to support that opinion, or if I impose it more forcibly, I will be revealing that I do not have the intelligence to realize that I am insisting that I know something I cannot read: your thoughts. If instead I explain the reason for my opinion, I will be providing you with the objective criticism that will allow you to take advantage of my observation of your performance.

Of course, before you can take advantage of criticism, you must be strong enough, or secure in the source of your affirmation, so that you are seeking information honestly, not just confirmation that you have done well. You also must be prepared to use the information you obtain from the criticism to improve your understanding or adapt your expression of it. You must know your objective to be stimulated to think and grow. To do this, you must first know how to immunize yourself, as was discussed in the last chapter.

If you think about it, the worst thing another person can do to you is to leave you to wallow in your ignorance, letting you believe that your performance is adequate. Then, when you attempt to express that opinion again in a more difficult or unforgiving situation believing it to be acceptable, you will be unpleasantly surprised by your unexpected failure, or destroyed by the rejection that will accompany your performance. The best thing another person can do for you, therefore, is to offer you a critical opinion. It may not always feel good. In fact, the initial reaction is for you to protect yourself by ignoring the comment. If you do this, you will be no better off than if you were left with no opinion at all. Of course, the most frequent type of criticism is subjective. You therefore must always be able to explore and consider every subjective criticism, even if you have to make a strategic retreat and lick your wounds before attempting to explore the conditions that led to the criticism. A person who gives subject criticism may simply be asking for an invitation to offer his or her different opinion. For me to say your action is foolish, am I not stating that I am seeing it from a more intelligent position? Am I not itching for you to seek that more intelligent perspective from me? If you are self-affirmed, you can explore my opinion just to get more information for your personal erudition.

Always be prepared to look at the two factors that can be adapted. Again, we cannot emphasize enough that you must know your objective. If all you want to do is to survive the situation, it may not be necessary to ignore the criticism; you probably will never have to deal with it again. However, you must remember that if it occurs again, you will be no better prepared than you were this time. You will have to re-experience either the failure or the criticism that tells you that your performance can be improved.

If you have your own growth and development as your objective, you will accept criticism as an ingredient for that growth. You know that your opinion on any issue cannot cover the whole problem. You know that your performance is, at best, a poor representation of all you are able to reveal. You know that any criticism is more an accurate assessment of the areas of an issue that you have not addressed, either in your consideration of it or in your expression of your opinions than it is a statement of the other person's prejudice. Therefore, you first will consider criticism as a mirror of your performance, not of your understanding; this allows you to determine where your inadequacy lies. If it is in your performance, you can attempt to restructure it, again seeking the feedback of criticism to polish it. If it is in your understanding, you either can reassess the issue or take information from the person who obviously has a different perception of it. I remember a situation that happened to me as a young intern in Canada. I was feeling misplaced in a new country with no friends and no connections. However, on my ward there was a senior staff member, a woman, who was so kind and caring and who went out of her way to make me feel comfortable. I was so taken by her warmth that I wanted to compliment her and told her how homely she was. I really meant that she made me feel at home. Of course she saw this as an insult and was peeved. Her criticism was well-directed, so I was able to correct not my intent but my expression of it.

Second, you will accept that you cannot address every aspect of any issue. You will know that there is a point when you can accept the presence of the criticism without necessarily needing to consider its input. Then you will express your opinion, knowing that it may not be perfectly acceptable to that observer, but knowing that it is as far as you are willing to take it.

ASSESSING THE ACCURACY OF A CRITICAL OPINION

There is a double variable that makes the contribution of a critical opinion more complex than seems likely. This is because a criticism is the expression of another person—a person just like you. If there can be a variation in both your perception of an issue and your expression of the opinion you will have made on it, so too can the other person experience similar difficulties. Whenever an issue is made complex by the interplay of two sets of variables, the easiest way to analyze it is first to examine one presuming the other to be stable, and then reexamine it with the other freely active. This is something you do regularly: you measure the movement of anything relative to yourself with the presumption that you are still. Then you introduce your movement to allow you to get a truer perspective of the other. We can do the same with our assessment of a critical opinion.

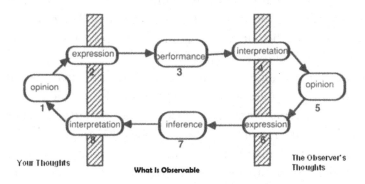

Figure 13. The Cycle of a Critical Opinion

First, let us presume that the opinion of the other person is an honest assessment of your performance, an objective criticism. That opinion then acts as a mirror of what you are revealing of yourself. In Figure 13, this is represented by the inference (7) being an ideal representation of your performance (3). You cannot see how you appear on the outside because your view from the inside is influenced by your knowledge of what you want to reveal, so the mirror gives you an added advantage. You then have what can be an accurate assessment of how you perform. Now, you have two pieces of information: what you want to reveal and what you actually have revealed. You can compare them. If this feedback, a true measure of your performance, determines that your performance is inadequate, you know that its inadequacy is caused either by a flaw in your opinion (1) or a flaw in your expression of that opinion (2). If it is an accurate representation of your opinion, then the flaw lies in your opinion. That is, if (3) equals (1), and (3) is wrong, then (1) is wrong. You can reassess the problem using information gathered from the criticism to correct your perception of the problem or add to it.

Then you will form a new opinion, revealing it with the intent of reassessing your performance and, if necessary, correcting it again. If the feedback is not an accurate assessment of what you wanted to reveal—that is, if (3) is not equal to (1)—then (2) has distorted (1).

You know that the flaw lies in your ability to express your opinion. You need to attempt to express yourself more accurately. Again, you can use information from the criticism to guide the expression of your opinion so that it is revealed more accurately.

Now, let us presume that the opinion of the other person is affected by that person's variables, a subjective criticism. The opinion therefore is not an accurate representation of what you did. Before you can use this information, you must make it into an objective opinion. The person has expressed an opinion not on the accuracy of your performance, but on its value. You need to know not that your solution is wrong, but why it is considered to be wrong. You must invite that other person to be more descriptive in the criticism. You probably will be providing a forum for that person to elaborate not on the reason for drawing that conclusion but as to why you are considered to be unable to formulate a correct solution. This may not be comfortable, but the intent is not to accept that other person's determination of your intelligence or that person's inferences on your capability at face value. Rather, it is to get information on those aspects of a problem you have failed to consider in your performance. Remember your objective: to grow, not to seek affirmation or pursue survival.

You know that you cannot consider everything. You know that you do not always wish to consider everything. You know that you sometimes want to influence the change that you may see occurring in something. You know, therefore, that the feedback may not just tell you why you have been inaccurate. It also may tell you the limitations of the other person's considerations. Then that invitation to the other person to continue to criticize you either will reveal new information to you on the subject, or it will reveal the limitations imposed on that other person by his or her defences. With that information, you will be able to make an assessment, either of your further involvement in the subject or of the importance that you will give to that person's criticism. In order to accomplish this, you must be able to disassociate yourself from the person's attempt to deride you.

Here is a true story that may explain this complex condition. I once assessed a young lady who had been having tremendous difficulty at work. She worked in Toronto as a storyboard editor in a large advertising firm. Her first statement revealed only her frustration: her boss was

American, and he hates Canadians. Of course this only revealed that there was a problem; it was not an accurate assessment of the source of the problem. As I questioned her about her job, she revealed that she had been working on a large account for more than three months. At this time, the customer was thrilled with her output. Yet when she presented it to her boss, he simply stated that it was inadequate and wouldn't work and that she should go back and redo it. I taught her to immunize herself first and then to take this as subjective criticism. She should go back to her boss, leaving herself open to further criticism just to get useful information. I assured her that her boss was just another human being with limitations. She must manage him.

The following week she returned much happier. She revealed that she had been working on a product, Downy detergent. Apparently there was an attempt to market a new detergent under that name. She had come up with a great advertisement that the customer liked. When she asked her boss to enlighten her, he revealed that in the consumer's mind, Downy meant soft and fluffy. Her ad for the detergent conflicted with that message. So it was not that she was wrong but that she was wrong for an aspect of the task that he saw and she did not see. Apparently for this conflict or perhaps for some other reason, the product was shelved.

You must know that the only thing visible about you is your performance, not your conscious ability. You must also remember that as that conscious energy, your strength is not in what you already know, but in your ability to create knowledge. You cannot be condemned for not knowing; you only can be condemned for not trying to know, and that of course occurs if you ignore the critic or silence the opposition without first considering whether he or she has been objective in his or her assessment. Only when you do that, and only after you have considered that new aspect of the whole condition or the subjectivity of that other person's opinions will you have earned the right to discount that opinion if that is the appropriate direction, and you can proceed with the assurance that you have given full respect both to yourself and to the demands of the task.

Sometimes you have to pay more attention to the critic than to the one who unconditionally accepts your performance, even if that criticism destroys what you believe to be true. Just remember Hans

Christian Anderson's story of *The Emperor's New Clothes*. The only opinion that was valuable to the emperor was that of the child who honestly shouted that the emperor was naked, whereas all his courtiers lied about the fine texture of the invisible fabric in order to save their skins.

SUMMARY

The admonition to be self-accountable does not mean that you always must be working, that you always must be so self-disciplined that your responsibility for relating to everything and everyone from the perspective of learning never stops and that you always must be looking only for the next problem. Even as you do express yourself, you also must be willing to enjoy the fruits of your labour. It means that you must give account of yourself maturely, that you do what has to be done and be prepared to deal with the consequences. It means that you must realize that other people may not always manage maturely for their part, and that their defences will cause them to leave more for you to do than you ordinarily will be required to do, or even cause them to attack you for doing what you are prepared to do if it makes their responsibilities more demanding. It means knowing that you sometimes will be condemned for your performance, but that you will use that to your advantage. It also means that your performance sometimes will be sufficient to deal with all the immediate problems that arise from a task. Then you will enjoy all the benefits and pleasures that will come your way as a result of your successes. You will enjoy the comforts that you can derive from the material environment. You will enjoy your healthy body and all the pleasures it can bring. You will enjoy the satisfaction that compatibility with the people you have learned to understand can bring you.

You will do so, however, with an awareness that change is happening in invisible areas of each of these. You will enjoy them without becoming complacent and expecting them to be there always. Whenever the things you have earned to provide for your comforts are lost or become uncomfortable, you will accept that manifestation of change as a natural event and either go on to other things or accept it. Whenever you recognize an unaccustomed discomfort, pain or illness, you will not be surprised by it or panic because of it. Rather, you will see it as a natural event that calls for your attention to deal with an immediate problem and go on to enjoy new and different pleasures your body can give you. Even if the news is bad, you also will be okay because you will have understood that your job is not to be, but to build yourself while being. That is an unpredictable amount of time. You just must use productively whatever you get of it.

Whenever the people with whom you have been compatible act strange or reject you, it will not surprise or destroy you. Rather, you will see their actions either as a message to you about changes within you that you can address or as changes within them that allow them to be different, to accept different things. You will expect that their personalities will grow, and you will provide them with different perspectives. This will be an invitation for you to get to know more of their hidden parts, more of their new personalities, and to grow with them.

Stress, a problem in modern society, will be less visited upon you because you will have learned to use a fast-paced world to advantage by adapting to the pace of these changes, accepting that in doing so, you always will be the proselyte, always being willing to learn to do things because they have been presented to you, not measuring your worth by expecting that you already should be able to do what has not yet been presented. Loneliness, a problem in modern society that occurs when you need the support or friendship of others, will not be visited on you because you will be the source of support, not its recipient. You always will have what others want, the ability to give consideration and share understanding, instead of looking for those others to share it with you and scaring them in the process.

Success, efficiency and accomplishment will be easier for you to achieve because you will have learned to have a clear objective and the self-accountability to reach it. Now, you must be able to share this with those who look to you for direction and assistance, or to those whose fears and defences may cause them to burden you with their demands and frustrations. You also must be able to pull yourself out of a rut if you have already fallen into one of distress, addictions or unhealthy behaviour. This treatise, having shown you how to be better prepared for change and disruption, will not be complete unless it also shows you how to apply this knowledge to restore others when they are managing poorly, and restore yourself when you are the one in need for restructuring. It gives this direction to you because you are truly the only one who can help yourself.

In my practice, when I attempt to assist another person to come out of a drug or alcohol habit, or to manage and unhealthy mood or behaviour, I always lead them to manage themselves. I will not attempt to stop people from drinking, but I will show them how to build the strength to decide how to stop themselves from living in and practising an unhealthy behaviour. Beyond this chapter are discussions that pertain to these three areas of personal angst. They show how to apply this understanding in a practical manner. You may read them for general information to help someone you care about or to help yourself in a private and discreet manner.

CHAPTER 8

BEING A MANAGER

PERHAPS THE MOST DEMANDING responsibility anyone can have in today's society is that of taking the mature position and managing from one's own resources when the task is difficult, poorly defined or in a state of turmoil. This is management, the act of being accountable to oneself for the completion of a task. Even greater is the responsibility of relating to other people from a mature and knowledgeable perspective, or guiding, training or managing them with authority and consideration. This is because every task is subject to change, even as we are addressing it, making our best efforts appear ineffective. It is also because as each person is influenced by these ever-changing conditions, his her response imposes a new direction to the change, making it more complex than before. All this happens because we live in a vast and complex environment, so vast that the other people can be affected by parts of the environment that may be totally alien to our experience, and so complex that even those parts that are familiar to us will have areas that we cannot see. It is this combination of the individuality of people and the complexities of the challenge that makes managing from authority or even relating to other people a difficult and frequently unrewarding experience.

Yet you do it. You may be managing people in a business organization, guiding children in a family or training students in a school. You may be responsible for the well-being of people in a community or clients in an office. You simply may be the person who takes the more responsible position in relating to another person such as a spouse, a friend or a colleague. You do this not because you have more advanced skills or more than adequate preparation than these other people. Sometimes, you arrive at this position because you are a little more experienced at a particular task or more familiar with a particular event than the people around you. Sometimes you are just a little less confused, tired or deflated than that other person or those other people. In any case, you must be able to recognize that the most frequent cause of disharmony, hostility or stress in any relationship between two or more people is the inability of one of the people involved in a confrontation to take the mature position and approach the unknown and unfamiliar aspect of the situation without feeling threatened, or to consider the other's perspectives without resentment. If you see management imbalance or stress as a condition that exists when what you have to do exceeds what you have for doing it, you will recognize that relating to people or managing them can easily be regarded as the most frequent way of reaching this imbalance.

In other words, one person must be willing to take charge and guide the other person in order to manage the confrontation or the common responsibility. Even if you are not in a traditional position of management, by taking the mature position in a relationship, you will have accepted the responsibility of managing the other person. This can be an unfair burden on you: The complexities of the common environment affect you just as harshly as they do the other person. The desire to be respected without compromise is as important to you as it is to the other people. Yet if you wish to succeed in the people management task you have chosen to do, or which you have inherited by virtue of your position, you must be able to have, as your main objective, the development of that other person or those other people into more capable and more productive members of society or of the unit in which you function. Then their influence on common conditions will be rational rather than defensive, their contribution helpful rather than destructive. First, however, you must be able to manage your own challenges capably even though these challenges are no less complex than those the other people have to manage. You must be able to be a resource for the people who look to you for guidance, assistance or consideration even though the problems they have to manage are rarely greater than or coincident with yours.

This may seem to be a difficult or impossible task. You must remember that you live in a world of people. The whole direction of everything you do, everything you plan, is influenced by how it allows you to relate to other people. Thus unless you can relate to people from a position of greater insight and understanding, their fears and the defences they use to counteract these fears will become excessive burdens for you to bear. Unless you can nurture them into being fully responsible for what they do and how well they succeed, they will always be there to demand more of you, drain you or leave you with the responsibility for their unfinished tasks.

The extra work that may be required initially in order to either motivate or educate the people with whom you live, work or play may be seen as an investment toward your greater peace of mind. If they can acquire a greater awareness of the problem, and if they are motivated to accept responsibility for managing it, then they can propel themselves into being more competent than you may have anticipated and so manage a common task more efficiently, or approach the confrontation with less hostility. Then the communications you will have established with them will suppress future problems before they arise, because these people will more likely approach you with early difficulties or discuss weaknesses with you rather than compound their problems with the effects of their frustrations.

In short, the role of the more responsible person or the person in the more responsible position is to be a leader and to know how to lead when conditions are strange or in turmoil as well as when they are familiar or stable. Whether or not you want it, there are times when you must assume the role of the more responsible person. It is up to you to do it efficiently and effectively. Even if you are simply taking the mature role in your relation to another adult from an intimate stance, you have accepted the role of manager, albeit for a temporary period.

MANAGEMENT: THE OBJECTIVE OF THE RESPONSIBLE PERSON

If you are going to manage a task, you will take control of that task and guide it with skill and authority toward a specific objective. If that task is a problem that is easily identifiable, and the objective is one that is easily reachable, you will be able to manage it effectively without too much bother or difficulty. If the task is even a little more complex, or the objective a little less reachable so that a tool or machine is required to take the task to the objective, you still can manage it as long as you have developed the skill and expertise in using that tool or machine.

However, when the task is the productivity and capability of another human being (subordinate, adolescent or client), and the objective is such a complex factor as the efficient management of some part of this vast and constantly changing common environment, success becomes a little more elusive. When the tool or machine for reaching that task (the person's capabilities) is also the independently activated skills, training and ambition of the person himself, management becomes governed by a totally different set of rules. It no longer can be the simple application of one rule that has worked somewhere else; neither is it the attempts to seduce the person with prizes that may have attracted someone else. Rather, it is the ability to approach each person as an individual and each task as a complex interplay of multiple factors to be managed, not by pretending that one or the other can be made to be stable, but by attempting to understand them as they change.

If you believe that the task of managing other people lies in being able to manipulate them as implements for you to reach the common objective, you also will see that success is made complex and frequently impossible by the very independent nature of the implements. If, however, you see the task of managing or relating to people as guiding these other people into managing their responsibilities themselves, or into producing effective solutions that can be shared and applied to the common responsibility, you will perhaps be more prepared to solve the two most difficult aspects of this management problem: those of identifying the task and using the tools.

Since at this point you are interested in how the other person is able to manage the problem, your challenge is not the problem but the person, namely that person's capacity for managing the problem. This is something you cannot measure. You cannot measure where any single person begins. You cannot measure how far that person may have developed. You know only that each person begins at point zero and that each person progresses at an independent rate. That person's capabilities are hidden, known only to himself.

As a responsible person, you have a task to accomplish, but the task has not been properly defined because you cannot be sure where your starting point is, or even whether you will have completed the task. In addition, even this ill-defined task of guiding other people into becoming more capable or productive is further compounded by the independence with which they may activate their skills and desires. The tools—that is, the skills, knowledge and motivation of the people themselves—that you must use to help them manage a problem effectively are not accessible to you.

The human being is a self-driven force. He cannot be turned on and off, or intentionally guided as can be done with a machine like a motorcar. The human being cannot be loaded with immediately relevant information and used to manipulate that information as can be done with a computer. The human being is so independent that regardless of how urgently you may need his performance, you cannot simply make it happen. You must wait for that person to want to produce, and to accept responsibility for the management of the task. It is this combination of the undetermined task added to the inaccessible tools that makes people management the most difficult management task there is.

THE CHALLENGE OF MANAGEMENT

Perhaps the most difficult part of any marriage is the need to relate to a spouse after the honeymoon is over, after the excitement of sexual and emotional gratification has been fulfilled. It is the time when new challenges are stretching each person differently. Children, financial demands, time demands from work or travel, and illness, either of the adults or a child, all impact each spouse differently. What is more is that each person sees the depletion to self of these added burdens and expects the same level of support and encouragement from the spouse to whom they once gave all of themselves. Now the spouse is also just as depleted, but each one does not know the extent of the other's depletion. All that is seen is that the other is not giving, now that one needs him or her. It builds frustration and resentment.

Perhaps the most difficult part of business management is getting other people to pull their weight and make a rational contribution when conditions change. But people, especially those in subordinate roles in business, would rather deal with a sameness, a stability in what they have to do. It is far too difficult for them to rely on a cognitive capability that should be the supreme capability of the human being. It is possible that this cognitive capability might have been underdeveloped, neglected in its development or restrained or repressed in its use. Then they will place greater reliance on physiological strengths to supplement or even act in full replacement of cognitive capabilities. In some cases, physiological assets may be described as muscle memory; in other cases it may be described as learned skill. But when conditions change—a major one at the macroscopic level or a minor activity at the microscopic or invisible level—and a different process of management is required, they either cannot function, or they try to force the proverbial square peg into the round hole. They force an established routine into a new or transformed condition.

Change in business is not just the major procedural restructuring that impacts all employees. More often it is the constant daily challenges of dealing with product, market, machinery, support services or customers, each of which has its own invisible activities that require cognitive and thus constructive problem-solving. And this must occur—if not at the subordinate level, then at least at the management level and filtered down to the subordinates.

Change in families is not just the infidelity or neglect or quarrels that ensues and destroys trust. These are the aftereffects. Change occurred before these acts become manifest. It is the constant daily struggles when pressures at work deplete the energies for use at home, personal feelings of incompetence, rejection, fear that pervade all aspects of life and can never be discounted.

Change, in all its forms and at all levels, can paralyze an employee, disrupt a marriage or challenge management to reach for and apply that superior attribute of every human being: the cognitive strength. To this end, change must be understood and become the stimulant to progressively more profound management skills.

THE OBJECTIVE OF MANAGEMENT

The ultimate objective in the management of any task is usually the attempt to improve its presentation—or the way we see it, anyway. In a similar way, the ultimate objective in managing another human being is the attempt to improve his or her presentation of his or her skills and understanding. This translates as improved productivity in business, improved social awareness in families, improved consideration in friendship and improved educational skills in schools. The main asset of the human being is that person's ability to make a contribution to the world by formulating ideas and expressing them. In short, people must be productive. People are not born productive, however. We are born with the *capacity* to be productive. When that capacity is nurtured, the human being becomes more than an extension of a person with greater vision, of a business or of society in general. He or she becomes a self-driven source of information and perception.

If the ultimate objective of managing or relating to other people is to nurture their understanding of a particular situation and help them to be more productive, the task of management becomes the task of being a competent authority in the areas in which you must lead them, being able to communicate with them and being able to motivate them to share your vision and manage their tasks competently and independently.

It must be done in that sequence. Remember, you cannot reach the tools that define and reveal a person as a human being. You must reach people and stimulate them into using those tools—that is, their information, experience, skills and dexterity. You cannot store your information into other people or inject them with your skills. You must let them use the tools which they have and which you have helped them activate or improve, to apply themselves purposefully and accomplish the task. Of course, this means that you must be able not only to guide the other people, but to allow them full responsibility for accomplishing the task, you being only the facilitator to the development of their capacity for making that accomplishment. Thus the objective of people management is the development of other people, not using them as extensions of yourself.

If you can accept that your task in managing or relating to another person is the nurturing of that other person, and that in order to accomplish that task you need to learn how to reach and facilitate that person's independence, then you will have realized the most important difference between the management of a physical task and the management of people. The abstract nature of people as a task requires that you approach them with respect for their personal visions, recognition of their developed skills and understanding and faith in their potential as independent human beings. Of course, this means that on the other side of your desk sits a force that may already be a formidable asset, or one that can be nurtured into being such an asset with the proper respect and guidance.

Usually it is a cinch to manage people or to take the mature role in relating to them. Unlike the car or the computer, which needs your direct input in order for them to produce anything, people are self-driven and are theoretically capable of holding their own and managing the task with their own initiative. Theoretically at least, the management of people is the ability to delegate effectively and to let those self-driven forces complete their apportioned tasks. Practically, however, only a small segment of any group of people is so independently driven. The rest, for one reason or another, require that they be activated in order for them to function effectively. They then become a challenge to you—a challenge this dissertation is designed to help you manage positively and purposefully.

THE ALTERNATIVE TO MANAGEMENT

It seems that it is not always necessary for you to take the mature position and manage the people for whom you are responsible or to whom you wish to relate. For instance, you may take the alternative of finding the right person who will fit into the job easily, one who has desires and expectations that are coincident with yours or one who is able to anticipate your desires and strive to satisfy them. This can be extended from the boardroom into the bedroom, as in waiting or checking to find the right partner. Then you can discharge the person who is not pulling his or her weight and replace that person with another more competent person. You may send your defiant or obstreperous child to a distant aunt's or to a military academy for training and discipline. You may divorce your inconsiderate or incompatible spouse and seek a more compatible mate.

That is not the intent of this work, however. For one thing, it is difficult to find sufficient numbers of highly motivated and self-driven individuals to replace the poorly productive ones and expect that they will remain motivated as conditions change. For another, you will find that the new person will become just as difficult to manage or to relate to when conditions change further and surpass her developed resources. The only easy person to manage or relate to is the one who can adapt herself to the demands of the changing conditions. This is difficult to find in just anybody. However, it is easier to develop in a person, or have that person develop in herself. I have often instructed spouses who want to divorce their partner because of inconsideration that the requirement for adaptation and management is the same with the new spouse. It is just evoked for different reasons at a different time. The devil you know is often better than the devil you do not know.

THE CHALLENGE OF MANAGING OR RELATING TO PEOPLE SUCCESSFULLY

Many people are so easily inundated by the demands of today's environment that too many of them cannot continue to face these changing challenges with self-driven accountability and motivation. That is, they are often overwhelmed in more situations and for simpler challenges than may be the norm. They need to be managed. This is not to say that these people are unable to take charge and manage in other areas. The fact is that in this vast and complex environment, even the most capable people will, at some point, be challenged by situations that are outside of their range. When that happens, they will need consideration for their opinions or help to manage a particular problem. Obviously this also can happen to you. Sometimes it can happen to both people in a confrontation at the same time. The point, however, is that one person must decide to take the mature position and manage or guide the other. In this argument, that person is you.

This is your task if you are a parent or a teacher. This also is your task if you are a business manager who wants to have a job done efficiently and effectively. By and large, it also has become your task if you are in a confrontation with your spouse, associate or colleague, and if you want either to benefit from your association with that other person or avoid having to deal with her unnecessary defences.

Regardless of the area in which you manage or relate to people, you no longer have a choice. If you are responsible for other people's productivity, you must learn to manage them, not just expect adequate performance from them. If you are responsible for the management of a common responsibility in association with another person or other people, you must learn to manage these people, not just expect compatibility with them. You must learn to accept as your task not the common responsibility but the persons with whom you must face the common responsibility. You must know that just as the inefficient and defensive person can become productive and considerate, so too can the productive and considerate person be inefficient and defensive under different circumstances. Thus the task of managing and relating to people can be a dynamic and challenging one. This may be a stressful responsibility for some people, or an exciting challenge for others.

If you see it as a stressful experience, it may be because you see other people as extensions to yourself, with you being their driving force—an exhausting approach to the task of management, or one that loses out on the contributions of the other people. It may be because you see them as being capable yet lazy or stupid, and therefore they're an unnecessary burden when they require assistance or guidance; if this is the case, you must reassess your perceptions of people. If you see it as an exciting challenge, you are ready to relate to people positively and manage that association with efficiency and to greater mutual benefit. You then must be willing to learn how to acknowledge an immeasurable force even as it continues to grow or regress. You must be willing to help a self-driven force move forward even though it will not progress without help in starting, yet will not start if not given the freedom to continue on its own.

THE PREREQUISITE FOR SUCCESSFUL PEOPLE MANAGEMENT

If you are about to use a new machine or put together a new structure, the first thing you will do is to read the instruction manual. Before you unwittingly do something to destroy a delicate instrument, you will become familiar with the function of its parts. Before you decide to use it to do a particular job, you must ascertain whether it is designed for that job. It is the same with the management of people. There are two great differences, however. The first is that unlike a machine that comes off a production line and is designed to be similar to other machines of its type, each human being is a distinct individual. Every parent knows that each child is different from the other, even if two of them are twins. Every teacher knows that each child is an individual, even if he or she attends the same classes and is given the same homework as others. People are so distinct that whatever you may have learned about one person is completely irrelevant for another.

However, people are also private individuals. What they think, what they feel and what they are able to do are facilities that are hidden deeply within them and which they guard rather possessively. The instruction manual, therefore, is not easily accessible; it is privately retained within each person. The only way to get at it is to have each person reveal it to you. As you know, there are good reasons for people's protectionism. When people are challenged by a task, they know that whatever they do is going to be seen as a representation of their true capabilities for managing that task. When people are sure that their capabilities are strong enough to be revealed with pride, they will do so. However, when people are challenged to reveal capabilities that may be inadequately developed or inappropriate for the situation, then rather than show their inadequacies or be open to further criticism, they may restrain their opinions and expressions. These restrained capabilities are possessions that no one can extract from a person without his or her express permission. And people aren't willing to give that permission easily to just anybody, especially someone they do not know, with whom they may have a disagreement or who has authority over them.

As the person in the more responsible role, you are expected to manage a task that is different from every other task, one that responds to no obvious instruction manual and whose unique operations are completely hidden and inaccessible. There is no common pattern that helps you to determine how to approach a particular person or group of people and overcome the need for an instruction manual. There is no instrument that can allow you to read what other people know or what they are thinking. You therefore must be able to encourage them to reveal their unique attributes to you before you can relate to them without damaging sensitive areas. This means being competent in the field in which you are leading them, being considerate of their perceptions and opinions and being willing to assist them in nurturing their independence rather than trying to protect their weaknesses.

SUMMARY

You must recognize that by relating to a self-driven force, your first task is to understand the issues that they are trying to solve. To be such a resource in a changing environment, you must be prepared to expect more of yourself than basic experience. You must be willing to respect change and prepare yourself by confidently embracing new problems and new twists in old problems as they continue to invade your familiar tasks. Then you should educate yourself on how people tend to deal with similar interferences to their familiar issues.

The first stage in relating to people from a mature perspective is that you must be a competent resource. Understand your world as it changes, and be strong in conditions that are fragile or constantly changing. Understand people as they try to deal with a changing world, and be capable in areas that confuse and threaten them.

The second stage is that you must know that different people have different perceptions of the common issue. Although their opinions and expressions may be in conflict with those you believe to be right, they also are not wrong. You must be able to communicate with those people and be genuinely interested in learning their perceptions of the common issue and the opinions they may have formed from those perceptions. Then you must be prepared to adapt your opinions to include the new information as it becomes available to you, both from your examination of the issues and from your consideration of the other people's perspective. You need to espouse the first stage competently in order to manage this second stage.

The third stage is that you must recognize that people have the capacity to expand their visions of the common issue and to manage it independently. All they need is to access their tools of reason, judgment and past personal experience, and to use them to create new solutions and manage appropriately the previously unfamiliar or unknown situation. You must be able to motivate these other people to manage the issues that affect them. You may need to share greater options with them. You may need to help them overcome their fears and weaknesses. You may need to give them full responsibility for their successes and for the consequences of their failures. You may need to sit on your hands while observing their difficulties, letting them go through the exercise of wrestling with the situation in order to get the most information from it.

The main thrust of these discussions have been directed at placing you, the reader, in the position of final responsibility. You have been given information that allows you to manage independently, above the need for feedback or assistance from other people. This is not to encourage you to be superior to others or isolated from them; rather, it is to place you in the position of being more useful while also allowing you to have full control over your own successes. You know that you are attracted to people who are both capable and considerate more than you are attracted to insecure or selfish people. These discussions give you that opportunity to be the capable and considerate person to whom the other people around you will be attracted. They show you how to relate to these others, either at their level or as an advisor, helping them to become capable and considerate themselves. It is a known axiom that if you do not need something, you will not be disappointed by not having it. By learning to be independent in change, you will be strong at times when you will not get anything from the people around you. Affirmation can be a boost, but it is better to be strong first rather than need the affirmation to give you the strength.

CHAPTER 9

Understanding People's
Reactions to Change

PEOPLE ARE SELF-DRIVEN FORCES, and they must access their own skills and understanding to manage a task or display a capability. When they can access these, they do not need a manager or authority figure to use them or push them; they can function adequately on their own. However, people frequently restrain themselves because they fear they are unable to give account of themselves effectively. The unknowns threaten to engulf them and to cause them to fail or lose their dignity trying to prevent, hide or hide from failure. Then they look to another person in authority or reluctantly allow such a person to guide, enlighten, or motivate them. As a manager and more enlightened person, you are often called to this position. This is the process of leadership. To lead people effectively, you need to know how to understand people and communicate with them not only when they are willing to reach you, but when they are restrained because of their fears or because they have already established defences to protect themselves or hide from failure.

One temptation in managing or relating to other people when they are dependent on you to guide them is to use them as implements to accomplish your goals or to express your decision. Another is to expect that they should be able to manage without help, leaving them to be inundated by conditions that may be natural to you but tremendously frightening to them. Remember, when you do not know something, it appears large and formidable; when you understand it, it appears small and manageable. Yet it will not have changed—what changed was your level of understanding. Therefore, what to you may appear small and easy can be large and formidable to the uninitiated. You may be surprised when their fears and failures encourage them to be defensive or even hostile in conditions you see as easy or natural.

What you need to know is that people generally are capable of managing their responsibilities independently. They restrain themselves only when they feel that the demands of the task will overwhelm them. When they are surrounded by problems that are strange or unknown, they become afraid, and rather than expose themselves to failure or the revelation of their inadequacy, they will resort to the less personal defensive behaviour. As a manager and a person who has taken responsibility for guiding your tasks toward a specific objective, you know that our present era is replete with unknowns that reach everyone. You also know that these unknowns can cause problems even for you. It is not difficult for you to understand that the people who are perhaps less experienced or less qualified than you will have even greater difficulty managing issues that seem difficult to you, and that some of those that may be familiar or comfortable to you.

They will not tell you this; they only will use defences that will hide this inadequacy and protect their survival or allow them to save face. What you need to be able to do is help those people understand the task so that they will manage it with dignity. With that, you will be useful as a leader to the people who prefer the safety of the role of dependent. You also will be able to extend your reach as a manager by using the resources of other people to manage a common task more effectively.

You now need two ingredients to make this possible. The first is an understanding of how the unknowns are generated so that you can defuse the threats that evoke people's defences and get them to pull their weight efficiently. The second is an understanding of the defences people use so that you can reach behind them effectively without also unintentionally attacking those defences and threatening the dignity or self-worth of the person involved. You have learned to get the first. Now, you must learn to achieve the second.

A defensive response is not just an act of failure or its prevention; it is really a less efficient way of tackling a problem. We know from the preceding chapters that the human being is a cognitive force, but the human being is also an organic life force. We use similar physical skills and instincts, as do all other life forms. A lower life form will respond to a threat using the physical strengths to parry or confront the opposing force. The common conjecture is that of the fight or flight instincts. In the human being, I have added the defence of validation, which is magnifying the power of self through the support of or confirmation by some outside force. Thus an organic life form will attempt to even the playing field by weakening the opposition, running from it or magnifying the ability to confront it, depending on how the opposition is seen and how personal strengths are perceived. (Lower animals use herd instincts or physical attributes of ferocity.) These are physical approaches to management.

We talked in an earlier chapter on the emergence of the cognitive strength. Take the way a deer will respond in the wild to a sudden change in conditions. It has been observed to go through the fight or flight response. The deer hears a sound. The ears prick up. The nostrils flare. The hairs stand on end. The breathing becomes heavier. The heart beats faster and the muscles tense. The animal is ready for fight or flight. Let us suppose that a herd of antelope is grazing, and a lion comes by. The whole herd goes into a fight or flight response. The lion gives chase and catches one. Within a short time, the rest of the herd will simply go back to grazing because the threat is no longer imminent. The fight or flight response, initiated by the release of adrenaline, is defused. As these threats are sporadic, the body gets a chance to recover from the adrenaline-induced stress.

A human being, on the other hand, has a penchant for moving from one threatening situation to another, often with little respite. We do not go into an adrenaline-induced response with such totality. The antelope does not have the option of first checking what made the sound. He is disturbed and the body responds. The human being, on the other hand, will often examine the condition before reacting. Cognitive strength allows us to look at the source of disruption. It may be a familiar person. It may be a problem well within our learned capacity. It may be something we will be able to manage with a little deeper examination. If so, the cognitive strengths take over. Do you remember our discovery that something we understand can appear much less formidable than something we do not understand? Cognitive strengths are our greatest assets; physical strengths are our back-up. They are the shields in battle. They serve a purpose, but not as the main weapon.

Herein lies the rub. If cognitive strengths are our safest and strongest resource, does it not stand to reason that we will rely on them preferentially if we have them? Then, if we rely on physical strengths too often, too easily and too tenaciously, does it not mean that we do not have or perhaps do not believe we have sufficient cognitive strengths? So the use of physical defensive manoeuvres is actually the revelation of insufficient cognitive strengths. Thus it is not as much the expression of power as it is the revelation of weakness. As a manager, you need to be able to recognize the physical defences and know how to work with the true mental strength or weakness of the person. Let us examine the various ways physical defences can be used, remembering that they are only the variety of walls that hide the weakness of the true self. The bigger or stronger we make these walls, the weaker or more fragile we see our true selves. Unfortunately, the more successful these walls, the more fragile we remain, and thus the more dependent we will be on those strengths that work.

A Logical Examination of Defences

The most basic need of anyone is to survive. It is axiomatic that when something is destroyed, it ceases to exist as that thing. Inanimate objects have little choice and do not have a defensive response. Organic life forms do have defensive responses that have evolved, mostly instinctually, to allow them to defend themselves as physical existences. Like other organic life forms, people have to defend their physical survival. Unlike lower life forms, however, people also use their rational capabilities to address issues. People use perception, cognition and established information to create solutions. Therefore, failure of those solutions represents failure of the person as a rational, intelligent being.

People have two areas to defend: the survival of their physical bodies and the integrity of their rational mind. This may be termed a dualism of responsibility. To defend themselves from the threats of the opposing forces, they must address three different areas of the conflict: the opponent and two aspects of the self (the physical and the mental). However, because we are considering the defences people use and not the right people have to exist undisturbed, we do not have to be concerned with the cause of the disparity. It may result because the challenge is too severe for a normally capable person or that the person is too weak to deal with a problem that may be considered simple by any other person.

Logically, the human being will use the same reactive choices as would a lower life form when cognitive strengths are limited relative to the demands of the task. Let us examine them in some sort of category. On the y-axis, we will place the three natural defensive responses of aggression, evasion and association or validation. On the x-axis, we will place the two opposing forces of the external opponent and the self; we will divide the self into the physical and mental. This is what it can possibly look like.

DEFENSE TYPE	DIRECTED AT...		
	OPPONENT	SELF	
		PHYSICALLY	MENTALLY
AGGRESSION	Manipulate, Repress	Perfectionism, Self-Harm, Anorexia	Arrogance, Condescension
EVASION	Dismiss, Exchange	Defiance, Procrastination	Ignore, Avoid
VALIDATION	Peer Support, Obligation	Sensory Indulgence, Physical Extravagance	Egocentricity, Deception

Figure 14. The Defence Systems

In each of the boxes where the x- and y-coordinates meet, I will describe the reactive solution to the best of my ability. My descriptions will be limited, and you may agree with some and disagree with others, or have a better description. They are not meant to be exhaustive—they only attempt to suggest an interpretation. The important exercise is to be able to see the behaviours from an analytic position and categorize them so that other similar responses are not additional but different interpretations of the same concept.

We have three ways to apply the defence of aggression—that is, to the opposition, to the self physically and to the self mentally or emotionally. Similarly, there are three ways to apply the defence of evasion: to the opposition and to the self physically and mentally. Finally, the same subdivisions can be applied to the defence of validation. You may note that the three reactive responses of aggression, evasion and validation are chosen according to the way the person perceives the self in relation to the conditions she must face. Usually a person will use only one automatically, falling to one of the other two only when that one fails. For example, a person who naturally resorts to aggression will evade or even seek validation when the aggressive response fails. She will, however, go to the aggressive response again the next time there is a challenge that exceeds her cognitive capabilities. In the same way, a person who resorts to evasion can use the aggression or the validation response when evasion cannot be completed. Again, she will naturally revert to the familiar response when the next stress arrives. We will now look at each application and see some of the ways each one can be interpreted.

THE AGGRESSIVE RESPONSE

The aggressive response is one that attempts to even the playing field by either making the protagonist greater or making the antagonist smaller so that balance may be achieved. Aggression is necessarily not a fighting role; it simply describes the attempt to achieve balance by forcing a change in one or the other component, or in both. If B is bigger that A, and they are opposing each other, balance can be achieved by making A bigger or by making B smaller. If A consists of two parts, A1 and A2, then either one can be increased to achieve the balance. In human terms, the two aspects are the physical and mental or cognitive. We already know that the ideal solution is to build cognitive strength of understanding so that the person is better equipped to manage. But building understanding takes time and a concerted effort to examine the challenge and all its invisible components. In an acute situation, such time and effort may not be readily available, so an immediate albeit less effective option must be introduced.

AGGRESSION DIRECTED AT THE WORLD

This is the most readily identified type of aggressive response. Anger, hostility and control can be seen as perhaps the most visible ones. However, manipulation can be an important contributor, and it can be aggressive or passive. The notion of passive manipulation can be a misnomer because it is all but passive. It just isn't as obviously imposing as is aggressive manipulation. Instead, it is directed at other people's cognitive strengths. It can perhaps be better termed "persuasive manipulation." One cannot, for instance, manipulate a dog or cat persuasively; it requires the consideration of the recipient being manipulated. The change in behaviour is initiated by the recipient as a decisive response to the request or demand of the source. Persuasion takes time and requires the consideration of the recipient, so it is often an established behaviour. Anger, on the other hand, can be simply a severe, immediate or knee-jerk reaction to a situation that is imposing but cannot be defused using understanding.

So you see, an aggressive response is defined by the intent of the response, not by the impact. The intent is to reduce the opposition or steer the opposition into reducing itself persuasively. An aggressive response like bullying intends to minimize the opposition through fear and so create a docile or impotent environment; this guarantees a restrained impact from the opposition. Bullying works in a different way from hostility or manipulation. It is a concerted effort to destroy the confidence of the opposition by removing or reducing any belief in the value or strength of self.

All aggressive behaviour directed at reducing the contribution of the antagonist is evidence of the limitations of the protagonist. Thus they are revelations of the weakness of the doer, no matter how strong the physical impact may be. In fact the stronger the physical impact, the greater is the evidence of the weakness of the protagonist. Of course, an aggressive response is not only initiated to remove an immediate threat—it can also be a lifestyle. Manipulation may be so successful that there is little incentive to build personal strength. I have seen people who expend more energy structuring ways to manipulate another person into reducing their impact or providing a desired input than would be required to confront an issue proactively.

The natural reaction to the person who demonstrates an aggressive response is to resist or punish the person who has initiated it, but that can be counterproductive. If the aggressive response was initiated because the existing conditions have overwhelmed personal cognitive resources, will not the expansion of the impact of these conditions by resisting or punishing the person cause him to be even more overwhelmed? Then, if the reaction is to initiate an aggressive response, will that not be the same immediate response, albeit more severely? Thus the management of a person who resorts too often, too easily or too severely into an aggressive response cannot be to fight with the same defence; it must be done with the greater power of understanding. This is the intent of the *Understanding Change* approach we will discuss in the next chapter.

AGGRESSION DIRECTED AT THE PHYSICAL SELF

Here again we see there is an intent to reach immediate balance, this time not by reducing the antagonist but by expanding the strength of the protagonist. The self has two aspects, a physical and a mental, so we will deal with each separately. The physical self is the organic body. We use it to reveal what we have acquired in knowledge and creativity. What it reveals can be an accurate representation of what we think. However, because our thoughts are always private and will always remain so, it is possible to use the physical strengths either as a full representation of self or as a means of magnifying what we are able to do. We are the only force that can drive the body. Our muscles respond only to us, whether we use them to speak or to act. Aggression directed at the body then stimulates the body to show us in a way that enhances our performance. Perfectionism is a great example of this. A person drives himself to exhaustion just so he can perform physically what he believes he cannot do cognitively. He may not understand the depth of the challenge but is willing to push himself to meet an objective he determines will show him as capable, or reach one defined by the expectations of another person.

The aggression toward self can also be an act of punishment. Take self-harm: head banging, self-mutilation and anorexia are acts that punish the self for being unworthy. Though the analysis is directed at self as a cognitive force, the punishment is directed at the body as a representative of self. Anorexia can also be a way to force the body to reach an objective in appearance that confirms to some self-determined or distorted standard. A person who pushes the self can sometimes be seen as giving more than expected, but he is really giving less. The harder a person pushes the self to augment physically what he believes he lacks cognitively, the less efficiently he will perform. Added to that is the fact that while he focuses on making up for lost ground by placing effort on physical performance, he will be losing precious opportunity to develop better understanding. I give the example in my talks of a monkey taught to pick up papers and place them in a neat pile. The pile is in a room with an open window that repeatedly disturbs the papers. The monkey runs around picking up papers and gets exhausted. Wanting to help, you suggest to the monkey that you close the window. He dismisses you with the comment, "Window, schmindow. If you want to help, pick up papers." This example demonstrates that the overdriven person can easily lose the opportunity to build real strength and become neurotically focused on extending what does not work.

AGGRESSION DIRECTED AT THE MENTAL SELF

We can direct our aggression at stretching our mental strengths or imposing what we have. This may seem to be a contradiction to what I have espoused in this argument I call *Understanding Change*, which encourages you to build a strong cognitive existence. But each period of growth takes time and effort. We need to gather pertinent information, digest it and reexamine the objective with greater insight, prepared to get back to further exploration if needs be. What if you do not have the time? What if you do not have enough of the energy—that is, the energy of fulfilment or self-respect? What if you have so little information that to get going, you have to build from the start? Then the process of building self can be so time-consuming that you cannot give account of yourself effectively. You need to show an insight you do not have. If your lack is not visible to everyone, you can expand it immediately by demonstrating that you have what you really do not have. You use arrogance to show a capability that really is not there. Or you express condescension that attempts to minimize the opposition by displaying a superiority of self.

The aggressive application to the mental self cannot manipulate the mental self, because this is not a physical entity. It only exists in the manipulation of the representation of self; the productivity is ineffective.

The effort is so focused on making a presentation that whatever comes out has no real power. There is little time left to build self, and true capability still does not improve.

THE EVASIVE RESPONSE

Ah, the evasive response! It does not always mean running away from something. It also means running toward something. Running to an easier state because the other is difficult shows to what we are running, but what we are running from can remain undisclosed. Again, when two opposing forces are unequal, there is discomfort in both that can be eased simply by separating them. Since we are considering the human condition, the discomfort to be relieved lies within the person. The separation relieves the person of the discomfort temporarily. Of course, the evasive response is only an immediate survival tactic; it still leaves the person and that task in a state of imbalance. The hope is that the task will dissipate or will be no longer an issue to be managed. The real intent is to discover a reality that is more forgiving or accepting, one that allows existence without discomfort. With this latter objective in mind, it is easy to deduce the types of responses that will fall into the evasive category and the methods of attaining the end result.

EVASION DIRECTED AT THE WORLD

This is more a physical form of evasion. The responsibility is removed though not managed; there is no attempt to destroy or manipulate it as in the aggressive response. Instead, the attempt is to send it away to someone else or to another area of reality. Delegating a responsibility because one cannot manage it without also learning to manage it, or with the determination that it does not deserve one's attention, is a form of evasion. Take the simple quote that is used as an example of avoidance: "I don't do windows." This is a response directed at evading the task. It can be the refusal to do a menial task or a difficult one. Someone can direct attention away from a situation wherein lies a responsibility they cannot manage, so they are effectively separated from it. There is no attending physical manipulation of the task—it is left alone, simply avoided. An employer or senior politician can remove a challenging staff member rather than learn to manage differently, so dismissal can be a form of evasion. Divorce, separation and break-ups in relationships can also be viewed as the evasion of a situation one cannot manage.

These are natural responses to navigating through a difficult terrain. Why, then, are they considered evasion? True, these are natural. They represent evasion, however, only when they are used as a form of escape from a situation that can present itself again, or one that requires immediate management. To delegate scullery work to a maid is management. To avoid scullery work and let the contamination build up because one is above doing the job is evasion. Similarly, to dismiss mountain climbing as an exercise may be sensible. To refuse to learn it while stuck waiting for rescue is evasion. Evasion can also mean doing things by rote. The unwillingness to examine the nuances of a task and only apply oneself to it blindly according to a set system is also evasion; in this case, one still does not manage the task even if the application of a system allows one to discharge it. Evasion is unhealthy only because one does not allow the challenge of the task to stimulate one's mental or cognitive growth. The task will be done and the slack will be picked up—just not by the person who chooses to evade.

EVASION DIRECTED AT THE SELF PHYSICALLY

We can also evade not by removing or dismissing the task but by removing or dismissing ourselves from the task. In the same as above, though it was not there elaborated but only suggested, this can take the forms of running away from the task or running to another. I see this often when dealing with people who have strayed into unhealthy habits. Look at the logic. I can run away from a responsibility by procrastination or by defiance: I just will not do it. But I can also avoid a responsibility by choosing to be involved in an opposite interest. For example, a person can state that it is not that he does not want to go to work; it is just that he prefers to go gambling. It is easy to observe the types of actions that will fall into this category. On the one hand, we can look at the behaviours that allow us to move ourselves from a task by refusing the responsibility for it. On the other hand, we can look at those behaviours that allow us to evade a task by being involved in some other more pleasant or doable

I can mention a few, but with the formula mentioned above, you, the reader, will be able to decide where any other will fit. Procrastination, defiance, laziness and irresponsibility are various levels of walking away from a task physically. Irresponsible overindulgence in any activity that allows one to leave a task undone while participating in or advocating for a less productive exercise can be seen as evasion. Partying, shopping, gambling, sexual indiscretions and pornography are all activities that fit into this category.

EVASION DIRECTED AT THE SELF MENTALLY

This is a good one and is easily discovered. One can turn away from productive effort without removing oneself physically from a situation. Again, there are two parts to this segment, which are moving away from something and choosing to move toward something. Can you see how one can mentally disconnect from responsibility or the presence of a task? The responsibility can be a job, the management of a home or parenting children. It can be relating to a spouse. There are many people who live in a marriage that is maintained only by the financial, legal or religious dictums that define the union; meanwhile, there is no interest in the needs or desires of the other person. Doing a job by rote can also fall into this category: the physical performance is there, but no mental energy is associated with the act. What about people who prefer to talk with a sibling than with a spouse? They are also avoiding but are displaying a choice that can be excused as acceptable.

On the other hand, we can evade by removing ourselves mentally from the situation. The activities of getting drunk, using drugs that distract from taking responsibility or simply choosing to hang out with people whose interests are unproductive or self-indulgent—these are forms of evasion through mental dissociation. The negative consequences of any form of evasion lies neither in the activity nor in the fact that a responsibility is left unattended, but in the loss of mental growth and stimulation that ensues. Let's face it: Nobody is indispensable. Anything one person can do, another can do also, and sometimes even better. In Shelley's poem *Ozymandias*, the idea was portrayed that no matter how powerful a person is, Nature, depicted by the moving sands of the desert, goes on relentlessly. A person's removal of himself from a responsibility does not leave that responsibility unattended. Instead, it leaves that person none the wiser from the encounter. Our job is to grow ourselves. Evasion stifles that growth.

THE RESPONSE OF VALIDATION

With validation, balance is achieved in a quixotic way by confirming our capability even if it is not realistically appropriate. Validation is an appeal to be accepted *as one is* with no expectation to improve the self, at least at that time. Thus it is an immediate or short-term solution. This is different from aggression, where the effort is directed at forcing a state of balance, though still without self-improvement. Just as with the other two types of response, validation can be directed at the three components of life management, namely the external forces or antagonist and the two protagonists, physical strengths and mental strengths.

VALIDATION DIRECTED AT THE WORLD

The intent is to get the world as represented by physical environment and other people to accept us and validate our presence, so that we can feel comfortable within ourselves even when we are not in balance with our challenges. There is a plea to have the world adapt to us, and there are various levels through which this is manifested. Sometimes it is necessary in order to establish your credentials as a person with knowledge or credibility. This is necessary when a person is establishing a base from which one is expected to function. Such validation does not stagnate—not because it is defined differently but because it has been established only to determine a base. The person is expected to function above that base. Validation can also be the endorsement from a respected authority that one's intent can be trusted. These types of validation are significant and are used not necessarily to create a balance, but to provide an assurance to the other people who can be affected by the person's presence that her hidden attributes or contributions are worth consideration.

As with all good things, however, validation can be sought not to create a base from which you can rise higher but to form a ceiling beyond which you do not have to climb. Validation used to this objective can be stagnating or even self-destructive. For example, if it works, there is confirmation in your mind that you do not have to expand yourself further, if this is the type of validation you seek; what you have reached is already good enough. Then you may stagnate in your further growth with an assurance that is unrealistic. We have already determined that the whole purpose in life is to grow. This type of success can be disastrous.

On the other hand, if it fails, you may see it as a condemnation of you, and that can be disastrous, especially if it had been positive before. Of course, if a prior endorsement allowed you to stagnate with a feeling of achievement, the result can be a devastated feeling of rejection, in the line of, "You liked what I was yesterday; why don't you like me now?" In chapter 5 we discussed the concept of having a purpose to grow. There, we intoned that the measure of people is not what they have reached but whether they can continue to use creativity to *grow their mind*. Sometimes peer validation is falsely offered for some personal gain. *The Emperor's New Clothes* happens every day. You may receive validation that is false, either to gain your affection or to ridicule your status. Then validation is as fragile as the level of falsity with which it is offered.

Validation can also be structured on obligation. You may do something not in order to gain approval, but because you want to provide what you see as your advantage to another person for whom you may feel responsible. That may be a child or family member, a friend or perhaps even an impoverished person you wish to help. Helping is great if given as a sincere gift. I encourage my clients to be like the Lone Ranger: give and then leave before thanks can be offered. Obligation, however, requires an appreciation and a validation of sorts. It is easy to see the danger here. One can give to exhaustion, waiting for the validation that may never come. Then one can become quite disappointed or resentful when, after great personal sacrifice, the contribution is not appreciated.

VALIDATION DIRECTED AT THE SELF PHYSICALLY

You want to feel good; thus you may not want to experience any or too much discomfort physically. Discomfort, however, can be so subjective that there is no absolute measure of its severity. Do you remember the Hans Christian Anderson story *The Princess and the Pea*? To the real princess, brought up with the softness of privilege, pain is something foreign. Thus the simple discomfort of having a pea under 20 mattresses and 20 featherbeds was so painful to her delicate skin that she was bruised by what she described as a rock in her bed. How do we accommodate the body when there is perceived or real pain? We can do it in two ways: reduce the discomfort or increase the comfort.

We reduce the discomfort using any of a number of chemicals, from alcohol to street drugs, uppers or downers. The problem with using chemicals to desensitise the body's pain is a phenomenon called tachyphylaxis. The body is designed to overcome any invasion, including that of chemicals. Thus it develops counteractive chemicals or enzymes that act to reduce the effect of the chemical. Eventually, more chemical is needed to create the same effect. This can go on until a vicious cycle forms. The body can then become so distorted in its attempts to react to the presence of the chemical that it can actually create a disease state that then requires more of the chemical just to be able to function. At this stage, the use of the chemical is the only option to gain a state of normalcy for the moment, and an addiction is born.

On the other hand, we can increase the comfort by taking the body to activities that give physical pleasure. This is an extension of evasion directed at the self physically. The activity can stimulate one or more senses. Food can provide that option; so does sex, shopping, gambling, partying or pornography. Again, there can be an unwanted consequence. These can also be addictive, though not in the sense of creating a chemical change, but in evoking a state of dependency. Of course, they also create the *princess sensitivity* because the activity of a more pleasant state denies the body the opportunity to be toughened by the harsher challenges. This then institutes a greater need to be soothed, and a vicious cycle is initiated. A simple indulgence can turn into a lifestyle of extravagance. Such a lifestyle denies the self, the cognitive and creative power of the human being to be stimulated. Physical comfort is then often associated with mental boredom, a state that also invites the use of chemicals not for physical comfort, but for stifling of mental awareness. Drugs or alcohol can then be used purely to stifle mental awareness and mental activity that reveals only the emptiness of a neglected inner self.

VALIDATION DIRECTED AT THE SELF MENTALLY

Many people will not identify with this option, even if they espouse it generally, because they do not want to know that they may be seen to be egocentric, deceptive or pompous. These are negative assessments directed at the inner core of the person. Yet these are ways that may allow you to offer validation to self mentally when it does not come from external sources, or when you do not consider the feedback they offer.

The apparent objective here is to condone or inflate the value of one's cognitive capability or the value systems on which it thrives. Because these strengths or value systems are hidden within the metaphysical essence of self, it is possible either to exaggerate their importance or deceptively aggrandize their display. What exists is hidden, so the true value cannot logically be disputed. There is thus a confirmation that is not real, but it is one that allows a feeling of righteousness by stifling or minimizing any contradictions. There are two negative effects from their use, however. One is that they are fragile sources of validation that can tarnish or dissolve, leaving you vulnerable and sensitive to the more accurate assessments that have been forestalled previously. The second is that they validate only the product of self—that is, understanding or values. They do not validate creativity and so stagnate it. Therefore, the person who feels strong through conceit or deception is one who remains stagnant as life surges forward. The gap becomes larger, and the real purpose of life will not have been realized.

SUMMARY

You must remember that the use of value systems—whether they cause people to be rigid in their views or so wishy-washy that they cannot be dependable—does not define those people as weak or immature. We all use value systems whenever we need validation. Just because the value system used by another person is different from the one you may be using, that does not make that person wrong, or you right. It only shows those limitations within which you or the other people function.

I tell you this not to show you how to exploit people's weaknesses but to give a measure by which you can understand how far people can go without direction and when they will need assistance or guidance in order to increase their productivity, improve their efficiency or reduce their hostility. This is what you want to know about people in order to communicate with them effectively: the defences they use when they are threatened. When you know this and you know under what conditions they use them, you will have two important pieces of information. The first is how they reveal that they are being threatened. The second is the point at which they feel threatened.

The successful manager uses this information to relate to that person in the state in which she is most efficient, her secure reality. By knowing when the insecure reality has been introduced, it is easy to determine the outward limits of that person's secure reality at that moment. You must realize also that the smaller a person's secure reality is, the more readily that person needs to hide behind a defence. Therefore, the defensive person must be seen as the more frightened, less capable person rather than a person who is trying to attack or inundate you.

The important thing to remember is that it is not necessary for you to explore too deeply to establish why a person is using a particular defensive strategy. Instead, you must recognize its use and realize what that tells you. It tells you only that something is threatening that person and that she is functioning at her limits or in an insecure reality. Because a person is most productive in a secure reality, you identify that she is in an insecure reality only to know how to put her back in a secure reality and expect efficiency from her. The threat that introduces an insecure reality may be a common responsibility, a personal experience, or you. Your discovery is your invitation to step back, to allow that person the dignity of feeling safe the way she has attempted to do so. Challenging that defence or revealing that you know it to be a defensive manoeuvre causes that person to retreat even further to whatever defensive strategy she chooses. Sometimes, she clings to that strategy more tenaciously. Sometimes, she changes it to a more secure strategy.

Sometimes you may approach a person with honest and good intentions, and that person will respond defensively. It is tempting to react similarly and either berate that person for her arrogance or retreat and allow her to wallow in her ignorance. This may establish how wrong that person is to react so defensively to you—yet it gains nothing for you. All you will have demonstrated is that you can be as threatened by that person as that person can be threatened by you. Unless you can take the mature position and show that you can relate to her knowing her limitations, you are no better than the other person. In such a case, you are in no position to do what you felt you had the right to do—condemn that person's show of insecurity.

Take the mature position and immunize yourself. Recognize that you unwittingly may have reached that person at a point of weakness. Then relate to that person within her demonstrated limitations. Even if you have to apologize for something you did not intend, you still are freeing that person to be as effective as she can be and to relate to you more honestly.

This is not the complete picture; it is only the first approach, the attempts to earn the other person's respect. Until you do take this first approach, however, you cannot really be managing or leading the other person, be that person a child, an adolescent or an adult. Only after you have reached the person beyond that person's defences can you influence that person into being more capable in managing her responsibilities, being more independent or growing to be more effective and efficient in her duties.

CHAPTER 10

MOTIVATING PEOPLE TO ACCOMPLISH

YOU ARE A MANAGER. You know how to take charge and be responsible for the issues that affect you. You must know that by taking that position, your advice and direction will be sought by other people who are not yet able to be managers. They may be your children or your employees. They may be your friends and associates who respect your dedication and accountability and who are unsure about their own abilities to manage the advancing unknowns. As a manager, the people around you will less be those who can give you direction and assistance when you are overwhelmed than they will be those who need to rely on your confidence.

Even as a manager, however, you sometimes will need the support and guidance of another person. That is okay; it is acceptable even for capable people like you to be weak at times. You now know that this happens whenever you lose sight of your personal objective and use defences that are destined to fall short whenever the going gets rough. You will have fallen back on these defences because you are human. As a human being, you will fail sometimes and do things that your logic ordinarily will dissuade you from doing.

There is nothing wrong with having these human frailties. You already have learned to forgive yourself and rebound to take the helm again when you are required to do so. You also know that this tendency to fall back on your defences happens whenever you feel threatened by something that is greater than your reason allows you to assess and understand. Then your immediate need for protecting either your physical survival or your integrity wins over any logic you may have developed. It is natural that you will retreat to the protection of *your* defences and *your* value systems. You have seen this happen before. You know how long it takes you to be able to rebound from it even when you know what you should do, and when your logic tells you that you should not be concerned. You also have learned that you will have these moments again. Sometimes you will be forced to rebound alone from them. Sometimes you will have someone to whom you can go. This may be your boss, a friend or your spouse.

In fact, I believe that this is the real therapy of a good marriage. You have a spouse with whom you can enjoy a mature relationship when both of you are strong. When one is weak, the other may be strong. Your spouse can be the source of replenishment for you when you are weak, and there is no gender superiority. Then, when your spouse is weak, you may have the opportunity to be his or her temporary source of strength.

You have learned to accept that it is human to fail sometimes, and that you will do so more frequently when you start being the manager with a deeper range of responsibility, but that it becomes less so as you learn to rely on yourself. You can see how difficult it is for you even though you already have some of the resources you need to be fully self-accountable. Now, you must consider those people who do not have half the resources you have. If you have had to retreat to your defences as often as you have done, you will be able to understand that those people will have had to use theirs even more. There are many people who may have started life with so little nurturing that they have had to rely on their defences from the very beginning. There are people who may have been provided with defences or encouraged to use them with the erroneous assumption that they are the necessary tools for survival. They may have depended on these defences for so long that they rarely allowed themselves the opportunity to accept challenges and be expanded by them. Then they, too, will be forced to continue to retreat behind their defences more often as they become exposed to more change. However, they will do so without the benefit of knowing that there is an alternative, that they can take the helm and become managers too, if not of a full line of responsibility then at least of their own small area. While they do not know this alternative, they always will retreat whenever what they have to do seems greater than what they believe they can do. Many people may not even see their response as a retreat; to them it is simply their choice to move into their area of strength and they may even choose to go to that area with pride, often not realizing its limitations.

For many of these people, their fears are more the result of their not knowing that they have the resources to manage the problem than they are due to an actual paucity of resources. Their attempts to defend themselves against the challenges that bring these fears, however, can cause them eventually to have a narrow secure reality. Then the immensity of the pressures will become more real than imagined, and their stresses will increase even under normal conditions.

MANAGING PEOPLE: THE CHALLENGE

It is up to you to be able to help these people manage the responsibilities they have, if not for altruistic motives then at least for your own greater peace of mind. Your forward vision allows you to see more of the task that needs to be done and more of the variables that affect these tasks. You therefore can see so many potential consequences that to manage the task adequately or influence its change, you must bring to the forefront more things than you possibly can do alone. For your own continued successes, you must be able to utilize the talents of these people without also evoking their defences.

Second, when problems that you can see but that these people cannot are brought to the forefront, either naturally or through your instigation, these people will react to you as the source of the unnecessary problem. This will be an added responsibility, one that sometimes demands more immediate attention from you than the task itself.

Last, even if you do not bring the problem but allow it to creep up on them, they still will resort to their defences. Then they may reject responsibility for the problem, or they will manage it so inadequately that you still will be faced with a greater task than was there before. The mismanaged problem will be yours again.

For your own peace of mind, therefore, you must be willing to share your management skills with these people. You must accept that they will be able to manage if only they will believe that what they can do is good enough for what they have to do. Then they will not need to resort to their defences. It is up to you to help them expand that capacity, or at least make the demands more equal to it so that they will function successfully to the level they have chosen to extend themselves. You may even be able to help them grow beyond those limitations and be more capable people who will take their place with pride in your common environment.

You must know also that some people do not want to have a greater vision—what they can see already frightens them. They are afraid that if they look further, they will be even more threatened. Some people may be so complacent with what they have been able to manage that they will not want to lose the existing status quo, and so they refuse to consider any problem that may go away if they ignore it long enough.

If you want to be that more successful manager and either extend your reach further with the help of the people who can use your direction or prevent any unnecessary work that may arise from their defences against problems that they are not equipped to manage, then you must be willing to include in your management skills an understanding of how to manage and guide other people.

RELATING TO PEOPLE WITH THE
STRENGTH OF UNDERSTANDING

There are two factors to be considered when you are attempting to help a person manage. The first is the size of the problem; the second is the strength of the person. You must remember that your intent is to help the person, that conscious entity, to move beyond just surviving the problem and really manage it. Therefore, you are not concerned about shoring up that person's defences. He can do that better than you can. You are concerned instead about how what that person can do measures up to what he has to do.

You must remember also that every person is a conscious entity. That person must have the same objective of growth and development of creativity as you do. You also know that you can share your understanding and help the other person grow without losing any insight or momentum yourself. In fact, the mere activity of attempting to help another person gives you the opportunity to solidify what you know, or even extend it. Therefore, any attempt to help the other person manage by helping that person develop the creativity to manage helps you.

You know also that the human being automatically uses what he has been born to do: create insight. Yet each person's momentum of creativity can become stuck or slowed down simply because, at a particular moment in its development, that person's conscious energy may have been inundated with too large a challenge. Then the person may have transferred his attention to the development and use of defences rather than be destroyed trying to succeed. In short, that other person is not necessarily failing because he is stupid, lazy or weak. That person is failing because the insight developed to date is insufficient for managing the problem as it is presented, and the momentum of creativity generated does not allow a quick enough transition into the management of the new problem. This is a state that exists in all children. It hurts to observe a child labelled as lazy, stupid or weak when by definition that child is a person who has not yet developed the insight to allow him to deal with many problems comfortably. That child has to be managed into accepting that he can do the task.

This argument is the same for the adult dependent. Just because that person is in an adult body does not mean that he has developed the insight for the problem or confidence in his creativity as the physical development may suggest. You must remember that we are referring to the development of the conscious energy. That development is not coexistent with the physical development of the person. Thus, there is no need to label a person who is only showing a relatively limited insight defending his survival or integrity as lazy, stupid or weak.

I often offer a short visualization to illustrate this. You are going for a walk in a quiet suburb; it is a balmy summer day and everything seems deserted. Yet you know there is life in the area. You hear people's voices talking in their backyards although you see no one. You hear cars in the distance though the streets are deserted. While walking, you encounter a young boy about 2 years old standing on the sidewalk and crying. You approach him and ask what the matter is. In his language, he says that he was playing and his ball rolled over to the other side of the street. He is not allowed to cross the street and cannot get his ball. Though the streets are deserted, you understand his frustration and help him. You continue your walk and encounter another person on another sidewalk. He also is upset, but he appears to be about 21 years old. You ask him what the matter is, and he too states that he was playing and his ball rolled to the other side of the street, and he is not allowed to cross the street. This time you may find it difficult to understand his frustration. He is a man.

Sometimes that adult dependent is so only relative to the problem. In effect she may be totally unexposed to that problem that to you may be simple, while being extremely familiar with a different problem that you may find difficult. Unfortunately, however, that capacity to be able to manage a different problem often is not considered in the existing situation. Whenever this possibility arises, I always think of Albert Einstein as seen from the point of view of a fisherman, teaching him the apparently simple process of fishing off the coast of Newfoundland. To the fisherman, this is an easy task. To Einstein, who knows deeply the profound problems of physics that the fishermen does not know, it may seem formidable.

The intent in managing the other person, therefore, is to accept that she has the capability to develop the insight to manage the problem, but that at the moment her insight is insufficient to allow an adequate representation to the demands of the problem. Whatever that person does to defend herself is less important than your realization of the state that exists. It is only with that realization that you will be able to communicate behind the defences and help that person appropriately. Then she can give full account of herself and either extend your reach or reduce the pressures on you, even if it is less than you may have desired.

Considerations of Effective Management

The first consideration, therefore, is that to the person, there is a real or apparent discrepancy between what she knows and what she is required to do. People are self-driven forces, and what they can do is more related to what they believe they can do rather than what they really can do. This is the information you must use. It is information that is inaccessible to you unless you are able to have that person share it with you.

The second consideration is that while that discrepancy exists, that person will be more focused on defending herself from the apparent threat than in using the insight with which she is equipped to manage that part of the problem that she is required to manage. In other words, you may get no output rather than the limited output that person believes she can provide.

It is important that you relieve that discrepancy. You can do this in two ways. The first is to reduce the problem. The second is to increase the person's insight. After this, you have to help that person expand her insight so that you do not have to go through this process again. Of course, you can also provide support to her defences. For example, you may assist in their retreat, support an aggressive response and more. This may be termed *management by facilitation*. But neither of these options offers any form of constructive solution.

It is here that your knowledge of people as conscious entities comes in handy. You know that a person's insight is developed by that person's creativity, and that the creativity is stimulated by new challenges. You also know that the creativity fuelled by the affirmation of her capabilities can be shut down if she cannot rise above a challenge, and that this happens when the challenge is too demanding of the person. You do not know where in that chain help is needed. You therefore have to communicate with that person and gain access to that information.

There are two areas where you can help immediately, and two areas where your help will affect the long-standing productivity of the person. You may help the person for the reasons given above so that you can use what that person has to offer, rather than getting little or no output, and so that you can reduce the added problems that person can create if she is allowed to proceed undirected. Yet you still must be influenced by your knowledge that people are conscious entities. Their real value does not lie in their willingness to be extensions of you, but rather in their desire to do their part, to give of their unique insight. With these concerns in mind, you will see that the two areas in which you can help immediately are the areas where you bypass her creativity and help her equate what she can do with what has to be done. One way is to reduce the problem to be within that person's range. This can be seen as management by facilitation. The other is to increase that person's understanding of the problem. This is *management by education*.

You also will see that the two areas in which you can help the long-standing productivity of the person are the areas where you stimulate their creativity. Since there are two ingredients to the stimulation of creativity, the fuel of fulfilment and the challenge of the problem, you must consider both in the sequence in which they can be more useful or less harmful. The most delicate part of the person and the one that is least developed in the person who is a dependent is the ego, that person's self-esteem. One way in which you can stimulate the person's creativity is to provide affirmation for what the person can do. This may be called *management by affirmation.* The other way, when you are satisfied that the person is not just weak but is unwilling to extend herself, is to delegate the task, allowing the person to be exposed to the full pressure of the problem or the consequences that may arise from the mismanagement of it. For some people the responsibility to manage without help can stimulate a drive to be creative, or a revelation of the limits they are prepared to meet. This may be called *management by delegation.*

The ultimate intent of any form of management is to help the dependent person believe that she is equal to the task or is capable of managing it comfortably. The reason that management is needed is that the person does not believe that she can survive the demands of the task. The prerequisite for any form of management, then, is to discern that the person is in a situation wherein she may be threatened by the demands of a problem, and to be able to empathize with the person even if her method of conveying that message is by revealing irresponsibility, stress, laziness or hostility.

MANAGEMENT THROUGH FACILITATION

This is the simplest form of management. You do it with people like children, who you know to be inexperienced and devoid of appropriate insight. You do it with people who are relatively inexperienced in a particular situation and who will not be required to deal with that situation very often, or ever again. You do it with people who are required to give special attention only to one aspect of a task, like members of a special sports team or specialists in a particularly complex responsibility. Beyond what these people can do, they are not required to do more, for the moment at least. The task, then, is divided so that they will be challenged by what they can do, and that they will have little or no reason to have to address what they cannot do.

As you can see, this is not necessarily of any long-term benefit to the people who receive it. Great sports heroes discover this later in life when what they have been able to do is no longer required of them, and then they are expected to take their place in the world and deal with other general problems they have never before considered. Children discover that they will not be excused as children for all of their lives—at a certain stage, someone will require that they take fuller responsibility for the management of more than what they were required to do as children.

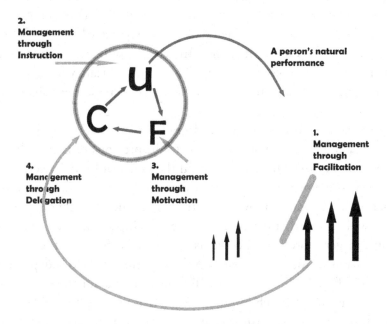

Figure 15.   The Four Types of Assistive Management

Yet, its immediate value both to you as the manager and to the person who gets a break from the excessive demands that may have suppressed their creativity cannot be denied. These people must use this opportunity to take a little more of the task and extend themselves to learn to manage it. Children must be encouraged to use it, not to remain secure behind their parents' protection but to have the respite that then allows them to get a little more exposure and develop a little more momentum. The world is tough. The break a person gets when you facilitate them is only a temporary measure. You cannot manage this way too long. As problems become more unstable, the parts you may have to do in order to facilitate your dependents can become larger until you become inundated with work that should have been accomplished by those other people. Parents who are too accommodating discover this long before their children become adults.

The point is that it is acceptable, and even advisable, to facilitate as a method of management because it allows you to get at least part of the task accomplished. It also allows you to have a base from which you can proceed to the next level of management. Nonetheless, you must use it only as a temporary option, believing that people—even dependants—have the capacity to grow beyond what they know so that they can do more than they are capable of doing at the moment. Then you must proceed to the next level and educate your dependents to be able to manage more of the task and increase their share of the common responsibility.

Of course, you must proceed gradually. If not, then by allowing too great an increase, you will revert to the previous situation where the other person needs to retreat behind the safety of his defences.

If this happens, it will be necessary for you to be the facilitator for that person again. Remove the extra part of the task and delegate only that which the other person is capable of doing adequately. Remember, you can get more from people as self-directed forces if they have the permission to focus on what they believe they can do independently, instead of having to act as unwilling implements for the expression of your solutions. With children, it means that you must provide reduced challenges while expecting them to be a little more accountable every day. Too often, well-meaning parents who are afraid to hurt the child do more damage through overprotecting that child from the challenges they are afraid to give him than they can do by challenging the child to stretch a little beyond what he can do at the moment.

You must know, however, that you can cause just as much harm by stretching your expectations of any child without also providing ample opportunity for facilitation. In childhood, growing can be seen to be like walking up a set of stairs. The risers are short with gradually increasing heights; the steps are wide, giving ample time to savour the last rise yet growing steadily narrower as the child continues to develop. Perhaps the most important responsibility in parenting is to progressively prepare our children to be comfortable and capable in a demanding world, not to protect them from it or expect them to grow into that state of comfort automatically with their chronological age.

Life: higher risers and shorter steps, for the erudite as well as the innocent

In the management of adults through facilitation, the same rules hold. Some adults may function at the level of children. This is not to discredit them; they may have been allowed to focus so singularly on a particular aspect of their development that, in the wide world of reality, they truly are children. Some of these people can be most respected for their unique knowledge in their specialty. You must help these people when they become your dependents, even if that happens only for a short time, by facilitating their gradual exposure to the areas where you can lead them. The emphasis is on the firm but gradual exposure of these people by giving them only those problems they accept that they can manage while also attempting to increase those problems in small increments.

MANAGEMENT THROUGH EDUCATION

The next level at which you can approach the management of people, again with your focus on achieving an immediate balance between what they can do and what they have to do, is to provide them with information that is useful for their immediate, efficient management of the task. As you can see from the exact nature of the requirements, this already is becoming more difficult. You are required to know what their specific needs are; otherwise you may be providing information that duplicates what they have while not satisfying what they need to know. This can cause the person to retreat more firmly behind his defences and to refuse to consider your next attempt to provide him with information.

It is here that you need communication. You must respect what that person knows. You know that he knows something. You only do not know what he knows or how much of it is relevant to the issue at hand. The only way you can know is if that person chooses to reveal it to you, and that person will choose not to reveal it if he believes that it will confirm an inadequacy that you may use to condemn him.

THE RULES OF SUCCESSFUL COMMUNICATIONS

The first rule in communicating with another person is to do so only if you can be genuinely interested in knowing what that person understands of a common issue. The second rule is to be genuinely interested in using that knowledge to help the other person expand his insight. You can only be that genuine if you first have a good understanding of the task and the insight to show that you can manage it competently and confidently.

There is a third rule, and that is to be willing to consider that the other person may be reacting to an aspect of the task that you also do not understand but that you do not see—and therefore do not fear. Then you must be able to be strong, not only because you have answers for that which you can see, but because you have the ability to formulate answers for that which is also unfamiliar to you.

If you do not heed these rules, and you show disdain for that person's understanding or retreat to a defensive position when he reveals a greater threat, you may cause that other person to return to the security of his defences instead of helping him become better prepared to manage the task appropriately. If you wish to understand what may be troubling that person, you must be prepared to accept that he is functioning in a totally different world than the one you can see, even though it is part of the environment you believe you may be sharing with that person. You must understand that he will be taking the information you have given him and applying it to a problem that you may not even understand fully—and if you do, you may not know the way it presents to that person or what the consequences may be to him.

An adolescent, for example, may need to deal with a problem with his peers that, on the surface, you do not accept as being of any great significance. Yet you cannot assume that just because you too have gone through the apparently similar stage of adolescence your solutions will apply to his situation. You have to realize that the solutions you may have acquired in dealing with your peers may not work for him, just as his solutions will not work for you in your situations.

The pace of change guarantees that the world of any tomorrow will be more demanding than the world of any today. The world of any adolescent can be more challenging than was a similar period in their parents' life. This of course holds true for any generation. This is as true for workers in a business. Apparently similar problems do not challenge them in the same way they challenge management. Their world, even with the same set of responsibilities, differs greatly from that of management.

You therefore must see that person's vision of his problem through his eyes. To get that, you must drop pretences and show concern. You must drop disdain and show interest. You must drop fears and show confidence. No one can resist the opportunity to share the ideas he has formulated if he believes that those ideas will impress or be useful to someone who is knowledgeable and competent himself. In other words, you must show that you need his ideas. You cannot be genuine about that show of interest if you do not accept that the other person may have a perception of the issue that truly is different from what you can see, and therefore it can be no less important than what you know.

Now, with the awareness of the problem as it pertains to the other person, and with the willingness to accept that the solutions that may be useful to you from your perspective may not also be useful to the other person, you are better able to offer a solution that is more appropriate to that person's needs. The simple formula for management through education, therefore, is this: what the person has to do, minus what the person is able to do, equals the information you must share with that person. Only when you are satisfied that you have that specific information, and when you are prepared to share it as slowly as that other person's momentum of creativity will allow, can you truly presume to be managing through education.

MANAGEMENT THROUGH AFFIRMATION

Now, you are prepared to manage other people by stimulating them to accomplish independently. You already may have taken care of their immediate needs, either through facilitating the task or through educating the person. What you need to do in order to relieve yourself of the continued obligation to care for their immediate needs is to help them access the strength to create solutions that are appropriate for the problems as these problems unfold before them.

You know that as long as the challenge is increased in small doses, and people have the inner strength to address the new parts of the problem, they can create the understanding necessary to deal with the task. You have seen to the first variable, first by facilitating the task and then by offering them information. The only requirement, if they are accountable enough to want to manage the task, is for them to have the inner strength to drive their creativity.

You cannot assume that just because some people have been successful, or because they have managed a difficult problem effectively in the past, they will always know and believe that they are capable. You cannot assume that because some people are receiving feedback about their successes in one area of responsibility, they have the flexibility to extend it to their management of other things. People may have knowledge and capabilities, but they may not always accept that they do. They still may be stuck in the cycle that requires recognition, acceptance, approval or respect from others in order for them to know that what they are is good enough to be what they can be. They need affirmation.

They need affirmation for their value as human beings. No matter how much a person wants to be appreciated for what he can show, there is a burning desire within every individual to be appreciated for his intelligence, his ability to think and create solutions. The beautiful woman wants this. The wealthy financier wants this. The presidents and governors want it. It is for this feedback of affirmation that many people will display their visible attributes or their developed insight, even if those assets they are offering have little to do with the problem they are required to manage.

It is up to you as the manager to recognize that if you need your people to function effectively, you must be able to affirm them, not just for the physical strength or appearance, nor an understanding that is inappropriate for the immediate task, but for their ability to create new ideas and express them confidently. You must know that the asset you affirm is the asset that people will offer you. You affirm brawn; they will show brawn. You affirm stamina; they will display stamina. In a changing world, you need people's creativity more than you need just brawn or stamina.

You must be able to affirm those people for creativity. Even when they seem to want affirmation for less personal attributes, you can be assured that you eventually will get more from them if you insist on seeking their opinions and affirming them for their ability to create those opinions. Yet if they believe that they already have offered you their best asset, you will have to use it as the only area available to you on which you can provide feedback prepared to encourage them to extend it at the earliest opportunity.

In other words, you must be willing to prime the pump—that is, give the affirmation to start the creativity so that you will be able to affirm the effects of the creativity at your next meeting. You start by offering genuine appreciation to them for whatever they are willing to give of themselves, especially if you can determine that even a small part of it resulted from their use of creativity. It may be their best asset; it may be what they think you deserve to be given at the moment.

EARNING PEOPLE'S TRUST

You must realize that you are the one under examination. You are the one who is seeking to be trusted. If you want to get the most from people, you must be prepared to earn that trust and use it to nurture them to their highest potential. They cannot do it alone. If they could, they would not need your help now. If you are going to give that help, you must do so willingly and honestly. If you are not willing to give that help, you must be prepared to deal with the immense backwash that will occur as rapid change causes even the skills of the most highly trained people to become redundant in short order. To earn that trust honestly sometimes requires that you make a comparative assessment against your own ability or that of a similar person. You are more likely to be believed if you can assure them that what they can do exceeds what you can do on that topic, especially if you are a person whose opinion they respect. Of course, you will be laying it on too thickly and lose that respect if you try to show that whatever they can do is better than what you can do. All they need is a reassurance that some little thing they can do is comparatively important. You must recognize that they already know that it is not great; therefore, trying to elevate its value inappropriately may not work, either. You sometimes have to convince them that their knowledge has some valuable applications, and use it honestly, before they will believe that you are not just putting them on.

Once you have started this, you must share further affirmation only for growth. Remember that is your primary intent. Do not lose it. Be prepared to expand your expectations, but do so in small increments. You can lose credibility if you affirm everything needlessly. You can lose that person's real potential for growth if you do not expect a little more the next time. However, you can also lose your gains with the person if you increase your expectations too rapidly.

Conversely, your credibility will soar if you can give affirmation honestly and appropriately. This is contrary to the theories of unconditional love, which focuses on offering affirmation regardless of performance. It does nothing for people's growth; it only reassures you that you have helped them survive for another day, or maybe less. How will they perform without your energy? The giving of affirmation does not suggest that it will stay. When they need it next and still cannot get it themselves or receive it from someone else, how will they perform?

This focused management we advocate, perhaps allowed to be called conditional love, has a specific objective: motivating people to become more capable and independent. For your own good and that of the other people, recognize the inherent limitations in unconditional love. You may return to facilitation if necessary; you may revert to attempting to educate the person. But give affirmation with a firm objective. If you give it just to make people comfortable, you are not helping them. You are setting them up for a tremendous fall. If you do it to earn people's appreciation, are you not being the dependent and seeking affirmation from those who need it from you more urgently? If you do it just to earn your brownie points for heaven, perhaps you should reassess your interpretations of theology.

If, after you have done all of this, those people still are unwilling to accept any more responsibility, only seeking repeated affirmation for a resource they may have acquired in the past for attributes that they may have inherited, or for assets that they may have been given, then you must be willing to stop giving that support. They may cry louder than before. They may accuse you of dishonesty. You must accept that you have done your part. You have given them the opportunity to use the fuel you have so generously shared with them to stimulate their creativity and accomplish more. You must be prepared to manage them as people who are too complacent to take responsibility for addressing the task and who are satisfied getting affirmation for whatever little they can offer. They have been able to survive offering the barest minimum so far. They have always had someone to pick up the slack and cover for them. You must be able to manage above that. You know that they can only grow by accepting tasks they would rather not do. You therefore are required to help them grow by giving them responsibility for those tasks even if you have to allow them to experience the full thrust of the consequences that the mismanagement of that task will evoke. You must be willing to delegate even if it evokes their failure.

MANAGEMENT THROUGH DELEGATION

You have helped people by making their responsibilities easier. You have shared the insight and understanding that is yours so that they can escape the tremendous pressures that can shut down a poorly developed creativity. You have given them the encouragement and appreciation they may have needed to restart that creative momentum. You must know when you can do no more. There will come a time when they must be encouraged to shoulder their own responsibilities and deal with the consequences. The worst thing you can do for them and for yourself, at this stage, is to continue carrying them. You must let them face the real consequences. They must be allowed to face the pressures and know what is required of them. This is the only way you can respect people as real human beings. If not, you will be treating them as less than human, as machines that can do no more than you give them the fuel to do.

If, however, a person prefers to be protected, to be given the solutions and is satisfied just being a tool for you or for any other manager despite your attempts to stimulate his growth, there is very little more you can do. That person will have chosen his path. You at least tried. There will be no need to advance your management of that person to the level of delegation. Then your management will revert to that of facilitation. You cannot continue to educate or affirm a person who is unwilling to take the reins and go for himself.

Sometimes you cannot give up, either because the person still will be there leaving his responsibilities undone, or because it is a child for whom you cannot relinquish your responsibility. You need to help that person be a person by taking responsibility for causing that person to grow beyond what he seems to have decided to accept. Sadly, many of these people will continue doing only as much as they need to do just to survive because there always will be someone to buffer their consequences in the mistaken assumption that they are saving that person from experiencing a severe discomfort. Instead, they are only succeeding in stagnating that person's growth.

I remember a person who spent more than two years trying to help a woman get a special, subsidized apartment because she was afraid that her ex-husband might harm her. This person felt that this woman's need was serious because she was able to convince him that she truly was afraid for her life. In the end, he failed. When he did, the woman simply went on; she had little choice but to go out on her own and get a job to pay for her own apartment. By doing so, she was able to do for herself what another person would have prevented her from doing: being responsible for herself. Eventually she met someone and remarried. This may not have happened had he succeeded in stagnating her in his attempts to overprotect her.

In the case of a child, other adults or society in general will unwittingly overprotect that child out of fear that he is unable to think or create solutions for complex problems. With the other adult, it is the person who knows how to get sympathy who usually cries the loudest. It is the one who cries the loudest who will convince people that he is the neediest. This is a form of survival through using the sympathy and consideration of others to the extreme. If that person is able to succeed in using the manipulative defence, the relative strength of his secure reality will diminish, and he will be threatened by more of the natural events that will have evolved. Then that person will need to use that defence even more desperately, creating a vicious cycle that spirals him into mental stagnation.

If you truly want to help a person grow, you must be prepared to give that person the opportunity to create his decisions. You know that the only impediment to a person's use of his creativity is the immensity of the task, inundating and eventually depleting the fuel of fulfilment. You therefore must be prepared to remove parts of the buffer just as you were prepared to remove parts of the problem by introducing the buffer in the first place. This is the act of gradually exposing a child to the demands of the modern world. It also is the act of exposing an adult so that such a person can be more useful to the organization or community as the stresses of change continue to become more pervasive and more demanding. You are offering buffered exposure at a progressively diminishing level.

You will have to be self-affirmed to do this because you may be seen not as allowing something that will have happened if you did not prevent it in the first place, but as the source of an unnecessary problem or consequence. People do not see the real consequence that their limited visions do not allow them to see; they see only the problem you have instigated or allowed to happen. You know this is a reduced or buffered exposure. Remember that though the increment may be small to you, it still represents a large increase to the person to whom it still represents an unknown. Then the resistances of the other person will more be directed at you rather than at the source of the pressure.

The following examples will serve to illustrate what can be a method of management that may be considered to be too different from those we may have learned to use, either because we accepted them in deference to our teachers, or because we developed them in defiance of the experiences we may have had to endure.

Example 1. The unproductive adult. An adult in your charge refuses to offer more than the bare minimum despite your attempts to help and encourage her. As a result, that person continues to do a poor job at managing her tasks. Nothing happens, but your greater vision tells you that you are saved only by circumstance. Something disastrous should have happened already. What do you do? You cannot wait for the repercussions to appear before you do something. You have attempted to facilitate, educate and even affirm the person. Now you must be the source of controlled consequences. You must provide a consequence that is less than what may happen, but greater than what is seen as appropriate to the person. This is a buffered consequence.

That person will be motivated to reassess her performance at the task not because of her greater understanding of the demands of the task, but because of her fears of the consequences you represent.

Example 2. The defiant child. Your child plays in the street. You know that there is a grave danger to this, which the child does not have the vision to understand. Facilitating the child is limited to what you can do when you are with him. You can request speed bumps. You can divert traffic. You can stay in the street with your child so that you will be able to forestall the danger before it happens. (Do not laugh at these solutions. Some people do go through such trouble.) Yet if you do so to the level that it becomes safe, you will be giving that child greater evidence that you are worrying unnecessarily and that there really is no danger. And of course, you will be stagnating his growth.

Trying to educate him does not go far because he can logically discount all your arguments. The child believes that because there are no cars visible to him) at the time he is playing, there is no danger. Even when cars come by, the child may reason that the drivers slow down and stop when they see the children. Your child does not have the experience to know about drunk drivers or people who are distracted by personal worries. You even try to affirm the child for other successes. You may emphasize your approval of his occasional decisions to play in the backyard or in the park while showing disapproval for playing in the street.

Whatever you do, the child still plays in the street. The real consequence is that your child may be killed. You cannot let that happen. Therefore, you decide to be the source of buffered consequences. You impose a discomfort on the child for disobeying you. This may take the form of a spanking, firm enough to make the point without being a harsh punishment. The idea is not to hurt the child unnecessarily; it is to provide proof that there is a consequence to his mismanagement of the issue. Instead of a spanking, if the child is old enough to let this be applicable, it may take the form of a removal of privileges.

In the perceptions of the child, this buffered consequence will be considered to be a severe discomfort. Only you will know that it is a less severe discomfort than the one the child cannot see—being hit by a car. That child will be motivated to manage the situation appropriately not because he understands the gravity of the problem, but because he understands the consequences that will come from you.

Contrary to some people's fears, this will not alienate the child against the parent. In fact, it allows any affirmation you may share for some other act to be more believable. The child knows that you are being honest, if only because you have demonstrated that you will show your displeasure when you do not accept something else (conditional love?).

Example 3. The difficult adolescent. Adolescence is perhaps the most difficult time in anyone's life. It is the time when the body is going through so many changes that adolescents become confused about who they really are and where they really are going. It also is a time when their parents and other adults still see them as children, whereas their peers see them as adults who should have full authority over their own lives, rarely knowing which is right. As an example, parents see them as about 2 years younger, and their peers see them as 2 years older. That makes a four-year gap that introduces confusion and resentment. They are pulled in opposite directions. Defiance therefore seems to be a natural behaviour for any adolescent because the solutions for one area of their world will always conflict with the problems in another. If, however, you will remember that this is the period of breaking out, a period of discovery when the world of people, places and things that he will have to face becomes more a part of his life than is the more familiar world of the parent, you will begin to see a reason for the defiance. Their world is beginning to take on more immediate importance than the world of their parent's dreams, hopes and ambitions. Ideally, the transition should be gradual. You will find, however, that in this era of rapid change, the demands from his peers or from the work he is required to accomplish become so great so quickly that he is easily inundated. Then he will develop defences just to deal with these extreme stresses.

There are, therefore, two considerations you must make when dealing with what you may see as a defiant adolescent. The first is that the behaviour may be an appropriate solution for the pressure from a world you cannot experience, but one that is more important to him than the one you can see. The second is that it may just be a defence required to survive in that world. If it is the former, you are well advised to respect it but to encourage the adolescent to expand his concerns to include the world beyond those immediate demands. If it is the latter, it becomes necessary for you to help that person deal with the issues that threaten him in a more creative manner. You differentiate between them simply by trying to see the problems through his eyes.

First, be genuinely interested in understanding his world, and make the effort to show that interest. We discussed this in the section under management through education. Second, encourage the youth to reveal his fears and concerns without letting them feel foolish or disrespected for their views. It is only when you truly can understand the stresses imposed on him by his world that you will be in the position to offer a solution that draws from your more developed creativity. It is only after you have accepted that there are unique problems he has to face, after you have made an effort to understand them and after you have offered a solution that has been refused that you can assume that there is an inappropriate behaviour.

If he wants to follow through with the behaviour regardless of your efforts to educate him on the unseen consequences or circumvent the need for a defence with honest affirmation, you may have to allow him to experience the consequences and manage them. Too many parents harm their adolescents by protecting them from consequences that should influence their behaviour. Sometimes you may have to offer a buffered consequence in order to discourage the person from doing what he intended and so activate the greater consequences that might be extremely harmful.

In the management through delegation, you may be seen as inconsiderate or even pedagogic. If you are self-accountable, you will accept this without prejudice and continue to manage your responsibility with maturity and dignity. Just as it is wrong to do something that attempts to show accountability while creating a greater problem underneath, so too it is wrong to let another person suffer the emptiness of stagnation just so that you can appear to be generous on the surface.

The four stages of effective management—facilitation, education, affirmation and delegation—do not always have to be applied in that order. Sometimes it is necessary to assume that your dependents are mature thinkers and that they can do the job when it is given to them; then you may delegate at first. By doing that, you will have given them the opportunity to display the level at which they can function comfortably. By their defences, you will recognize which persons will need facilitation, which group will benefit from education and which will require affirmation. Then you can be flexible enough to manage each person appropriately for his or her abilities, and so get the most from people as the individuals they are.

SUMMARY

To manage effectively, there are two main points you must bear in mind. The first is that everyone is created equal. You know, however, that everyone grows at an unequal pace, depending on the affirmation she may have received to fuel her creativity and on the challenges she was given to stimulate it. A healthy balance of these two can allow anybody to develop the momentum to be a successful manager. The second, therefore, is that it is never too late to provide this balanced growth.

Sometimes you have to give what may seem to the observer to be an imbalance. At some stages you may be seen to give too much affirmation for the amount of the task. At other stages you may be seen to give too much task for the amount of affirmation. However, you know that the only way one can correct an imbalance is through the provision of a compensatory imbalance. To the casual observer, every person should be equally capable to every other person. If someone is not, then he is perceived to have stagnated as a result of his own disinterest. You must believe that it is not so. What may seem to be too much affirmation can be a drop in the ocean for the needy person. What may seem as too much responsibility may only be the accumulated discards of the irresponsible or unaccountable person.

As a manager, you must create the vision for those who are too busy surviving the present to have a vision of the problems and consequences that lie ahead. That vision must allow you to have a plan for where you must take these people.

As a parent, your duty is to lead your dependents into being capable adults, not to keep them as happy children; to teach them to be strong, not fight their battles for them. Yet you must be prepared to stand behind them, to buffer them so to speak, so that they will have consequences but not as severe as the world will throw at them. In effect your job is to teach them and prepare them to deal with a difficult world, not protect them from its demands and impositions.

As an administrator, you need people who can eventually function independently and grow to meet the demands of the task, not tools that are simple extensions of yourself. If you approach management of others this way, it will not necessarily make you popular. It will, however, make you effective. You will be doing what you can see as necessary for the greater good of the people you have been given the responsibility to manage. Your vision also must take both the task and the person into account. Just as people do not have the vision for the changes that must be addressed in the tasks, they also do not always have enough vision for the changes that must be addressed in their own needs. You must be the source of their productivity as well as being the source of their well-being. Just as you must push, you also must assign the breaks that they may not have the self-management to take.

Remember, to your own self be true. To what you accept as the other person, be honest.

Finis Coronat Opus (The end crowns the work).

APPENDIX A

HOW STRESS AFFECTS PERFORMANCE

AS A MANAGER, YOU will not only have the responsibility for stimulating yourself and others to move forward, but often they, and even you, will have to come up from states of despair, burnout or stress to a normal level before you attempt to move forward. This appendix will attempt to explore stress using the *Understanding Change* model to understand and manage it.

Stress can be defined as the distortion of the internal structure of an object by the imposition of an external pressure. Yet human beings experience stress, often without apparent distortion, because any distortion can be so hidden that it is not easily recognized. We are blessed with sensitive receptors that alert us to injuries in any part of the body, to allow us to protect it. We are often made aware of distortions of even modest levels long before they are represented externally. Thus we can experience a stress when an organ system is only slightly affected by the pressures imposed from outside. It is also partly because the human being is also a sophisticated mind. This entity can also be stressed. When stressed, it is a distortion that can no more be measured than thought itself, so the stressed mind can experience the stress but cannot manifest it externally to even the most astute observer. An observer is relegated to visualizing his own perceptions of a described stress and assuming these to be the experiences of the other.

It is not difficult to see that since the body is composed of various organ systems, a stress can be induced by one organ system acting as the external factor to another organ system. A distorted liver, for example, can create such pressure on the circulatory system that heart disease can ensue. In the same way, a distressed mind can act as the external force on any part of the body, creating a stress response even when a recognized external pressure does not exist. It is an established fact that worry can distort the blood pressure so that heart disease may ensue.

Obviously, a stress can be prevented either by reducing the external pressure if it can be defined, or by strengthening the internal structure. In the body, structure can be strengthened with the use of a balanced diet and rest. Sometimes the specific weakness can be discovered and treated. Then the diet can be supplemented with recognized nutrients or medications. Also, the rest can be augmented with a short-term use of tranquillizers. In the mind, structure can be strengthened only with education or appropriate and well-directed advice and the challenge to apply oneself to a task. However, since stress in the human being can be highly subjective, assistance in preventing it is not always appropriately directed. The sufferer must therefore learn to be the healer. And the sufferer can be the manager, supervisor or parent as well as the child or subordinate. This treatise is intended to provide the sufferer with some tools to become the healer of her own stresses and to provide the manager with the means to understand and assist the sufferer.

UNDERSTANDING STRESS

In a mechanical model, an object—say, a box—maintains its wholeness (integrity) because internal forces are balanced against external pressures. In the case of a box, the internal forces are the tensile strengths of the fibres (wood or paper). The external pressures are the weights, humidity and temperature that are imposed on the structure of the box. The box is designed with sufficient tensile strengths to withstand the pressures consistent with its use. If, for example, a weight greater than the box is designed to bear is placed on the box, the internal fibres become stretched, distorted or even broken. In other words, the box is stressed. (Do not laugh—this term, originally coined as an engineering term, was imported into the psychological model only recently.) Such stress can occur whether the external pressure is an increase of weight, humidity or temperature. Sometimes the distorted tensile fibres manifest externally as a distortion of the box. Sometimes the box appears undisturbed, only to fall apart with any added pressure.

This process is not very different for the human being. We have the equivalent of a tensile strength. In our bodies they are the biochemical and physiological activities that maintain the integrity of the body. In our psyche, they are the emotional strengths of courage and wisdom that define our integrity as a person. Thus the human being can have two levels of stress, that of the body and that of the mind. Unlike the mechanical object, however, these structures are highly complex and dynamic. Distortion can be more readily introduced into a dynamic system than in a fixed one. In addition to the mechanical structure of each organ system, there is a dynamic balance between the biochemical and physiological activities of the various organ systems of the body. This balance is necessary for the performance of the body as a whole. A distortion of the balance can be as destructive as a distortion of any of the organ systems individually. Similarly, there is a dynamic balance between the strengths of courage and wisdom that gives rise to the performance of the mind. Wisdom gives courage and courage nurtures wisdom. When they are not in balance, a distortion—that is, a stress on the integrity of the mind—can arise.

Let us first consider the body. Stress in the body can be initiated when external pressures distort the balance that is held between the separate organ systems by the biochemical or physiological interaction. Thus the distortion produces illness or pain, sometimes manifested as an identifiable disease, sometimes not manifested externally (for example, feelings of malaise or headaches). In a similar way, the mind can be stressed by external events that challenge the internal strengths of wisdom and courage. An event that arises from activities that are beyond present experience can stress the psychological strength of wisdom.

On the other hand, events like rejection, criticism or uncertainty can erode the strength of courage and cause similar psychological stress. Then the mind manifests its stress internally with emotional pain and externally as behavioural maladaptation. Of course, just as with the box or the body, the mind can be internally stressed without this stress being externally manifested, and a simple pressure may be all that is needed to have a total breakdown. In a world of such immensity that is so easily reached with modern technology, it is hardly surprising that a person's wisdom can be exceeded by events that could not possibly be experienced earlier by that person. Similarly, in these times of change, the pressures of uncertainty, and with that rejection and criticism, can so easily arise that even the most resilient person can be weakened.

It is important to know this as a person with mature self-accountability. First, it can happen to you. You only see or feel the manifestations, but you must also be able to identify the source so you can address the effect more appropriately. Second, it can happen to people whose performance or well-being impacts you. They may not understand the dynamics of their stress. It is up to you as a manager to be able to understand the nature of their stress and guide them through a process they do not understand with the courage derived from your greater insight.

Our first observation is that the internal disturbance that is a stress on the integrity of the psyche can affect anyone anytime. Even a visionary leader is not immune to these stresses. The wise can, at times, be as easily wounded as the ignorant. Our second observation is that the internal disturbance can be prevented through strengthening the internal forces of courage and wisdom. Then, just as healing the body aims at restoring biochemical and physiological balance and not simply removing the pain, so must we be able to direct our management of mental and emotional stress at the restoration of the internal strengths of wisdom and courage, not just pacifying the emotions or redirecting the behaviour.

MANAGING THE STRESS EXPERIENCE

We are able to manage the stress effects on the body to a limited degree through proper diet, rest and exercise. We cannot prevent a disease from occurring, but to a limited degree, we can treat many diseases and restore the integrity of the body. When we refer to stress, we usually refer to psychological stress or stress of the mind. This is not easily reached, diagnosed or treated. This is the most disturbing stress because regardless of whether it manifests a measurable stress on the body, it is so close to our awareness that it demands immediate attention. The Understanding Change model focuses primarily on mental stress and the only effective way it can be addressed—through strengthening personal resolve and personal confidence. It will recognize that such stress is not a measure of a person's weakness, but it is a reminder of our general ignorance in a world of vast uncertainty and instability. Stress of the mind, therefore, is an inevitable experience for anyone with a desire to reach beyond existing limits.

The stressed mind cannot be healed by treating the behavioural maladaptation it manifests through the body. The traditional approach to "fixing" the wounded psyche through suppressing the emotional pain with drugs, and measuring success through observation of behaviour changes, can thus be self-limiting, misleading or ineffective. Remember, Freud once thought cocaine to be the wonder drug. Heroin was once included in some over-the-counter remedies. Diazepams and now serotonin enhancers are claiming this position. Yet we can see from past experience that the psychological distortion apparently returns after seeming to respond to our manipulation of the secondary biochemical distortion or our suppression of the emotional pain. We must consider that the human psyche is closely associated with the human body. A distressed psyche will attempt to compensate for its distortion by straining the resources of the body. Anyone can attest to the biochemical or physiological distortions that can arise from worry, anger or fear. In fact, it is not altogether different from the back pain that can arise as the body compensates for an injured leg. As a result, a psychological distortion can evoke a biochemical or physiological distortion. We must not be fooled into believing that by treating a concomitant biochemical disorder, we have also healed the distressed psyche.

Let us learn, therefore, to treat the psychological distortion for what it is: a natural stress of the psychological integrity caused by external events that are larger than the internal strengths of the individual at that time. Of course, every measure is relative. The event may be unfairly large relative to a highly developed wisdom. Similarly, wisdom may be extraordinarily small relative to a naturally evolved event. We cannot provide wisdom to another; people must be directed and encouraged to procure it themselves. We cannot provide courage; people must be taught how to develop it within the conditions in which they function. It is these challenges that make the process of people management not only difficult for the well intentioned supervisor, counsellor or parent, but fair game for those with delusions of being able to provide the better answer. In fact, no one can create the ideal solution for another. There are no 10 easy answers to being a better manager of any of the pressures, whether from life, business or relationships. The person must create his or her own answers. The only help we can give is to guide people, assuming that they are not chronically disturbed but are simply made unwell by the pressures from an external event they do not have the internal strengths to manage. As a result, let us see how we can both reverse a psychological distortion that is established and control the evolution of a new one before it begins.

PSYCHOLOGICAL IMMUNITY

It is necessary, therefore, for us to accept that in a world of imposing immensity and persistent change, we cannot contain the external pressures; we can only attempt to expand the internal strengths we need to face those pressures. As human beings, we will always be bombarded by the immensity of work and the uncertainty of life to a degree greater than our developed strengths can resist. Rejection and criticism will always reach us. Therefore, we must have the internal strengths to resist greater pressures than we can do automatically and easily. To expand our internal strengths, we must first realize that no one is so experienced that his wisdom will embrace all events that can arise. Wisdom, a quality we do not possess at birth, can be created progressively if only we can harness the courage to analyze events as changing paradigms, look for the patterns within those paradigms and understand them as they appear. Courage is the variable we must protect or immunize; this cannot be achieved if courage is derived from external sources either of success, acceptance or prescribed motivation because these external sources are secured within changing paradigms. Courage must be self-initiated, nurtured from a measure of self that cannot be eroded by the uncertainties of life. Again, we go back to the thrust of *Understanding Change*. But how do we measure self?

As a measure of self, wisdom is always insufficient relative to the vastness of new events or the new twists that will consistently arise in old events. As a measure of self, the performance of our body and its appearance are qualities that cannot endure. A tiny virus or a simple injury can negate our best prepared presentation. As a measure, our acceptability is unpredictable. Our friends cannot always be there, and when they are, they cannot always be focused on our needs, or they will measure us against standards that are inappropriate to our efforts.

Instead, we must learn to measure ourselves by the product of our efforts, and our efforts only produce one thing: wisdom. It is the application of wisdom that appears to produce an effect in this world; yet the effect is never lasting. Wisdom is the only product that endures. It is only the vastness of our world and the variability of its presentation that make wisdom appear to be depleted. Consider having to fix a broken chair, for example. Your initial impulse is to fix it. This is your apparent product. Yet the first thing you really do is assess the damage. Stop there. Only one thing has been produced at this point. It is the insight you have derived from assessing the event and developing a way to fix the damage. The broken chair has stimulated you to produce insight, a product that is so intangible that we dismiss its importance.

Now, let us go on. You apply that expanded wisdom to the chair and fix it. Two products have been created; yet only one endures. This is the wisdom not necessarily as a readily identifiable unit, but as an important ingredient to future events. You do not remember, for instance, the importance of the first time you read the letter A in the alphabet, yet it has stayed as an important ingredient in all of your future uses of language. It was small, but it contributes so much to everything you do. On the other hand, the chair stays fixed for only a limited time; it will fall apart again, perhaps to challenge another person. We, the human beings, are minds. We produce wisdom.

We must learn, therefore, to see ourselves as intelligent beings with sophisticated bodies, not as sophisticated bodies with intelligent minds. Then we can learn to measure ourselves by how we use our intelligence. If we have the wisdom to manage an event, we must recognize that our intelligence created it. If we do not have the wisdom to manage a particular event, we must conclude that our intelligence can create it. Courage is then based on our use of our intelligence, a facet no one else can measure. Once we can learn to recognize this, we can free ourselves from the fragile external measures that can so easily reject us. It is these fragile measures we once determined to be greater than us that make us fragile. It is our self-directed measure of growth that determines the security of our internal strengths. This is true self-esteem, not to be confused with esteem derived from external recognition of success, smugness with one's level of wisdom or conceit regarding one's inherited qualities. True self-esteem can allow one to create a solution and rise above oppression even when one is stressed by an external pressure or when other support systems are in short supply.

Thus, education aimed at learning to strengthen our true self-esteem does not have as its prerequisite an unwounded teacher with a multitude of applicable solutions. In fact it really does not require a teacher, just a person with true insight into the relentless instability of this world and their competence in gaining personal independence from this instability. The aim is to empower yourself to find your own answers, not seek an external source of inspiration or enlightenment. This does not require long sessions with a counsellor or great brilliance on your part. It does requires the belief that your real objective in life is not to form and shape the world, but to be formed and shaped by its challenges as growing minds and not fragile bodies. Such an objective can then truly reach your ultimate goal of modifying behaviour through healing the stressed mind, the generator of all behaviour. It can thus also go the extra step of minimizing future stress by strengthening the internal forces of wisdom and courage through the practice of self-accountability and self-determination. It is only through a proper understanding of the inevitability and unpredictability of change that we can address ourselves at using our greatest asset, our creativity, to explore new challenges and to keep doing so by truly *Understanding Change*.

Understanding Change is a technique that does not aim at relieving emotional pain or simplifying a complex society. Rather, it is directed by the understanding that the world will always change of its own accord. That change is the energy we use to stimulate and develop ourselves.

I once had to interview a young man who was convicted of possession and use of a banned substance, cocaine. The young man was defiant and uncooperative, but he had to go through the process because it was required by court. His take was that the correctional system had it all wrong because cocaine was a drug he would use daily if they would allow him. He liked the experience when he was high and hated both the withdrawal and the experience when he was natural, or not high.

As we began to talk, he stopped me and asked me whether I had ever been high. I told him that I never used drugs and only occasionally used alcohol but to a limited degree. He looked at me and dismissed me by stating that I had no capacity to help, assess or advise him. He challenged that I could not talk knowingly or even disparagingly about an experience I never had. I responded that it was true. I could not talk about the drug experience, and I also could not condemn it except from a medical perspective. However, I knew about how to be satisfied, content, believe in myself and like myself. "You see," I told him, "people use drugs and other activities to distract themselves from having to face existential pain, emptiness or weakness. When that is filled, there is less need to have to fill it artificially, and the call to be distracted is even less pronounced. I have experienced existential pain and emptiness; it is the birthright of every human being. I have also learned how to get existential satisfaction, and what's more, I have learned how to keep it when all else seems to be falling apart. That is all that I want to explore with you, and perhaps teach you." We were then able to communicate a little more effectively, though he still remained cagey and suspicious for much of the interview.

This exploration is what my work has been focused on developing. It is the argument I hope to present in this book. I will not be discussing the pressing issues for which you may wish to have solutions. I want to present to you a logical and scientific argument about how we as human beings can live in this world of chaos and unpredictable change without either falling apart or using the spurious means we have discovered to divert ourselves from the responsibility to build existential strength.

The idea is to show the reader, without resorting to religious or philosophical principles (but respecting them), that it is our invitation and duty to discover ourselves and build ourselves using the chaos of life as the energy for that transition. Thus, it will introduce and discuss arguments that may seem irrelevant on the surface but are essential ingredients for you to build your own understanding of that ethereal concept of the human essence, and to use it to personal advantage. For example, it is like learning to drive a car. One of the ingredients is to understand how the car functions. It may seem to be a waste of time; after all, what you want is to learn to steer and brake. But that understanding will come in handy not only if there is a breakdown, but in the day-to-day management of your driving. It becomes an unconscious act, but it is a necessary ingredient you must explore on its own.

Once I was challenged by another counsellor that it is our duty as counsellors to fix the person, not just guide the person to fix himself.

Dr. Albert de Goias

He suggested that, when his car is broken, he takes it to a mechanic and lets him fix it. When his body is injured, he takes it to a doctor and lets him fix it. Therefore, when a person is emotionally ill, he comes to us to have us fix him, and that is our job. He stated that whether we do it as a doctor with medications, as a support worker with empathy or as a counsellor who helps them with basic needs, it is our job to do it.

My response was that a mechanic has knowledge about mechanics that can be applied to any car because, with small differences, a car is a car. He also has the advantage of being able to open the hood and look inside. The doctor also has knowledge about anatomy and physiology that can be applied to any human body. He may not be able to open the hood to look inside, but he can do so with sophisticated instruments, and he can take a sample and send it to the lab for analysis. The human mind, however, is singular. Each person is so unique that the most astute psychoanalyst or counsellor does not have preexisting knowledge that can be applied to a particular person. Even if I know your family, that knowledge cannot be applied to you—you are an individual, and I cannot open the hood to look. No instrument can measure a person's thoughts or feelings, not even through the analysis of neurons in the brain. Therefore, I cannot "fix" another person. I can, however, teach a person to "fix" himself. It is far easier to provide you with insight about life and about yourself, no matter how complex this may seem to be, than it is to "fix" that which can never be accessed physically.

This book will take you on a journey. There is a sequence from the definition of the manager as that of being responsible and mature to the examination of life in a progressively deeper process, from the superficial to the abstract. The idea is to help you disconnect from the material world and define yourself in a more profound way: as a thinking force that cannot be physical. To do so, you must go through the apparently unnecessary examination in chapters 5 and 6 of the physical, though basically invisible, nature of matter and the abstract nature of the human essence. Only with this understanding, but not through having to remember it, can you get to appreciate the powerful nature of your existence and the invitation we all have to develop ourselves as spiritual entities. In short, we must be born of spirit. The admonition is not that we are born of spirit, but that it is our responsibility to be born of spirit.

Until we do that, we really are not more than sheep living to live, not to do.

You may need to read those two chapters more than once to be able to get the message. Remember, the objective is not to give you solutions, but to get you to rise to the challenge of creating your own solutions. Yes, it may seem to be hard at first, but it becomes wonderful and stimulating as you go through it. At the other side, you may wonder how you lived without having that ability—not the information, but the ability to see the abstract, examine life with objectivity and love yourself for more than the external identities given by your name, your connections or your body, all of which are transitional. These external identities are just the seed capital. We all get them, though with different values for each. We can only use them to build what is eventually ours, and until we do, whatever we have is not truly ours.

The aim of the book is not to give solutions or to entertain. It is to get you to think differently and deeper, even if you already do. The truly deep thinker always knows that there is always another angle he could not have seen and can appreciate being shown. Hopefully, at the end you will be able to say, "I see things differently. The book didn't show me. In fact, it all came from me. I cannot point to any particular statement or suggestion that has impacted me, but I do think differently, and I have a full and independent ability to appreciate me."

BIBLIOGRAPHY

Baars, Conrad W., and Anna A. Terrure. *Healing the Unaffirmed*. New York: Alba House, 1972.

Bohr, Niels. *Atomic Physics and Human Knowledge*. New York: John Wiley & Sons, 1958.

_____. *Atomic Theory and the Description of Nature*. New York: Cambridge University Press, 1934.

Bourke, Vernon J. *The Pocket Aquinas*. New York: Washington Square Press, 1960.

Broad, C. D., J. McTaggart, and Ellis McTaggart, eds. *The Nature of Existence*. Cambridge: The University Press, 1921.

Bronowski, Jacob. *The Ascent of Man*. London: Macdonald Futura Publishers, 1973.

Davis, Allen F., and Harold D. Woodman. *Conflict and Consensus in Modern American History*. D. C. Heath and Company, 1984.

Dawkins, Richard. *The God Delusion*. New York: First Mariner Books, 2008.

de Goias, Albert. "Individual Development within a Dualistic Paradigm." *Modelling and Simulation* 14, School of Engineering, University of Pittsburgh, 1983.

_____. "Individuality, Dualism, and the Perception of Performance In an Insecure Reality." *Modelling and Simulation* 14, School of Engineering, University of Pittsburgh, 1982.

Descartes, Rene. *Discourse on the Method and Meditations.* Translated by F. E. Sutcliffe. Suffolk: Penguin Books, 1968.

Everett, N. B. *Functional Neuroanatomy.* Philadelphia: Lea & Febiger, 1971.

Freeman, W. F., and J. Watts. *Psychosurgery in the Treatment of Mental Disorders and Intractable Pain.* Springfield: Charles C. Thomas Publisher Ltd., 1950.

Gleick, James. *Chaos: Making a New Science.* New York: Penguin Books, 1987.

Haldane, Elizabeth S., and G. R. T. Ross. *The Philosophical Works of Descartes.* New York: Cambridge University Press, 1979.

Haley, Jay. *Advanced Techniques of Hypnosis and Therapy: Selected Papers of Milton H. Erickson MD.* New York: Grune & Stratton, 1967.

Hawking, Stephen W. *A Brief History of Time.* New York: Bantam Books, 1988.

Hume, David. *Dialogues Concerning Natural Religion.* Edited by Nelson Pike. Indianapolis: The Bobbs-Merrill Company Inc., 1970.

Martin, Bernice. *A Sociology of Contemporary Cultural Change.* Oxford: Basil Blackwell, 1981.

Sartre, Jean-Paul. *Being and Nothingness.* New York: Washington Square Press, 1956.

Schlipp, Paul Arthur, ed. *Albert Einstein: Philosopher-Scientist.* London: Cambridge University Press London, 1982.

Selye, Hans. *Stress without Distress.* New York: Lippincott, 1974.

Walker, Evan Harris. "The Nature of Consciousness." *Mathematical Biosciences* (February 1970): 131–78.

INDEX

A

abilities, 31, 44, 181; *see also* strengths
  accessing, 185
  belief in, 208, 210
  visibility of, 167
Abraham, 63
acceptance, 6, 26, 197
accomplishments, 25, 46, 117, 118
accountability; *see also* performance
  benefits to, 153
  in expression of skills, 149
  and failure, 160
  flexible priorities, 154–58
  misrepresentation, 150
  and objectivity, 150–51
  to others, 149
  requirements for, 153–54
  to self, 151–54, 168–69
  to a standard, 149, 150, 151, 152
achievement, 24, 25, 26–27
adaptation, 1, 2, 140
  to environment, 17, 18, 67
  in marriage, 179
  of opinions, 182
  of performance, 153, 154
addiction, 132, 169, 199
adolescence, 215, 223–25
affirmation, 32
  cycle, 36, 37
  giving appropriately, 218–19
  management through, 210, 216–17
  need for, 35–38, 106

need for as vulnerability, 115
  self-, 103–7, 115–18
aggression, 189, 190
  directed at physical self, 192–93
  directed at the world, 191–92
  at mental self, 192–93
  response, 190
aging, 44, 95
alcohol, 131–32, 137, 196, 199
Alexandria, Egypt, 64
altruism, 127, 205
Andersen, Hans Christian, 168, 198
anger, 102, 191
animal instincts, 17–18, 24, 187
anorexia, 192–93
antimatter, 74
appearances, 27–30, 192
approval, 26, 105, 111
Aquinas, Thomas, 102
artificial intelligence, 19
The Ascent of Man (Bronowski), 13, 81
astrology, 62, 64
atoms, 69, 70
attention, 89
attributes
  at birth, 42
  developing strengths, 29, 32
  flexible, 32–35
  limitations of, 31
  loss of, 30
  personal, 30–32
  reliance on, 29
  visible, 27–30

awareness, 3, 4, 15–16
    at birth, 21
    of bodily functions, 6–8
    of other people's thoughts, 10, 11, 15
    of physical environment change, 3, 4

B

Babylon, 63
background, 28, 29, 52
bacteria, 67
balance, 2, 67, 190, 197
Ballistic Research Laboratories (US Army), 23
beauty, 27–30
behaviour
    control center for, 85, 86
    defensive, 186, 189
    disorders, 85
    with maladaptation, 229, 231
    unhealthy, 169
Being and Nothingness (Sartre), 23
beliefs, 52, 64, 66, 121
Bible, 65
Big Bang, 23, 70
birth, 27
    attributes at, 42
    disadvantaged at, 29
    family circumstances, 29
    inheritance, 29
    knowledge at, 21
body, 6–8; *see also* breaks
    abusing, 131
    appearance, 27–30, 192
    dependability as asset, 95
    deterioration, 20–21, 83
    healing, 6
    health fanatics, 127
    muscular movements, 7
    nurturing, 135–38
    relation to mind, 22–23, 83, 85
    using effectively, 130–31
Bohm, David, 21
boredom, 3, 199
brain, 86–87

cerebral cortex, 88
chemicals, 89–90
damage and mental function, 87
EEG patterns, 91
electrical activity, 91
frontal lobes, 88
lobe structure, 87–88
medulla, 88
neurons, 88
percentage used, 88
brain waves, 12
breaks, 117
    and burnout, 133
    discipline, 133
    and efficiency, 130, 133, 134
    how to take, 133–34
    how to use, 134–35
    need for, 132, 133
    provided by substances, 131–32
    when to take, 132–33
Bronowski, Jacob, 13, 81

C

capabilities, *see* abilities
car and driver, 23, 86
ceremony, 152
challenges, 11
    adapting to, 17
    avoiding, 45
    complexity, 171
    conquering, 17
    and creativity, 44, 45
    difficulty levels, 47, 139
    insight into, 30–31
    overly extensive, 48, 106, 207, 211
    persistent, 48, 112
    resting the task, 140–41
    stimulation of, 45, 125
    strategic retreat from, 116, 117, 118
    ubiquitous, 129
    using, 138–39, 139–40
change; *see also* adaptation; sources of change
    accepting, 140–41

areas of, 3
awareness of, 3, 4, 15–16, 168
buildup to, 2, 4
in business, 176
constant state of, 74–75, 141, 159
daily, 1, 2
facing, 2, 139–40
in families, 176
forcing, 190
influencing, 143
in modern times, 48–49
pressures of, 49–50
reality of, 1–3
running from, 1
self-perpetuating, 69
turning away from, 2
chemical dependence, 199
children
consequences for, 54, 222, 226
facilitation of, 211–12
how relates to world, 115
IQ testing, 32–33
labeling, 207
lack of needed insight, 207, 210
need for guidance, 151
need for parental approval, 105
overprotecting, 212, 220, 226
parenting, 171, 196, 212–13
problem solving ability, 47–48
taking on responsibility, 211
teaching, 34
Christianity, 121
The Church, 62, 65
cigarette smoking, 131, 132, 137
class structure, 52
coffee, 131
cognitive strengths, 187–88
expanding, 193
relative to demands of task, 189
reliance on, 174–75
colours, 72–73
comfort, 43, 199
comfort zones, 1
commitment, 125–28
communication, 11, 53–54, 177, 214

distortion, 132
rules for success, 214–16
showing genuine interest, 182, 214, 215, 217, 224
with your body, 132, 137
communities, 51–52
competence, 44
complacency, 28, 44, 99, 206, 219
computers, 19, 156
conceit, 200
condescension, 193
confidence, 44, 46
conflict, 188–89
conscious energy, see human thought; mind
consequences, 54, 152, 158, 226
buffered, 221, 222, 224
contributions, 20, 101, 177
to all areas of responsibility, 126–27
request for, 111
contributors, 113
Copernicus, 65
courage, 232
creation, 70
creativity, 12, 13, 18
challenging, 44, 45, 139, 143
fueling, 44, 45, 209
growth in, 97
self-recognition, 106
credibility, 197, 218
criticism, 181
accepting, 153, 161–62, 163
assessing accuracy of, 164–68
ignoring, 163
objective, 161, 162
subjective, 161–62, 163, 166
using to advantage, 161–64
crystals, 66–67, 70

D

David (Michelangelo), 141
Dawkins, Richard, 22, 23
Dead Sea Scrolls, 19

deceit, 200
decision making, 19, 152, 156, 158
defences
    of body, 6, 7, 10
    against fall from grace, 31
    falling back on, 203, 204
    focus on, 208–9
    mind integrity, 188, 189
    against opposing forces, 188–89
    of physical survival, 188, 189
    supporting in others, 209
defensive behaviours, 186
    inefficiency of, 186
    retreat into, 203–5, 214
    type and direction, 189
defiance, 195, 196, 222, 223
deities, 62, 63, 152; *see also* God
dependency, 199
Descartes, Rene, 85, 86
detachment, 81
development, 29; *see also* growth
    as a conscious energy, 97
    early, 30
    stuck, 31
discomfort, 60, 198–99
    consequences as, 222, 223
    relief through evasion, 194
disease, 67, 68
disrespect, 121, 224
diversity, 52
divorce, 1, 178, 179, 195
dogs, 18
dreams, 13
drugs, 196, 199, 231
dualism, 22, 85, 188

E

early development, 29, 30
education, 209, 214, 216
effectiveness
    of management, 208–10, 225
    in self-expression, 185
    use of body, 130–31

use of other people's perceptions, 144–45
use of people-challenges, 143–44
using immediate challenges, 138–39
efficiency, 104, 106, 138
    and taking breaks, 130, 133, 134
ego, 26, 146, 210
Egypt, 64
Einstein, Albert, 25, 56–57, 71
electromagnetic energy, 71
emotional eating, 137
emotions, *see* feelings
The Emperor's New Clothes (Andersen), 168, 198
English Channel ferry disaster, 154–56
environment
    physical, 3–6
    protection against, 31
    volatility, 49, 50
essence, 22, 24
evasion, 189, 190
    directed at mental self, 196–97
    directed at physical self, 195–96
    directed at world, 194–95
    negative consequences, 196
    response of, 194
evolution, 18, 50, 86
exhaustion, 49, 142
    mental, 21, 22
    physical, 21, 22, 132
existence, 23, 73, 84
expectations, 51, 150, 197
experience, 30, 144
eyesight, 4

F

facilitation, 177, 209, 210–13
failure, 2, 45, 203
    considerations missed, 159–60
    fear of, 185
    hiding, 185
    learning from, 160, 161
    protecting self from, 185

real, 160
rebounding from, 203, 204
responsibility for, 182
of solutions, 160, 162, 188
using to advantage, 158–61
fall from grace, 31, 153
familiarity, 1, 2
families, 28, 29, 176
fatalism, 81
fear, 44, 62
  defensive reactions to, 186
  of unknowns, 44, 60, 62, 66, 185
feedback, 26, 32, 146, 154, 165; see also
    criticism
  cycle, 44–46, 47
  effects of change on acquisition,
    54–56
  immunity to, 115, 121
  paradox, 41–42
  prerequisites for, 46–48
"feeling good," 26, 27, 32
feelings, 132, 134, 176
  chemical sources, 89
  expression, 1
  hidden, 1, 181
  location of, 84
fight or flight response, 187
flexibility, 153, 154–58
fluidity, 6
Freud, Sigmund, 85
frustration, 11, 166, 169, 173, 175
fulfillment, 26, 27, 32, 43
  growth in, 97, 100, 102
  investing, 106
  in a secure reality, 45

G

Galileo, 65, 66
Genesis, Book of, 65
germ theory, 68
Gevins, A.S., 91
God, 23, 99
  acts of, 122, 123, 124
  blind allegiance, 122–23, 152

fear of, 65
  image of, 63, 100, 102
  loving, 121
  nature of, 101–2
  praying to, 118, 124
  as punitive, 62, 67
  as source of change, 69
  trinity of, 102
  wrath of, 62, 67
The God Delusion (Dawkins), 22
"good enough," 24, 26, 32, 43, 198
growth, 43, 46, 139
  assessing, 103–5
  helping others achieve, 221
  ingredients for, 102–3
  momentum, 94, 95, 97–99, 103,
    105
  opportunities for, 107, 119, 124,
    127
  purpose to, 98
  stifling, 197
  as ultimate objective, 97–100, 119

H

happiness, pursuit of, 26–27
Hawking, Stephen, 23, 70
health, 8
hearing, 4, 89
heart, 86
Heisenberg principle, 74, 141
heliocentricity, 65
Heraclitus, 5, 74
heritage, 28, 30
home base, 42, 197
homes of the future, 5
homogeneity, 51
Homo Sapiens, 19
honesty, 217–19
hostility, 172, 186, 191
human body, see body
human cells, 67, 70
human condition, 22, 24–25, 25
human potential, 24–25, 26, 32, 106, 143
human thought, 8–11, 18; see also mind

awareness of existence, 15
expression as source of change, 10, 12, 15
hidden nature, 9–10, 14
measuring, 12, 84, 92
necessity of, 14
power of, 12–14, 15
problem solving, 11, 12–13, 14
sharing, 14–15
during sleep, 13, 92
humility, 112, 116
hydrocephalus, 90

I

ideas; see also solutions
applying, 55
contributions, 20
measuring value, 55
original, 19
identity, 21–24, 28
as a conscious energy, 93–97
definition of a person, 83–84
stability of, 80–81
idols, 63
ignorance, 4, 15, 62
and fear of God, 62, 63
wallowing in, 163
imbalances, 8, 172
inadequacies, 111, 159, 165, 181
inanimate objects, 17, 20, 24
incentives, 31
independence, 105, 175, 177, 183
individuality, 180
indulgence, 136, 196, 199
industrialization, 51
inner strength, 44, 49
Inquisition, 65
insecurity, 43–44, 152
insight, 21, 30–32
acquisition, 32–33, 32–34, 120
asking for help, 116
at birth, 21
creation of, 94–95
expanding, 103–5

insufficient for challenge, 207, 208
inspiration, 11
instincts, 13, 17, 18, 187
instruments, 51, 66
caring for, 135
five senses as, 61
magnifying, 66
particle affects, 72, 73, 74
person as, 150
sensitivity, 73, 74
state of change, 74–75
for studying stars, 65
for subatomic particles, 70
intellect, see mind
intelligence, 18–19, 25, 32, 126
intergalactic clock, 65
inventions, 17
invisible changes, 3–4, 5
invisible particles, 68–69
IQ tests, 32
irresponsibility, 153, 195–96

J

Jesus, 152
judgment, 104

K

Keynes, Maynard, 158
knowledge, see insight

L

languages, 50, 52
leadership, 151, 185
learned responses, 18
lifestyles, 199
light, 71, 72, 76–77
lightning, 70
limitations, 24, 112, 144, 167
logic, see reason
Lorber, John, 90
losses, 2, 96, 109, 196
love, 121, 218

M

management, 171; *see also* accountability; performance
by affirmation, 210, 216–17
alternative to, 178–79
challenge of, 175–76, 205–6
in changing environment, 176
of defiant child, 222–23
delegation, 178, 194, 195, 210, 219–21
difficult adolescence, 223–25
by education, 209, 214, 216
effectiveness, 208–10, 225
by facilitation, 177, 209, 210–13
motivating others, 173, 177, 178
objective of, 172, 176–78
of own challenges, 172
physical approaches to, 187
prerequisites for success, 180–81
replacing people, 178
as stressful *versus* exciting, 180
successful, 179–80
of task *versus* people, 173–75, 177
tools for, 174, 175
types, 209–10, 211, 225
of unproductive adult, 221–22
managers, 171–73; *see also* defences
communication, 173, 185, 214–16
as competent authority, 177, 181, 182, 214
defusing threats, 186
dependence of others on, 185
developing others, 172, 177
as driving force of others, 180
earning trust, 217–19
leadership, 185
relating to others, 173, 179–80, 182, 185–88, 190, 206–8
as resource for others, 172, 181, 182
role responsibilities, 173–75
as useful contributor, 113
manipulation, 191
marriage, 1, 125, 175, 196, 204
material possessions, 28

matter, 66, 67, 68, 69, 70–71; *see also* particles
basic entity, 92
destruction of, 78
instability of, 80
structure, 77, 78
maturity, 113
measurement, 69, 78; *see also* instruments
change due to, 72, 73
by effects, 87
human thought, 12, 84
nature of immeasurables, 73–74, 79–80
meditation, 118, 134
Mendeleev's table of elements, 91
mental awareness, 199
mental dissociation, 196
Michelangelo, 141
middle class, 52
mind, 41, 44, 92–93; *see also* human thought
and body, 22–23, 83, 85
capability, 25
destruction of, 118
locating, 87–92
nature of, 93–97, 118–19
as physical entity, 87
search for intellect, 85–87
molecules, 68
momentum, 94, 95, 97–99, 103, 105
monism, 22, 23, 85

N

natural selection, 22, 86
Newton, Isaac, 25, 77
nourishment, 43, 146
nurturing, 43
the body, 135–38
capacity for productivity, 177
of independence, 177, 181
others as sources of information, 146–47
the task, 143
nutrition, 135–37

O

objectivity, 121–25, 150–51
obligation, 198
onion skin effect, 70
opinions; *see also* perceptions
    adapting, 182
    assessing accuracy of, 164–68
    consideration for three entities, 123,
        124–25
    consideration of others, 122, 146,
        150, 179, 181
    expression of, 146, 161
    forcing on others, 144
    honesty of, 146
    personal suppression, 147, 150
overindulgence, 136, 196, 199
overpreparedness, 142–43
overwhelming challenges, 48, 139, 179,
    186, 192, 203
Ozymandias (Shelley), 196

P

pain
    desensitization to, 199
    emotional, 88, 229, 231, 234
    perception of, 198–99
    suppression, 231
pain threshold, 6
parents, 29, 105, 212, 226
particles
    affect on instruments, 72, 73
    discoveries of, 68, 69, 70
    effects of measuring, 72, 73
    emission of, 72, 73
    instability, 73, 74
    interrelations, 73, 76, 77
    light as, 71
    motion, 76–77
    smallest, 70, 73
peace of mind, 119, 122, 173, 205
"people challenges," 143–44
"people change," 8–11
perceptions, 9, 89

considering others, 172, 181, 182
    evoking, 143
    nurturing people as sources of,
        146–47
    and opinions, 161
    resting other people's, 145–46
    suppressing, 150
    use of other people's, 144–45
perfectionism, 141–42, 192
performance, 104, 120, 193
    adapting to change, 154
    assessing critical opinions, 164–68
    repetitive tasks, 125
    as representation of self, 161, 163
    to a standard, 150, 151
    using criticism to advantage,
        161–64
    using failure to advantage, 158–61
personalities, 169
perspectives, 113, 124; *see also* opinions
photons, 71, 72
physical comfort, 199
physical environment, 3–6; *see also*
    universe
physical strengths, 188, 192–93
Planck constant, 74
planets, 65
pollution, 5
polytheism, 62, 63, 64
post-tetanic potentiation, 7
potential, 24–25, 26, 32, 106, 143
prayer, 118, 124
precedents, 54
predictability, 76
preparedness, 2, 11, 16, 142–43; *see also*
    unpreparedness
presumptions, 12
pride, 116
priests, 62
The Princess and the Pea (Andersen),
    198–99
princess sensitivity, 199
priorities, 154–58
privacy, 147, 181
problem solving, 17

procrastination, 140, 195, 196
productivity, 51, 179, 180
    capacity for, 177
    improving in others, 174, 176, 209
    replacing under producers, 178
psychological immunity, 232–37
Ptolemy, 64
puerperal fever, 67–68
purpose, 118–21

Q

quantum particles, 71, 74, 77, 78, 91
quark particles, 70, 73, 92

R

randomness, 6
reality, 55
    of change, 1–3
    insecure, 43–44
    of matter, 77
    of modern change, 48–49
    secure, 41–43
    versus symbolism, 75–79
reason, 17, 32–35
recharging, 22, 38, 43, 117, 118
recognition, 26, 31, 41
rejection, 43, 111, 163, 198
relationships, 31, 195
    between big three entities, 123
    of child to the world, 115
    confrontations, 145, 172, 173, 179
    of responsible adult to world, 117
    taking mature position, 145, 172
    understanding others, 206–8
relativity, 71, 72
relaxation, *see* breaks
religion, 52, 84; *see also* God
    restrictions due to, 62, 64
    separating from science, 69
resentment, 117, 172, 175
resourcefulness, 41, 42, 205
responsibilities
    accepting, 126

delegating, 194, 195, 219–21
    as manager, 173
    mental disconnection, 196
    physical removal from, 195
    as self-accountable person, 152, 157
    shared, 172, 174, 179–80
Rutherford, Lord, 70

S

sameness, 2, 5, 175
Sartre, Jean Paul, 23
scientific discoveries, 66–71
security, 41–43
self-affirmation, 112, 115–18
    advantages of, 105, 107
    and asking for help, 116
    recognition of creativity, 103–6
self-drive, 149, 150, 161, 175, 178, 208
self-esteem, 26, 210
self-expression, 1; *see also* opinions
    accuracy of, 166
    of capabilities, 150
self-harm, 192
self-improvement, 95, 120, 197
selfishness, 119, 125–26
self-protection, 163, 181
self-worth, 20, 30, 186
Semmelweis, Ignaz, 67, 68
senses, 3, 4, 78, 89
Shakespeare, William, 94
Shelley, Percy B., 196
sin, 102
sleep, 13
socioeconomic class, 52
solid matter, 66, 67, 68, 69
    as illusion, 76–77
solutions
    applying, 55, 151–52
    creation, 188
    failure of, 160, 162, 188
    offered by others, 55
soul, 22
sound, 4, 89

sources of change
  behaviours of entities governed by, 74–75
  God, 69
  rules governing activity of, 71–73
  search for, 66–71
spouses, 11, 175, 178–79, 196, 204
stability, 3, 5, 69
  identity and, 80–81
stagnation, 49, 63, 106
  tendency toward, 94
  with validation, 197–98, 200
stamina, 27–30, 28
standards, 151, 152, 153, 161, 232
stars, see astrology
strengths, 27, 28, 29, 114
  cognitive, 187, 188
  physical, 188
  and response to threats, 187
stress
  adrenaline-induced, 187
  causes, 153
  effects on performance, 227–28
  management, 134–35, 230–32
  understanding, 228–30
successes, 45
  affirmation from, 42
  control over, 183
  measuring, 55
  responsibility for, 182
  savouring, 48
Sumerians, 64
sun, 65
survival, 17, 18, 20, 96, 188
symbolism, 75–79

T

tachyphylaxis, 199
taking charge, 113, 114–15, 118, 129
talents, 30, 42
tasks, see challenges
theory of relativity, 71, 72
threat responses, 186, 187
throwaway society, 5

time management, 128–30
transportation, 52–53
true to self, 128, 226
trust, earning, 217–19

U

uncertainty, 74, 141
unconditional love, 218
understanding, see insight
uniqueness, 20–21, 121
universe; see also matter
  birth of, 23
  exploring, 66, 75
  extent of, 79
  as heliocentric, 65
  measuring, 78, 79, 84
  time frames, 75
  unknown, 60
  views of by early man, 61
unknowns, 46
  approaching, 172
  fear of, 60, 66, 185
  understanding, 60, 185–86
unpreparedness, 29, 56, 80
  for change caused by people, 9–11
  for changes in physical environment, 4, 80–81
Ur, 64
urbanization, 51–52
usefulness, 20, 122, 183
utopian environments, 5

V

validation, 187, 189, 190
  directed at mental self, 199–200
  directed at world, 197–98
  fragile sources of, 198, 200
  from peers, 198
  response, 197
  self-, 198–99
value, 20–21, 94, 101, 105
variables, 156, 164, 205
vulnerability, 2, 108, 115, 200

W

Walker, Evan Harris, 22–23, 92
weaknesses, 30, 44, 203
wealth, 28, 30, 95
weather, 68
Western society, 121
work
    dedication to, 126
    doing by rote, 195, 196
workaholics, 126, 146